Scientific Coaching for Olym

dedication:

In memory of my father (WP)

Willy Pieter / John Heijmans

Scientific Coaching for Olympic Taekwondo

Meyer & Meyer Verlag

Die Deutsche Bibliothek – CIP-Einheitsaufnahme

Pieter, Willy:
Scientific coaching for Olympic taekwondo / Willy Pieter/John Heijmans.
- Orig.-Ausg. – Aachen : Meyer und Meyer, 1997
ISBN 3-89124-389-8
NE: Heijmans, John:

Cover photo: Bongarts Sportfotografie, Hamburg
Photos and illustrations: Willy Pieter, London
Cover design: Walter Neumann, N & N Design-Studio, Aachen
Cover exposure: Qualitho, Lithographie GmbH, Essen
Exposure: typeline, Dagmar Schmitz, Aachen
Printed by Druckerei Queck, Jüchen
Printed in Germany
ISBN 3-89124-389-8

Content

PREFACE

This book is believed to be the second publication in a Western language (the first publication of the present volume is in German by Meyer & Meyer Verlag) dealing with the systematic coaching of taekwondo athletes based on scientific principles and research. Although taekwondo has grown to become an international sport with continental, world championships and, as of 2000, Olympic games, coaching the taekwondo athlete has, so far, for the most part relied on traditional views. This may be related to the lack of scientific training of most taekwondo coaches, the lack of scientific research in taekwondo, the reluctance of coaches to adopt opposing views, or a combination of these and other factors.

The authors have investigated taekwondo for the past several years with their colleagues and have attempted to introduce scientific principles in teaching this activity in the gymnasium (dojang) (1). Past and ongoing research have led to the present product: a book specifically written for the coach of competitive taekwondo athletes. This work is meant for those, who are dealing with adult taekwondo athletes. Although most of the principles and findings mentioned in this book are also applicable to coaching Junior taekwondo athletes, they are not the main focus of the discussion. Coaching young taekwondo athletes requires knowledge that is outside the scope of this book and would justify a separate treatise of the topic.

Chapter I, II and III lay the foundation for the remainder of the book. In the introductory chapter, chapter I, the rationale for this book is presented, while at the same time introducing the extensive research project that provided the data for some of the chapters. Chapter II covers basic training principles that will aid the coach in developing a training program for his/her athlete(s). Chapter III discusses the cyclic nature of training and how this may be applied to taekwondo training.

The next five chapters, IV, V, VI, VII and VIII, will detail the information that was presented in chapters II and III. This means that the various training components that were distinguished in chapter II will be integrated in the information discussed in chapter III. The following training components will be dealt with: endurance (chapter IV), strength (chapter V), technique (chapter VI), psychological (chapter VII) and tactical (chapter VIII).

The final two chapters of the book will cover two related and important topics. Chapter IX will cover basic anatomical information on the joints, while chapter X will discuss injuries in taekwondo training and competition. Anatomy is not only important in relation to technique and strength training, but it also has a bearing on injuries in taekwondo. Knowing how the knee joint is stabilized, for instance, will give the coach and athlete a better appreciation of the importance of measures to prevent injuries to the knee. In terms of technique training, knowing the (im)possibilities of movements in the elbow joint, will give the coach an indication what to tell the athletes when practicing the punch or how to strengthen the muscles surrounding the elbow joint.

A book such as the one before you, is not only a collaboration between authors, but is also based on work that was done by others. Whenever we derived our observations from research by other investigators, we acknowledged their contribution by a number in the text that is put between brackets. These numbers correspond to numbers in the References where you will find the complete citation of the sources.

Acknowledgements

Besides our colleagues and the American young and adult taekwondo athletes, who volunteered their time over the past few years, we are indebted to coaches all over the world, who were willing to answer our questions and discuss problems with us about their work with taekwondo athletes. We are also grateful to those athletes, who were kind enough to share their ideas, frustrations, fears and hopes with us. A thank you from the first author (WP) to the (past) secretaries and executive directors (the name of the latter may have changed at times, but the work that had to be done remained the same nevertheless) of the United States Taekwondo Union (USTU), who were a great help during data collection for the Oregon Taekwondo Research Project (OTRP), especially Michael Weintraub, Pam Janelle, Debra Kopp and Robert Fujimura. Pam and Debbie, a special thank you for all your support and the conversations we had. Robert, thanks for your help and concerns regarding the results of the project and subsequent recommendations. The feedback you all provided will contribute to the improvement of the project in the immediate future. Thank you to coaches Sang Chul Lee and Dae Sung Lee for recruiting and motivating the athletes to participate in the OTRP. Without the cooperation of coaching staff and athletes, no research in taekwondo would have been possible and, as a result, no knowledge would have accrued. Special thanks to (former) athletes May Pejo, Debra Holloway, Kim Dotson, Lynette Love, Sam Pejo, Tim Connolly and Doug Fuechsel for their suggestions and help. The USTU is to be commended for supporting the OTRP, while thanks is due to all tournament directors from 1988 - 1991 for their permission to collect injury data at national tournaments and Team Trials.

The former chair of the USTU Sports Medicine Committee, French Anderson, M.D., deserves a sincere thank you from the first author for his encouragement to start the OTRP. Thank you to Samuel Pejo, M.D. for his never ending interest in, encouragement and support of the OTRP as well as his invaluable help during injury data collection. Sam, I (WP) hope we will soon accomplish some of the goals we agreed upon in Greece. Marianette and Charles Bailey, thank you for your assistance, support and interest in the OTRP. Data collection at those tournaments for the injury component of the OTRP would not have been the same without you. As representatives of the parents of the young athletes we tested, Gary and Ann Hunsicker, thanks for your interest in the OTRP.

It goes without saying that the support and suggestions from (former) staff of the Division of Sports Science, United States Olympic Committee, in Colorado Springs, CO, were invaluable. Thank you to Jay T. Kearney, Ph.D., Head, Division of Sports Science; Steven Fleck, Ph.D., Department of Sports Physiology; Sarah Smith, Ph.D., Department of Sports Biomechanics; Shane Murphy, Ph.D., Department of Sports Psychology; the late Peter Van Handel, Ph.D., Senior Sports Physiologist; the computer staff, and all the research assistants and interns from 1987 through 1991.

Thank you to Tony D.H. Kim, D.P.M., Karl Heinz, M.S., George Fields, J.D., Eric Wegner, M.A. and Luigi T. Bercades, M.S., who were part of the coaching staff of the University of Oregon Taekwondo Club. They all provided the authors with valuable insight in the intricacies of coaching taekwondo. Thank you all for your friendship and sharing your knowledge with us. The authors are also grateful to Marja van Noort, MO-P, who was willing to express herself in a more physical sense in front of the camera, as were Monique Jellema, R. N., Drs. Roy Lufting, Roemer Trompert, Drs. Marie-José Borst and Anja Bonte, M.D.

On a more personal note, the first author (WP) would like to thank his brother, Frans, for his comments on some of the chapters and for showing the author in practice that an engineer and proponent of the hard sciences knows how to appreciate and value the inter-relatedness between art and science in taekwondo. Thanks is also due to Roy Lufting for his comments and suggestions on some of the chapters as well as for the numerous discussions on coaching (elite) taekwondo athletes. Gratefulness is extended to Marja van Noort and Paula Gaillard who, with more physical talent than they are aware of, reaped the benefits of psychological skills in taekwondo faster than they or others had anticipated and, as a result, confirmed the importance of the mental aspect in taekwondo competition. A special thank you to Guido Van Ryssegem, R.N., A.T.C., M.S., Martje Adams, R.N., Sam, Lisa as well as my co-author John Heijmans for being there when it was desperately needed and to Yongin Song, M.S. and Tony Kim for their friendship and trust during hard times in Eugene. Finally, and most importantly, thanks to Socorro and Andrea for their love, understanding and support.

The second author (JH) would like to thank Anja for her comments on and proofreading parts of the manuscript. Ben de Veen, M.D. and Mart Wieland, M.D. for their encouragement and helpful comments. Daniël van Neer for showing him that "impossible" is a relative concept. Jose Verhoeven, ballet teacher, for sharing the value of good coaching with him. Marc Jonckers, M.D. for his help and advice regarding some of the pictures in this book and the great time during the photo sessions. Prof. Dr. J. F. Wilmink and Prof. Dr. Harm Kuipers for providing the pictures on cerebral concussion and muscle cell damage, respectively.

Finally, thanks to Dennis Taaffe, Ph.D., Eric D. Zemper, Ph.D., Heather Bricken, B.S., Angela Ferrin, B.S., Carey Hilbert, M.S., Lisa Lochner, B.S., Luigi T. Bercades, M.S. and Eric Wegner, M.A. who, at one time or another, were with the University of Oregon, Eugene, U. S. A. and on the staff of the OTRP. Also thanks to Kathy Yeh, M.S. and Susan Ciraolo, Ph.D. for their help in collecting data for the OTRP.

Reference

1. Pieter, W. and Heijmans, J. (1989), *Taekwondo (W.T.F.) Stijlfiguren*, Haarlem: Uitgeverij De Vrieseborch.

CHAPTER I

INTRODUCTION

In recent years, taekwondo has evolved to an international sport and was recognized as a full Olympic sport in 1994. Originally from Korea, it was first presented as a martial art (e.g., 6; 8), although its historical claims (e.g., 6; 10) are suspect and highly debatable (25; 27). For instance, the *hwarang* group is typically depicted as being the Korean equivalent of the Japanese *samurai* (e.g., 6). The *hwarang* are also thought to have been at the cradle of what is presently known as taekwondo (e.g., 19). An historical comparison between the *hwarang* and *samurai,* however, shows that in terms of militarism as well as their influence on modern taekwondo, the *hwarang* definitely have not had a similar impact on Korean martial sports the way the samurai had on Japanese martial arts and, as a result, on Japanese martial sports (26). Extreme caution is recommended when reading accounts on the "historical" link between the *hwarang* and taekwondo, or even other Korean combative sports. Careful and objective historical research has shown that the *hwarang* (best translated as "flower boys") were "a band of adolescents of high purpose, who could not avoid being both religious and at least quasi military, sometimes very military, because that was the nature and need of the society in which they lived" (33, p. 46). They were most likely a group of young boys who were recruited to entertain the court with singing, dancing, poetry reading and the like (33; 42).

Taekwondo's development in the past 35-plus years has shown that its status as a martial art as expressed in the *do* part of its name, has all but disappeared. It was Draeger (11; 12; 13), who clarified the *do* aspect in the Japanese martial arts and, by extension, the Korean versions. According to Draeger, the classical conception of *do* activities is that of *do* as the Way (Chinese: *Dao*) to follow in life, while the new *do* activities (emerging after World War II) are the more westernized sport activities. Classical *do*, as opposed to new *do*, is imbued by philosophical perspectives from Daoism, Confucianism and Zen, while modern *do* is characterized by winning or losing in competition as governed by rules and regulations. From its introduction in the West, taekwondo has always been a modern sport, which is especially true for that specific brand of taekwondo that was a demonstration sport at the past two Olympic Games (1988 and 1992) and that will be on the regular program in 2000: taekwondo as propagated by the World Taekwondo Federation (WTF). It is precisely coaching WTF taekwondo athletes that will be the topic of this book, although proponents of like martial sports, such as karate, kick boxing and kungfu will undoubtedly find some valuable information contained in it as well.

Taekwondo Research

Coaching taekwondo athletes from a scientific point of view is in its infancy. First of all, scientific research of taekwondo has been scarce. Furthermore, taekwondo coaches are usually reluctant to abandon traditional ways of preparing athletes for competition in favor of a more scientific approach that may lead to better results. Both issues will be addressed in what follows.

Research in taekwondo until now has emphasized a biomechanical approach. For instance, the front kick *(ap ch'agi)* and the spinning hook kick *(twit tollyo ch'agi)* were thus far studied (1; 16; 17; 22; 41). Our research group analyzed the forward backfist strike *(dung jumok ap'e ch'igi)* from a theoretical perspective (23). Some biomechanical studies were concerned with the occurrence of injuries (7; 34), whereas the speed and force of selected taekwondo techniques were investigated by Sung et al. (38) as well as by Stull and Barham (36; 37). Research in other scientific fields that is relevant to taekwondo coaches has been conducted in the areas of sport psychology (e.g., 18; 21; 35), physiology (39) and motor performance (43).

Given the poor state of scientific research in taekwondo, a need was felt to start a large-scale research project to assess the athletic profile of elite taekwondo competitors. After a preliminary study, the results of which were published in national and international professional journals (23; 24; 29; 30; 31), the Oregon Taekwondo Research Project *(OTRP)* was initiated and headed by the first author (WP). The project was named after the geographical area where it was conceived: the University of Oregon in Eugene, Oregon, U.S.A. It was funded by the United States Olympic Committee *(USOC)* and supported by the United States Taekwondo Union *(USTU)*.

Oregon Taekwondo Research Project

As alluded to above, scientific research in taekwondo has been scarce in the West. Taekwondo research is being conducted in Korea, but only a few of us have access to or are able to read the results of these studies. If taekwondo is to grow as an Olympic sport, it will need to have its own body of scientific research, just like any other Olympic or international sport, to help improve the performance of its competitive athletes.

The OTRP covers a variety of scientific disciplines (28). All of the laboratory testing took place at the US Olympic Training Center in Colorado Springs, Colorado. Additional data were collected at various national and international tournaments. Although nutrition was a component of the project, no data have been published as of yet. The OTRP included the following research areas:

1.) Endurance
2.) Muscular strength
3.) Body fat
4.) Kicking speed and force
5.) Competition injuries
6.) Competition anxiety
7.) Psychological overtraining

The remainder of this chapter will give a summary of the various components of this research project, which is believed to have been the most extensive project of its kind in the U. S. A. or anywhere else.

Endurance

One factor that is important in taekwondo performance is rather obvious: endurance. Aerobic endurance refers to the energy system needed to do work in physical activities while using oxygen over a longer period of time, such as running 10 km. Anaerobic endurance refers to the energy system needed to do work in physical activities over a shorter period of time (less than one minute) without any major help of oxygen, such as sprinting a 100 m dash. Aerobic endurance is important to taekwondo athletes, because it affects how well they will be able to continue performing during the length of a bout and throughout several bouts in a tournament. Anaerobic endurance is important, because it is involved in short bursts of activity, such as in a series of rapid attacks or counterattacks. In the OTRP, aerobic endurance was measured while running for several minutes on a treadmill or cycling on a stationary bike. Anaerobic endurance was measured while pedaling at maximum speed for 30 seconds on a stationary bike (see chapter IV for further information on endurance).

Muscle Strength

Another factor that is relevant to taekwondo performance is muscle strength. Although most elite athletes in other sports in the U.S.A. and elsewhere are using strength training to gain a competitive edge, this form of training is still rather unknown in taekwondo. The muscle strength tested in this component of the OTRP involves the same muscle groups used in kicking, such as the quadriceps and hamstrings. The results of the tests that were completed on elite taekwondo athletes in 1987 showed that muscle strength during leg extension and flexion, as measured in the OTRP, was positively related to kicking speed and force (9).

In addition to its importance for improved kicking speed (up to the athlete's genetic potential) and force, increased muscle strength may also aid in the rehabilitation of injuries. Research has shown that there is a relationship between strength of the hamstrings and a return to training after injury (14). Individuals whose strength of the knee flexors was similar to or greater than the strength of their knee extensors could return to a higher level of training after injury than those whose knee flexor strength values were lower. Research on a variety of athletes in different sports has suggested that increased muscle strength of the hamstrings may also play a role in the prevention of injuries to this muscle group (e.g., 3; 4; 15). It is well known that the hamstrings are very susceptible to injuries in many athletic groups, including taekwondo (44).

Body Fat

Clearly, excess body fat may become a disadvantage for the taekwondo athlete. Not only will he or she have to compete in a higher weight division, but excess fat may also interfere with the athlete's ability to accelerate as fast as possible. In taekwondo competition, of course, the athlete has to be able to propel him/herself through space as fast as possible to avoid an attack, to initiate an attack, to start a fake, and so on. It will come as no surprise, then, that taekwondo athletes will try to lose fat to optimize their chances in competition. To calculate body fat, several measurements were taken in the OTRP, such as height, weight and skinfold thicknesses.

Before the false notion is created by coaches, who think that their taekwondo athletes should be as thin as possible to achieve success as a competitor, a word of caution is warranted. Nowadays, researchers agree that there is no unambiguous formula to assess fat content, especially in young athletes, as expressed in a percentage of body weight. Instead, sum of skinfolds is used. For a composite of athletes, optimal ranges of skinfold values and sum of skinfolds have been formulated (5). Athletes close to the lower limit of these optimal ranges are endangering their health and performance, while those close to the upper limit of the ranges will most likely fall short of their peak performance. As a result, the recommendation to try to achieve a lean physique only refers to a pattern of skinfold values within the optimal ranges, which are also sport-specific. This means that athletes do not need to compete with the *minimum* amount of fat possible to be successful. The optimal range for sum of six skinfolds (back of the arm, back of the shoulder, hip, abdomen, front thigh, and medial calf) for an amalgamation of female athletes is given in Figure I.1.

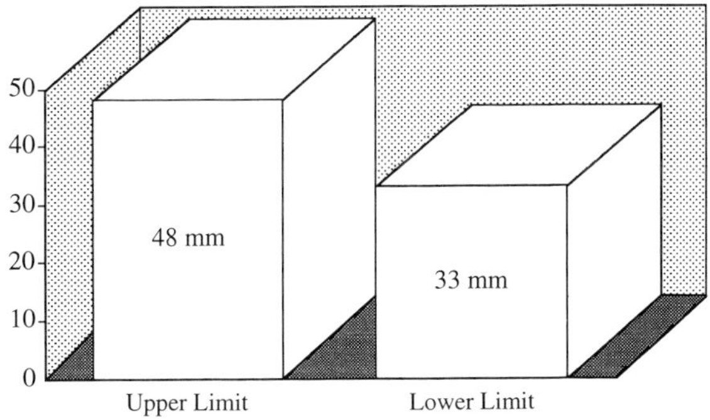

FIGURE I.1: Optimal Range for Sum of Skinfolds for Female Elite Athletes (After 5).

Speed and Force

This part of the OTRP consists of assessing the speed and force with which elite taekwondo athletes kick and punch. In this project, speed and force on impact of selected kicks and the reverse punch were measured with a dual-light beam system (to measure speed) and a water-filled heavy bag with a built-in force sensor unit (to measure force). These measurements are relevant to injury prevention and fighting tactics in taekwondo. Being able to bring the non-dominant limb up to par with the dominant limb as much as possible, in terms of speed and force, opens up a whole array of strategic possibilities that can be used during taekwondo fighting. With respect to injuries, the more the taekwondo athlete can alternate kicking with both legs, the less likely the preferred leg will get bruised, for instance.

In 1989, a new dimension was added to this component of the project. In addition to speed and force, a preliminary study was done to include the sum of reaction time (to a visual stimulus) and movement time, viz., performance time. Reaction time refers to the time it takes to start the movement (which was the roundhouse kick or the *ap tollyo ch'agi*) after the stimulus (a light) is given. Movement time is the time that elapses between the beginning and the end of the kick. High speed video was used to arrive at movement time. Preliminary results showed that there was hardly any difference in female elite taekwondo athletes between the right and left leg (0.70 versus 0.67 seconds, respectively) to reach the target (W. Pieter, Unpublished data).

Competition Injuries

The taekwondo athlete and coach alike should be aware of the importance of knowing more about the types and mechanisms of injuries in taekwondo training and competition. What needs to be stressed, however, is that in the OTRP we only collected reported injuries during competition. From the literature it is known that some 50 - 60% of martial arts injuries incurred at tournaments and during training sessions are not reported (2), which means that the injuries reported to the OTRP should be considered minimum numbers, especially the less serious ones, such as bruises and sprains. The more serious injuries, on the other hand, such as brain concussions and fractures will most likely be reported as soon as they occur (32).

With the increased participation of children and adolescents in taekwondo, extra care should be taken to ensure the safety of these young athletes because injury to this age group has the potential to stunt the growth of its members (see chapter X). For instance, overuse injuries as caused by repetitive training have recently been observed to occur in children and adolescents as well, as was already found in adults. One risk factor in developing overuse injuries in adults as well as in children and adolescents is related to sudden changes in the training load. Since the ramifications of overuse injuries in children and adolescents are more severe, coaches of young taekwondo athletes should be required to have some basic training in physical growth and development or to consult with a physician or specialist in growth and development on a regular basis regarding the effect of training on the growing organism.

Competition Anxiety

For some time now, it has been recognized that elite athletes can compete adequately at the national and international levels only if they also train their minds. Eastern European literature shows that a large part of their training is devoted to the psychological training of their elite athletes (e.g., 20). At the Olympic Training Center in Colorado Springs, elite athletes of other sports than taekwondo are working with the available sports psychology facilities and some teams, such as the skiers, gymnasts and figure skaters, have added a sports psychologist to their coaching staff. In order to assess the mental aspect of elite taekwondo athletes, a number of sport psychological tests was used in the OTRP. Some of the psychological measurements included in this project were overtraining (see chapters II and VII for more information about overtraining) as expressed by the athlete's mood profiles (see below) and competition anxiety. Anxiety is distinguished in *competitive trait* and *state anxiety. Competitive trait anxiety* refers to the tendency of an individual to react with high levels of tension to stimuli from the environment (competition, for instance) that are perceived as threatening. This reaction, then, is called (competitive) *state anxiety*. See chapter VII for a more detailed discussion of competition anxiety and psychological overtraining.

Psychological Overtraining

To assess psychological overtraining as expressed by the mood profiles of elite taekwondo athletes, the *Profile Of Mood States (POMS)* was used in the OTRP. The POMS is a scale that measures how the taekwondo athlete is feeling at the time the test is taken or has been feeling the week during which the test was administered. The following moods were assessed: tension, anger, depression, confusion, fatigue and vigor. The more overtrained the athlete becomes, the higher the scores on tension, anger, depression, confusion and fatigue. The score on vigor, on the other hand, tends to decrease dramatically when the athlete becomes overtrained.

Researcher – Coach-Interaction

In order for taekwondo to develop as a full-grown sport, it is not only necessary to do more research in the area, but it is equally important for coaches to be more open-minded toward the contributions of scientific research. For taekwondo's continued growth to happen, both the researcher and coach need to get a better understanding of each other's perspective. The following is meant to facilitate the discussion between the two and should not be taken as suggestions set in stone. Each individual circumstance has its own unique characteristics for which solutions need to be sought by the parties involved (i.e., the coach, the athlete and the scientist) to optimize the interaction between all concerned.

This section will briefly elaborate on what scientific research is about. It will discuss what its objective is, how it is done, how the subjects are selected and how to interpret the results and recommendations based on these results. It will finally address the issue of how the researcher and taekwondo coach may improve their understanding of each other.

Simply put, scientific research is an attempt to gain insight in reality without the interference of any subjective position regarding the issue at hand. This typically means that the researcher will quantify that part of reality that he/she is interested in: he/she will express reality in a number. For instance, if the scientist is interested in the difference in speed of a taekwondo kick between two athletes, he/she will not say "person A's kick is faster or slower than person B's kick", which would be a subjective statement. Instead, he/she will say "person A's kick has a speed of 13 m/s and person B's of 15 m/s", which would be a more objective observation.

After a number has been attached to a piece of reality, which in this case is the taekwondo kick, the scientist will then proceed and try to find out whether the first kick (13 m/s) can be said to be slower than the second kick (15 m/s) according to certain rules, which have been agreed upon by the scientific community. One such rule, for example, will make it possible for the scientist to decide whether the observed difference is most likely due to chance. If it is chance, the likelihood of finding this difference the next time will be small. If this difference is "real", the next assessment again will show person A's kick to be slower than person B's. In this case, the researcher will say that the kicks are "significantly different from each other" or "person A's kick is significantly slower than person B's". If it is chance, the conclusion will be: "there is no (significant) difference between the two kicks".

Unfortunately, what is significant to the scientist is not necessarily significant to the coach. For instance, there is probably no scientifically significant difference between a time of 10.0 seconds and 10.01 seconds over the 100 m dash. To the coach and athlete, however, this difference may mean the difference between winning or losing. Conversely, the difference between the two kicks mentioned earlier may be significantly different from a scientific point of view, but may mean nothing from a practical perspective. Therefore, the coach should be aware of what the scientist means by "significantly different" when he/she is presenting the findings of his/her research. It is up to the coach to decide whether the results are of practical significance and, as a result, meaningful to him/her and his/her taekwondo athletes.

Another factor that the coach should be aware of is that in order to arrive at objective data, the researcher has to control for irrelevant variables that may "dilute" the results (see below). This means that the investigator will try to keep as many of these variables as possible out of the picture. It is no wonder, then, that scientific measurements are usually done in a laboratory setting where the environment is more or less stable and under the researcher's control. Although this way of information gathering is a prerequisite for scientific research, it has a major limitation in that athletic performance does not take place in isolation. For instance, kicking speed and force of elite taekwondo athletes were measured in the laboratory with sensitive biomechanical equipment as part of the Oregon Taekwondo Research Project. Though the results are objective, kicking speed and force under controlled circumstances cannot entirely be compared to speed and force in an actual bout where the athlete's anxiety level, the opponent, the specific fight conditions, and so on, play a role to exert their influence. In a lab, there is no opponent, there are no fight conditions. In a sense, then, kicking speed and force in the lab are "pure" kicking speed and force without the aforementioned variables (anxiety level, opponent, etc.) that may "dilute" the results.

In addition to irrelevant factors being controlled for in the lab, there are also the questions of who were tested, how and when the testing was done. Ideally, the physiological, biomechanical or psychological variables that are thought to contribute to success in taekwondo competition should be assessed before or even during actual matches. Unfortunately, this is not always possible or even technically feasible. In order to be able to understand the athletic profile of taekwondo athletes, existing testing or conventional equipment or tools are employed in the laboratory. Sometimes, actual match situations are even simulated in the lab, such as reacting to a visual stimulus (light). In other words, the equipment used may not have been sufficiently adequate to assess a particular characteristic that is unique to taekwondo. As far as when the athletes were tested, it should be clear that there will be a difference between testing athletes before or after an intensive workout or in the middle of a series of workouts. Recommendations by the scientist, therefore, will always be carefully formulated, taking into account the aforementioned features of scientific research.

The question of "who were tested?" refers to the way the subjects for the study were selected. To get the most accurate picture of a group of taekwondo athletes would be to assess all of them. This, of course, would not be very realistic. Instead, what researchers do is select a smaller group of the whole population of taekwondo athletes, such as adult elite male and female athletes. What this means is, that any results and any recommendations derived from them are only applicable to that specific group. Generalizations to the whole population of taekwondo athletes, consisting of individuals of various ages and skill levels, are not always warranted and should be viewed with caution.

Having elaborated on the scientist's point of view, this chapter will conclude with some suggestions for the taekwondo coach. The following is based on work by Van Ingen Schenau and Whiting (40). In their discussion of the interaction between science and sports, the authors observe that coaches should be aware of how scientific research is done. This will make the coach more sensitive to the strengths and weaknesses of scientific research. As a coach, be more open to other approaches, while at the same time insisting on practical recommendations from the scientist. It is also advisable to read the literature on the most recent developments in taekwondo. Unfortunately, as was mentioned above, taekwondo research is still limited. However, reading relevant scientific literature in related areas, such as karate, judo, boxing, wrestling, and so on, may give the coach a clue how to improve his/her coaching. Reading the literature on other sports, such as running, swimming, and so forth, may yield valuable information for the taekwondo coach as well. Successful coaches usually observe coaches from other sports or read the literature on other sports to learn more about their own sport. Be honest about the things that one does not know. Do not think that you are the only one who knows something about taekwondo, or that you know everything there is to know about the sport. This also implies that the coach should try to educate him/herself, which may be done by going to seminars, workshops, symposia, instructor certification courses, and so on.

References

1. Ahn, B. H. (1985), *Kinematic and Kinetic Analysis of Taekwondo Kicking Motions,* Unpublished Master's Thesis, Purdue University.
2. Birrer, R. B. and Birrer, C. D. (1983), Unreported injuries in the martial arts, *British Journal of Sports Medicine,* 17, 2: 131 - 134.
3. Burkett, L. N. (1970), Causative factors in hamstring strain, *Medicine and Science in Sports,* 2, 1: 39 - 42.
4. Campbell, D. E. and Glenn, W. (1982), Rehabilitation of knee flexor and knee extensor muscle strength in patients with meniscectomies, ligamentous repairs, and chondromalacia, *Physical Therapy*, 62, 1: 10 - 15.
5. Carter, J. E. L. and Yuhasz, M. S. (1984), Skinfolds and body composition of Olympic athletes, In: J. E. L. Carter (ed.), *Physical Structure of Olympic Athletes*. Part II, Basel: S. Karger, pp. 144 - 182.
6. Choi, H. H. (1972), Taekwondo. *The Korean Art of Self-Defence*, Toronto: International Taekwondo Federation.
7. Chuang, T. Y. and Lieu, D. K. (1991), A parametric study of the thoracic injury potential of basic taekwondo kicks, In: K. Min (ed.), *USTU Instructors Handbook*, Third Edition, Berkeley: USTU Instructors Certification Committee, pp. 118 - 126.
8. Chun, R. (1982), *Advancing in Taekwondo,* New York: Harper & Row Publishers.
9. Conkel, B., Braucht, J., Wilson, W., Pieter, W., Taaffe, D., Fleck, S. and Kearney, J.T. (1988), Isokinetic torque, kick velocity and force in taekwondo, *Medicine and Science in Sports and Exercise,* 20, 2 (Supplement): S5.
10. Corcoran, J. and Farkas, E. (1983), *Martial Arts: Traditions, History, People,* New York: Gallery Books.
11. Draeger, D. F. (1975), *Classical Budo,* New York: Weatherhill.
12. Draeger, D. F. (1973), *Classical Bujutsu,* New York: Weatherhill.
13. Draeger, D. F. (1974), *Modern Bujutsu & Budo,* New York: Weatherhill.
14. Giove, T. P., Miller, S. J., Kent, B. E. et al. (1983), Nonoperative treatment of the torn anterior cruciate ligament, *Journal of Bone and Joint Surgery,* 65A, 2: 184 - 192.
15. Holmes, J. R. and Alderink, G. J. (1984), Isokinetic strength characteristics of the quadriceps femoris and hamstring muscles in high school students, *Physical Therapy*, 64, 6: 914 - 918.
16. Hwang, I. S. (1987), Analysis of the kicking leg in taekwondo, In: J. Terauds, B. Gowitzke and L. Holt (eds.), *Biomechanics in Sports III & IV. Proceedings of ISBS*, Del Mar, CA: Academic Publishers, pp. 39 - 47.

17. Hwang, I. S. (1985), Biomechanical analysis of dwihuryo-chagi in taekwondo, In: *A Collection of Research Papers in the 1st World Taekwondo Seminar*, Seoul: Kukkiwon, pp. 67 - 79.
18. Kim, C. (1991), *Perceived Motivational Factors Related to Initial Participation and Persistence in Taekwondo*, Eugene, OR: Microform Publications.
19. Kim, D. S. (1980), Sport and physical education in the Republic of Korea, In: W. Johnson (ed.), *Sport and Physical Education Around the World*, Champaign, IL: Stipes Publishing Company, pp. 383 - 398.
20. Matveyev, L. (1981), *Fundamentals of Sports Training*, Moscow: Progress Publishers.
21. Park, Y. D. (1981), *The Effects of Tension Recognition and Control of Beginning Taekwondo Instructors*, Unpublished Master's Thesis, State University College at Brockport.
22. Park, Y. J. (1989), *A Biomechanical Analysis of Taekwondo Front Kicks*, Eugene, OR: Microform Publications.
23. Pieter, F., Pieter, W. and Heijmans, J. (1987), Movement analysis of taekwondo techniques, *Asian Journal of Physical Education,* 10, 3: 45 - 58.
24. Pieter, W. (1987), Angst bij vechtsport, *Sport-Gericht,* 9, 3: 109 - 112.
25. Pieter, W. (1981), Etymological notes on the terminology of some Korean martial arts, *Asian Journal of Physical Education*, 4, 1: 47 - 52.
26. Pieter, W. (1985), Korean hwarang and Japanese samurai: a comparison, In: N. Müller and J. K. Rühl (eds.), *Olympic Scientific Congress Sport History Official Report,* Niedernhausen: Schors-Verlag, pp. 75 - 80.
27. Pieter, W. (1994), Notes on the historical development of Korean martial sports. An addendum to Young's History & development of tae kyon, *Journal of Asian Martial Arts*, 3, 1: 82 - 89.
28. Pieter, W. (1991), The Oregon Taekwondo Research Project, In: K. Min (ed.), *Taekwondo. USTU Instructors Handbook,* Third Edition, Berkeley, CA: USTU Instructors Certification Committee, pp. 160 - 165.
29. Pieter, W., Taaffe, D. and Heijmans, J. (1990), Heart rate response to taekwondo forms and technique combinations: a pilot study, *Journal of Sports Medicine and Physical Fitness,* 30, 1: 97 - 102
30. Pieter, W., Taaffe, D., Troxel, R. and Heijmans, J. (1989), Isokinetic peak torque of the quadriceps and hamstrings of college age taekwondo athletes, *Journal of Human Movement Studies,* 16, 1: 17 - 25.
31. Pieter, W., Taaffe, D., Troxel, R. and Heijmans, J. (1992), Quadriceps / hamstrings ratios of taekwondo club athletes and beginning tennis players, *Journal of Physical Education and Sport Sciences*, IV, 1: 31 - 39.

32. Pieter, W. and Zemper, E. D. (1990), The Oregon Taekwondo Research Project: part II - preliminary injury research results, *Taekwondo USA,* 3, 1: 24 - 26.
33. Rutt, R. (1961), The flower boys of Silla (hwarang). Notes on the sources, *Transactions of the Korea Branch of the Royal Asiatic Society*, XXXVIII, 1 - 66.
34. Serina, E. R. and Lieu, D. K. (1991), Thoracic injury potential of basic competition taekwondo kicks, *Journal of Biomechanics,* 24, 10: 951 - 960.
35. Skelton, D. L., Glynn, M. A. and Berta, S. M. (1991), Aggressive behavior as a function of taekwondo ranking, *Perceptual and Motor Skills,* 72, 1: 179 - 182.
36. Stull, R. A. and J. N. Barham (1990a), An analysis of movement patterns utilized by different styles in the karate reverse punch in front stance, In: E. Kreighbaum and A. McNeill (eds.), *Biomechanics in Sports VI. Proceedings of the 6th International Symposium on Biomechanics in Sports*, Bozeman, MT: International Society of Biomechanics in Sports and Department of Health and Human Development, Montana State University, pp. 233 - 243.
37. Stull, R. A. and J. N. Barham (1990b), An analysis of work and power produced by different styles in the karate reverse punch in front stance, In: E. Kreighbaum and A. McNeill (eds.), *Biomechanics in Sports VI. Proceedings of the 6th International Symposium on Biomechanics in Sports,* Bozeman, MT: International Society of Biomechanics in Sports and Department of Health and Human Development, Montana State University, pp. 225 - 231.
38. Sung, N. J., Lee, S. G., Park, H. J. and Joo, S. K. (1987), An analysis of the dynamics of the basic taekwondo kicks, *US Taekwondo Journal,* VI, 2: 10 - 15.
39. Thompson, W. R. and Vinueza, C. (1991), Physiologic profile of tae kwon do black belts, *Sports Medicine, Training and Rehabilitation*, 3, 1: 49 - 53.
40. Van Ingen Schenau, G. J. and Whiting, H. T. A. (1987), Wetenschap en sport, In: A. Vermeer (ed.), *Onderzoek van Menselijk Bewegen, Amsterdam: VU Uitgeverij*, pp. 37 - 53.
41. Wohlin, S. (1989), *A Biomechanical Description of the Taekwondo Turning Hook Kick,* Unpublished Master's Thesis, Montana State University.
42. Yi, K. D. (1979), Silla hwarangdo ui sahoehak chokko ch'al, *Yoksa Hakpo,* 82: 1 - 38.
43. Yoon, Y. J. and Pieter, W. (1996), *Skill level in taekwondo and selected measures of agility and balance in college age students*, submitted for publication.
44. Zandbergen, A. (no date), *Taekwondo Blessures en Fysiotherapie, Unpublished Thesis*, Twentse Akademie voor Fysiotherapie, Enschede.

CHAPTER II

SYSTEMATIC TRAINING IN TAEKWONDO

Introduction

Preparing taekwondo athletes for competition requires systematic and methodological planning of their training. Training may be defined as a process of stimuli that are goal-oriented and planned to enhance athletic performance. These stimuli are of a physical, psychological, technical and tactical nature. Physical stimuli are those that will bring about changes in physical appearance as well as in functional efficiency. In other words, training will affect the athlete's physique (less fat, more muscles), the athlete's bodily functions (more endurance, lower resting heart rate), and the athlete's flexibility. Technical training refers to optimizing taekwondo skills, such as kicking and punching. Tactical training involves plans of attack and defense to score a point before the adversary does. Psychological training refers to exercises that will facilitate improvements in self-confidence, concentration, as well as those that will lead to reduced anxiety levels. Figure II.1 shows the relationship between the various training stimuli. They are inseparable components of any training, but have been distinguished here for the sake of clarity.

Technical training needs a solid physical foundation. If the taekwondo athlete lacks the necessary strength, endurance or flexibility, he or she will not be able to execute the taekwondo skills as optimally as possible. Tactical training is based on physical, technical and psychological prerequisites (1). For instance, if the athlete is supposed to fake an attack before actually starting his or her offensive move(s), he/she needs the self-confidence that the fake plus actual attack will work to score a point. If this self-confidence is lacking, the fake will not be convincing and will fail. The athlete's plan of combat will also depend on his/her mastery of the various skills and his/her endurance. For instance, if the athlete is comfortable with the roundhouse kick only, he or she will most likely not include any other kick in his/her technique arsenal for competition. By the same token, if the athlete is lacking in endurance, for instance, he/she will make sure not to attack too long and/or too often.

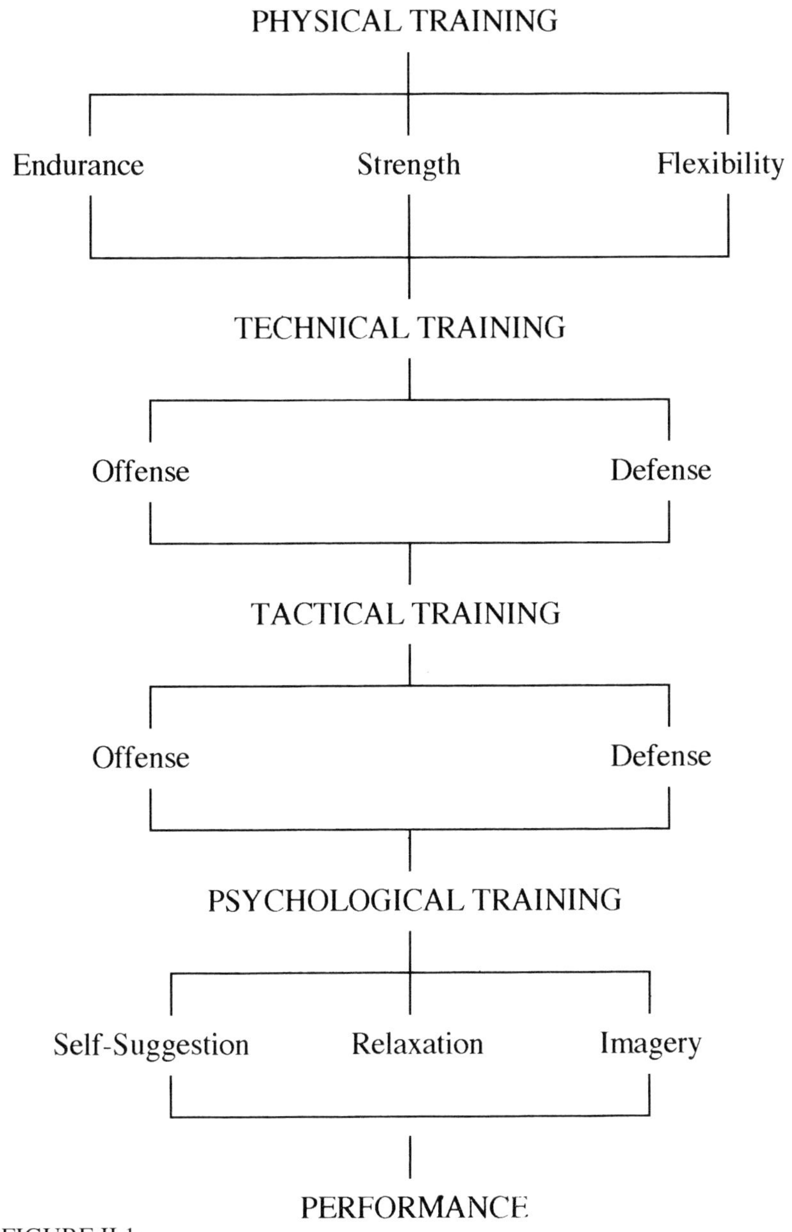

FIGURE II.1:
Preparation for Taekwondo Competition: Training Components (Based on 1).

Endurance and strength will be covered in chapters IV and V, respectively, while chapter VII will deal with psychological training. Chapters VI and VIII will detail the technical and tactical bases for taekwondo competition, respectively. In addition to these factors, others, such as flexibility, reaction time as well as movement time, will unfortunately stay out of the focus of this book. This is not to say that they are not important. On the contrary. They are definitely necessary to achieve success in competition. However, due to time and space restrictions, a selection of topics needed to be made. It was felt, that for the time being, the above mentioned variables should have priority, although flexibility will be covered briefly in chapter X.

Training always takes place according to certain goals (16), which may vary from winning a gold medal at the world championships to performing a taekwondo technique according to certain principles, to working out three days a week instead of two days. Training goals should be defined on an individual basis, which implies that training programs should be individualized. After the general goal has been determined, secondary goals need to be identified which in turn are broken down into contributing factors. For instance, suppose the general goal of training is defined as winning the national championships. In order to achieve this goal, the following secondary goals are identified: winning local tournaments and winning regional tournaments. The contributing factors are: technique development, speed, force, flexibility, psychological skills, tactical skills and (strength) endurance. Both the coach and taekwondo athlete ought to be aware that goals should be realistic and attainable. They should also be flexible, which means that in the event goals cannot be achieved because of an injury, for example, they have to be adjusted to meet the present situation.

To summarize, training is a way to improve the athlete's performance by means of physical, technical, psychological and tactical stimuli. It is done according to a certain method and is characterized by a systematic approach. Physical stimuli, such as running, lifting weights, kicking and punching, will lead to changes in physique, in the body's capacity to endure a specified work load, while technical and tactical training will result in a more efficient way of moving and scoring points, respectively. Psychological stimuli, such as a pat on the back, encouraging words, relaxation exercises, will lead to positive changes in the mental make-up of the athlete. Physical, technical, psychological and tactical stimuli are all intended to achieve a certain training goal, such as winning a gold medal.

In order to optimize the athlete's preparation for competition, the taekwondo coach needs to know how to stress the athlete in such a way that his or her health is not endangered. The coach needs to know how to manipulate work and rest periods to enhance the athlete's adaptation to training, which is called the training effect. For instance, running will improve the athlete's endurance, while strength training will improve the athlete's strength. These improvements are called training effects. To aid the coach with a more systematic approach to training, certain training principles need to be adhered to. These principles are: specificity, overload and progressive application (15). Training overload is accomplished by: frequency, duration, intensity and mode of training (5).

The principle of *specificity of training* dictates that the training overload the training components that are most important to taekwondo competition. For instance, when developing endurance in taekwondo, the workouts should be geared toward overloading the specific metabolic systems involved, i.e., a combination of aerobic and anaerobic endurance (see chapter IV). *Overload involves volume* (frequency and duration) and *intensity* of the training stimuli to bring about *physiological adaptations*. Overloading the specific metabolic systems should be done in a progressive manner that is *gradual* and *discontinuous* in nature (2). This implies that periods of high-intensity training should be interspersed with recovery periods of decreased volume and intensity, because it is during this time that adaptation occurs (2).

Applying the principle of specificity to taekwondo ultimately means that in order to prepare the taekwondo athlete for competition, competition-specific exercises need to be done. This sounds logical and yet there are still coaches (as well as athletes), who think that running to improve endurance a few weeks before competition should be employed. Running as a means of training will improve general endurance, be it aerobic or anaerobic, but will do little in the way of taekwondo-specific endurance (see chapter IV).

Overloading the system means that the training load should be increased to meet the new training status of the athlete. For instance, during strength training, the athlete is able to bench press 60 kg. After one or two weeks, a training effect will occur in that the athlete will have gained strength. In order to accommodate for this strength gain, the load should be increased by 5 kg, for example, given the same number of repetitions. If the object is to gain in strength, the system (i.e., the muscles) has to be overloaded. If the object is to maintain strength levels, no overload is necessary. Overloading applies to any of the factors trained, be it strength, endurance, speed, or concentration.

Progressive overload that is discontinuous in nature has to do with alternating work and rest periods. The training load, which should increase progressively, is applied during the work periods, whereas the training effects take place during the rest periods. If the interplay between work and recovery periods are not carefully planned, the athlete will become overstressed which will eventually lead to a decrease in performance and even health problems (see Recovery and Taper-Off below). Both the work and rest periods may be manipulated by alternating heavy and light workouts and by short or long periods of rest. However, the recovery periods should not be too long, since any training effects may disappear that way. Figure II.2 shows the interaction between training or workload and recovery.

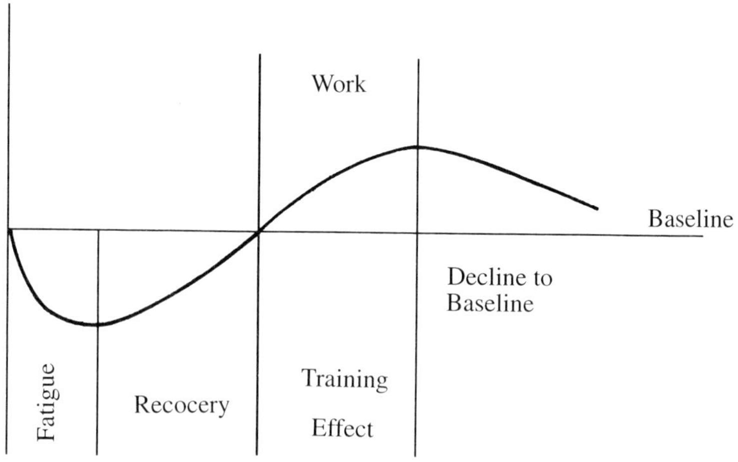

FIGURE II.2: Interaction between Workload, Recovery and Training Effect

A certain workload will temporarily lead to fatigue, which, in turn, will have a negative effect on performance. After that, recovery will set in and lead to a higher performance level than before, which is the training effect. The new training load should be applied during the time the training effect occurs and preferably at the highest point of this effect. If no training stimulus is applied, performance will deteriorate until it reaches the level before training started (see also Recovery and Taper-Off).

Frequency of training refers to how often the taekwondo athlete trains. It is usually expressed in terms of days per week. A minimum requirement to get a training effect is to practice three days a week. For elite athletes, this minimum requirement is not sufficient anymore, unless it is used to recuperate from very intensive workloads. For a taekwondo athlete, frequency typically involves four to six days of training. Depending on the time of the season, the athlete may choose to do three days of general conditioning and three days of taekwondo training. Later, the athlete may switch to five or six days of taekwondo training and a minimum of general conditioning training to maintain acquired levels, such as general strength.

Duration of training refers to the duration of a single training session, but also to series of training sessions. For instance, a typical taekwondo training may last for two hours, while running to improve aerobic endurance may have a duration of 30 minutes.

Intensity refers to how "heavy" a training session is. Depending on the exercise, intensity may be expressed as *heart beats per minute* (bpm) (figure II.3) or as a certain *resistance* to move, such as in strength training. Intensity may also reflect the number of *repetitions* a weight is lifted, or the *number of laps run*, or the number of repetitions to run a specified distance, such as ten times the 100 m dash, or *the time* exercised.

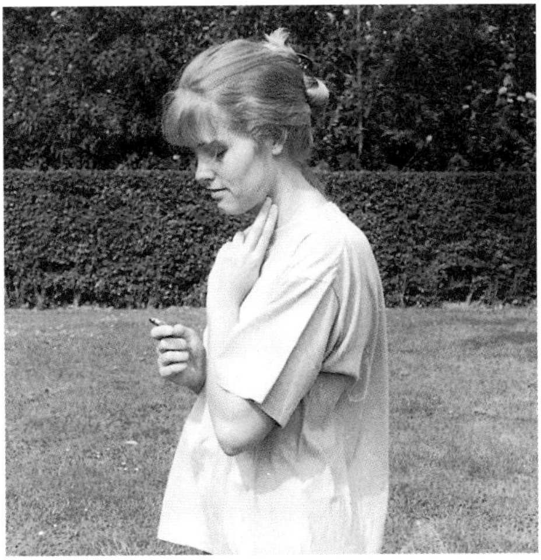

FIGURE II.3: Taking Heart Rates

When using heart rates to represent training intensity, the Karvonen formula is typically employed (5). This formula requires the athlete or coach to assess the athlete's resting heart rate and his/her maximal heart rate. Maximal heart rate may be found by subtracting one's age from 220. The relationship between the athlete's age and his or her maximum heart rate is depicted in figure II.4.
The Karvonen formula is as follows:

$$HR_{ex} = HR_{rest} + \% \, (HR_{max} - HR_{rest})$$

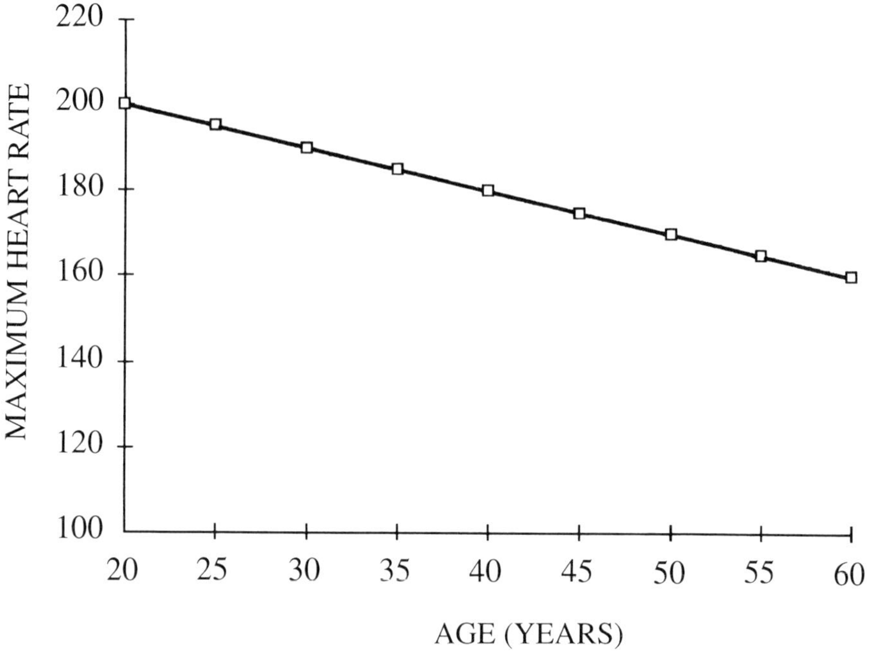

FIGURE II.4: The Relationship between Age and Maximum Heart Rate

where HR_{ex} = exercise heart rate and HR_{rest} = heart rate at rest. Heart rate at rest may be taken before training by having the athlete lie down in a supine position for about ten minutes after which the heart rate is taken. It may also be taken in the morning before getting out of bed, in which case it is sometimes called the morning heart rate. Applying this formula to taekwondo training would give the following exercise heart rate for a 20-year old athlete with a resting heart rate of 60 bpm, a max HR of 200 (= 220 - 20) and training at 70% of max HR:

$$HR_{ex} = 60 + 0.70\,(200 - 60) = 158 \text{ bpm.}$$

Mode of training is simply the exercise employed to bring about any training effects. For instance, to improve aerobic endurance, running, swimming or bicycling may be used as the mode of training. To improve kicking force, taekwondo will be the mode of training, while improvements in strength may be done by engaging in a strength training program.

An example of the training principles as applied to taekwondo training is shown in table II.1.

TABLE II.1: Example of Training Program for Pre-Season

WEEK 1 – 3			
Frequency	**Duration**	**Intensity**	**Mode**
Monday	-	-	rest
Tuesday	15 minutes	75% HR_{max}	running
Wednesday	2 hours	75% HR_{max}	taekwondo
Thursday	15 minutes	75% HR_{max}	running
Friday	2 hours	75% HR_{max}	taekwondo
Saturday	15 minutes	75% HR_{max}	running
Sunday	2 hours	75% HR_{max}	taekwondo
WEEK 4 - 6			
Frequency	**Duration**	**Intensity**	**Mode**
Monday	-	-	rest
Tuesday	20 minutes	75% HR_{max}	running
Wednesday	2 hours	80% HR_{max}	taekwondo
Thursday	20 minutes	75% HR_{max}	running
Friday	2 hours	80% HR_{max}	taekwondo
Saturday	20 minutes	75% HR_{max}	running
Sunday	2 hours	80% HR_{max}	taekwondo

A more detailed explanation of a table like this will be given in subsequent chapters. For now, the following will suffice. It is assumed that the athlete will work out six days a week, once a day. It is also assumed that the athlete will work on general endurance in the pre-season and on taekwondo skills on alternate days. The frequency of training, then, is six days a week, once a day. The duration depends on the mode of training. If general (aerobic) endurance is the objective, the mode of training may be running (running would be more specific to taekwondo than swimming, for instance), in which case the duration per training session may be 15 minutes, not including warm-up and cool-down. Taekwondo training is set at two hours per session. The intensity of running is arbitrarily chosen and set at 75% of the age-predicted maximum heart rate (HR_{max}) according to Karvonen's formula. In this example, the intensity for the taekwondo training is also set at 75% of HR_{max}. Since the training overload has to be progressive, the duration for the running part was increased from 15 to 20 minutes after three weeks, while the intensity remained at 75% of HR_{max}. For the taekwondo part, the duration remained the same, but the intensity was increased from 75% to 80% of HR_{max}.

Although training has to be progressive in order to result in any training effects, there will come a time that improvements will start to show a levelling-off, preceded by smaller increments of improvement compared to the beginning of training (see figure II.5).

In other words, the longer the athlete is in training, the more difficult it will be to improve performance. As can be seen from figure II.5, over the same amount of time, less training effect has resulted from training during period II compared

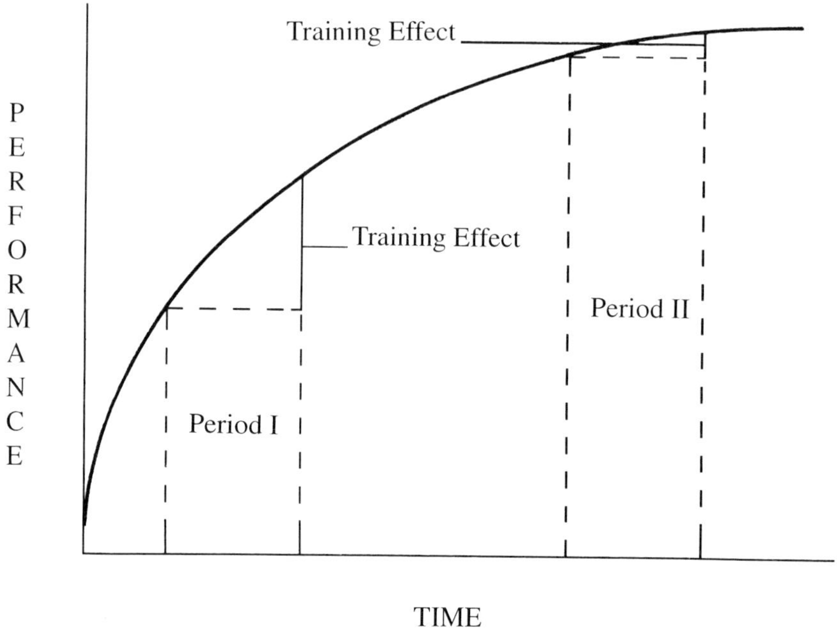

FIGURE II.5: The Relationship between Length of Training and Training Effect

to period I. The coach will have to be very creative in manipulating the training stimuli and training principles that will lead to the desired training effects. A strength program using different machines (e.g., free weights, nautilus), and endurance training on a different surface (e.g., instead of running on a track, the athlete may choose to run on the beach) are two examples of how this may be done.

Recovery and Taper-Off

Recovery

As alluded to above, the main goal or purpose of training is to improve one's performance during competition. The aforementioned principles of training are based on the knowledge that the human body adapts itself to the situation it is subjected to. In order to achieve a training effect (or, in more technical terms, *overcompensation*), the athlete surrenders his/her body to ever greater demands. The interaction between work and recovery periods and the importance of adequate rest are illustrated in figures II.6 - II.8.

In figure II.6, the workload is applied *after* the training effect is on the decline, which will result in a performance level that will be an extension of the previous level, i.e., the training load did not have any training effect whatsoever. Instead, the next workload needs to be applied during the period of the training effect. If it is applied after that, it will not lead to any increased performance.

Figure II.7 shows the vital importance of adequate rest. If the stimulus is applied before the body is fully recovered from the previous training load, the result will be a decrease in performance. No training effect occurred.
If the workload is systematically applied *before* adequate rest, the result will be a burnt-out athlete, who will not only experience a decrease in performance, but who will also have a higher chance of getting injured, which in turn will interfere with the athlete's training: a vicious circle that can only be broken by forced rest (see also chapter VII and section on Overtraining below).

Figure II.8, finally, displays the adequate interaction between workload and recovery that will lead to increased performance. The training effects will get a chance to be cumulative after the appropriate timing of the training stimuli. The training load may also be increased to lead to the desired effects, which could not be done in the previous two cases.

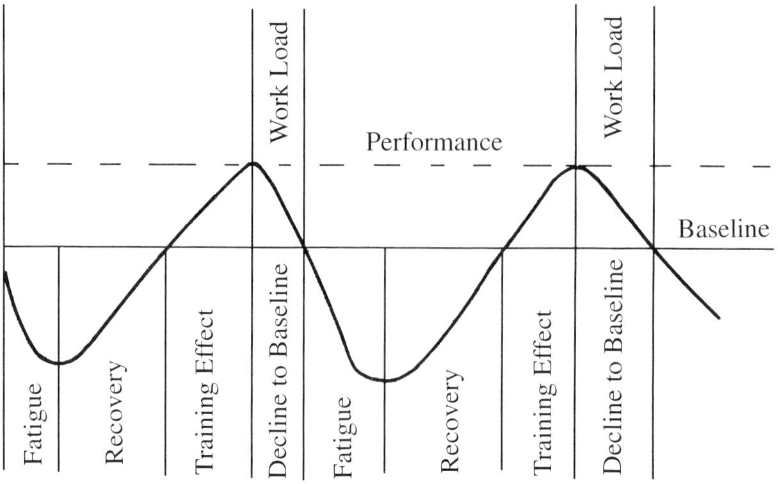

FIGURE II.6: Workload Applied after Training Effect Has Disappeared

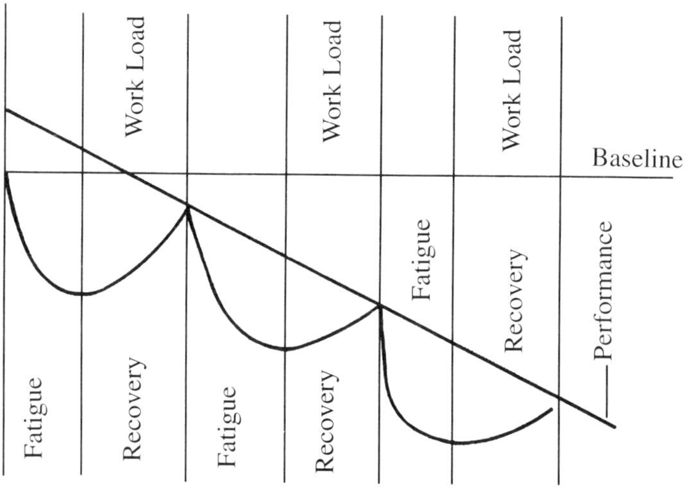

FIGURE II.7: Workload Applied before Adequate Recovery

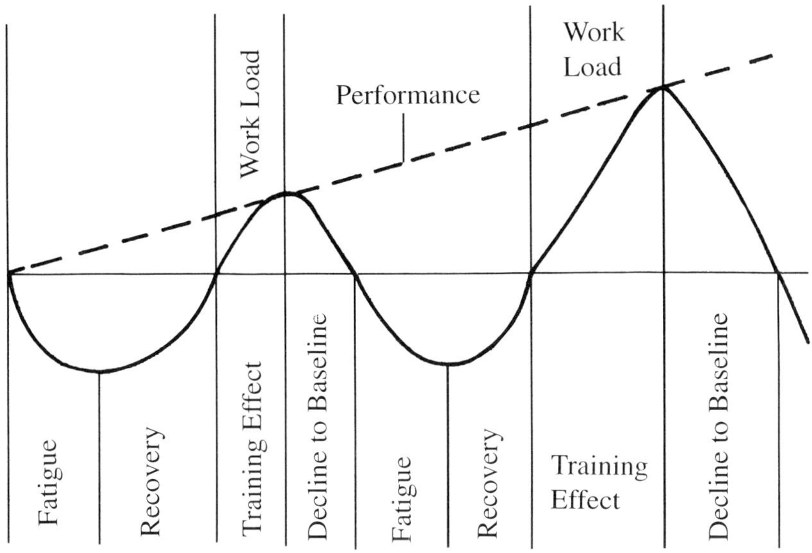

FIGURE II.8: Appropriate Timing of Workload and Recovery

Unfortunately, it is not possible to indicate the precise duration of the recovery periods. First of all, the recovery depends on the preceding training stimulus. A strenuous workout will need a longer recovery than a workload that was done at a low intensity. For instance, after an aerobic workout at 75% of maximum HR, a relatively short recovery period will suffice. After an intensive anaerobic workout at 95 - 100% of maximum HR, however, a much longer recovery will be needed. Of course, the training status of the athlete also plays a role here. Secondly, the recovery period depends on the athlete. If the athlete is still tired from the preceding workload, regardless of its intensity, a longer recovery may be in order. Thirdly, job-related or study-related stress may influence the recovery periods as well. Personal factors and sickness also exert their own specific impact on the recovery process of the athlete. A rule of thumb is to advise both the athlete and coach to listen to the former's body. If the athlete does not feel 100%, a decreased workload should be applied. A list of possible signs that will help the coach and athlete alike in determining when it is probably not appropriate to apply the training stimulus is presented below (see section on Overtraining). Another preventive measure is to alternate heavy and light workouts (see table II.2).

TABLE II.2 Alternating Heavy and Lighter Workouts During In-Season

WEEK 1 - 3

Frequency	**Duration**	**Intensity**	**Mode**
Monday	-	-	rest
Tuesday	2 hours	70% HR_{max}	taekwondo
Wednesday	2 hours	75% HR_{max}	taekwondo
Thursday	2 hours	95% HR_{max}	taekwondo
Friday	2 hours	80% HR_{max}	taekwondo
Saturday	2 hours	75% HR_{max}	taekwondo
Sunday	2 hours	95% HR_{max}	taekwondo

Heavy and lighter workloads can also be used during any single training session. For instance, on Tuesday one could choose to alternate the exercise heart rate between 65% and 70% of HR_{max} during the 2-hour training session.

The suggestions below have been made to aid in determining the most adequate recovery period. In general, a *full* recovery period is recommended in the following cases (13):

training of the athlete's coordination;
training of maximal strength;
after subsequent tournaments;
technique training;
training of speed, reaction time or explosiveness.

It is also possible to start the next workload after a partial recovery period, which would be indicated in the following cases (13):

training of speed-endurance;
training of strength-endurance;
training of general and specific endurance;
training of willpower.

So, if the objective of the taekwondo athlete's training, during the pre-season, for instance, is to work on his/her techniques, the coach should make sure to adhere to full recovery periods. This means that technique training is characterized by long periods of rest and short periods of work. If the goal of the workout is to develop both speed and endurance, partial recovery periods may be employed. In other words, relatively short work periods interspersed with relatively short periods of rest. It is impossible to be very specific about the exact time frame of both periods of work and rest. They all depend on individual circumstances. A possible example would be to exercise for 30 seconds and have a rest period of one minute and a half during technique training. To develop speed-endurance, a ratio of 30 seconds of work and 30 seconds of rest may be used. Recovery periods may vary in duration and intensity. They may be active or passive. Active recovery is preferred, since this is the best way to get rid of any waste products in the blood.

A good example of the effect of inadequate rest on performance is shown in figure II.9. Before the first training session, the athlete had some socio-psychological problems, which had led to a sleepless night before the day of the workout. As can be seen from the graph, the athlete's recovery heart rate on that day (day 1 in figure II.9) was way too high. Instead of scheduling a training session the next

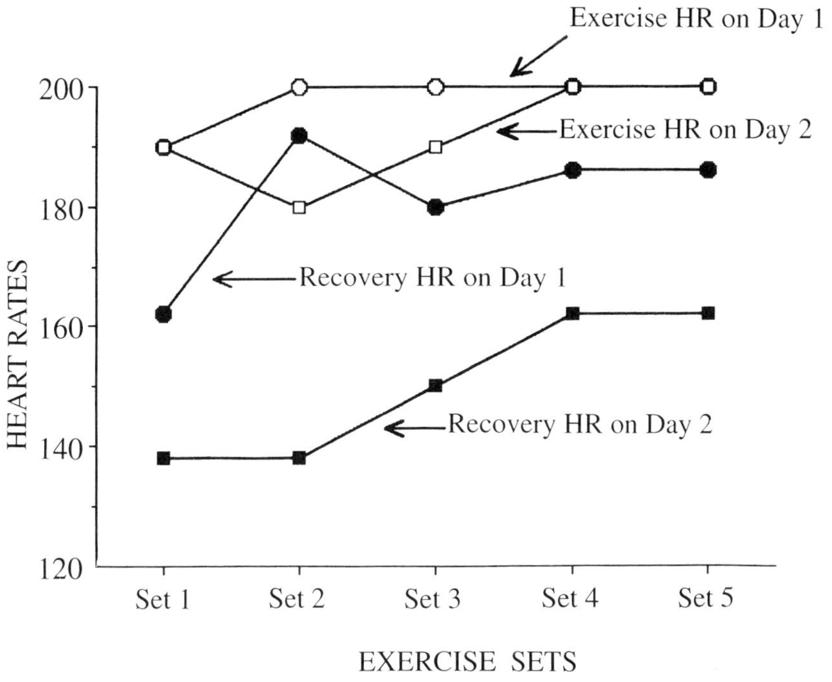

FIGURE II.9: The Effect of Inadequate Rest on Performance

day, the athlete was given the day off in order to rest and to attend to the problems. After that, another training session was scheduled (day 2 in the graph). Clearly, the recovery heart rates were much better. The graph, in addition to the entries to the athlete's training log (not reported here), also shows the effect of environmental factors on athletic performance. In this particular case, the environmental factor was the support group or rather, the lack thereof.

To summarize, there is a delicate balance between work and rest in the athlete's training. IT IS DURING THE RECOVERY PERIOD THAT ANY TRAINING EFFECT WILL OCCUR. If the workload is applied after the training effect has disappeared, the resultant improvement in performance will be annihilated. If the training stimulus is applied before the athlete has had a chance to recover from a(n intensive) workout, performance will decrease. Alternating heavy and lighter workouts may be employed to ensure an adequate interaction between training load and recovery. Depending on the training objective, full or partial recovery periods may be utilized.

Taper-off

The crucial role of adequate rest lies at the basis of the phenomenon of tapering-off. Prior to competition, a taper-off period is implemented to give the athlete a chance to recuperate from intensive workouts, to give minor injuries a chance to heal and to facilitate peak performance. *The taper-off period is characterized by reduced training and, a few days prior to competition, even no training at all.* Depending on the individual situation, the taekwondo coach may decide to taper anywhere from between one to two or even more weeks.

Most coaches feel uncomfortable including a taper-off period in their training program, thinking that any gains from months of hard work may be lost in a matter of days or even hours. However, the effects of detraining are less severe than one would tend to think. In fact, research has shown that swimmers experienced an improvement in performance after reduced training as well as an increase in muscular strength (17). Of course, this does not necessarily imply that the same effects will also be observed to the same extent in athletes from other sports. In order to give the taekwondo coach a better appreciation of the effects of reduced training, results from research pertaining to detraining will be presented next.

Inactivity showed no significant effects on loss of muscular strength up to four weeks after cessation of training. Reduced training does not seem to have any major effects on anaerobic endurance either, although complete inactivity, such as immobilization (e.g., total body cast) may affect this type of endurance within the first two weeks (17). Since the taper-off period for taekwondo athletes is not characterized by complete inactivity, this finding is not relevant for taekwondo coaches. Speed and agility are less affected by training than strength, for instance (17). Therefore, potential losses in these two variables will be even less than for strength or anaerobic endurance during the taper-off period. Flexibility, however, should be maintained year-round, since it is lost rather quickly as well as gained rather quickly. It should come as no surprise, then, that flexibility is maintained throughout the taper-off period. Aerobic endurance will deteriorate faster than any of the other training factors, even within some three weeks after bed rest (17).

Any decrease in aerobic endurance during the taper-off period will be negligible, though, since the taper will consist of reduced training and only a few days of no training, which are not exactly similar to three weeks of bed rest. During the off-season, however, aerobic endurance should be maintained as much as possible. The "loss" during the taper-off period will not be as dramatic as some taekwondo coaches seem to think, so that the athlete's fine tuning for his or her peak performance should not be affected appreciably. The longer the athlete's preparation for competition, the longer it will take to lose the gains from hard training. A taper-off period from between seven to ten days prior to competition, depending on the individual situation, would be advised for taekwondo athletes. STRENUOUS TRAINING DURING THE WEEK OF COMPETITION IS DEFINITELY NOT RECOMMENDED.

An example of a taper-off period is shown in table II.3. It is assumed that the taper lasts for ten days and that the first day of competition is on a Saturday and that Friday is used to travel to the competition site. Remember that the taper, just like the training program, is individualized. If one has to be at the tournament site a few days before competition starts, the coach should take that into account when designing the taper-off program. Also, travelling by air will affect the athlete differently than travelling by car.

The first few days of the taper may consist of stretching, warm-up kicks and/or low-intensity taekwondo workouts. Two to three days prior to competition, the workout may only consist of stretching. As can be seen from table II.3, the total duration of the taekwondo workout has been reduced to 90 - 60 minutes instead of two hours, with a further reduction for stretching three days before competition. In other words, the taper in this case consists of a reduction in duration as well as in intensity.

TABLE II.3 Example of Taper-Off Program

Day	Duration	Intensity	Mode
Wednesday	90 minutes	60% HR_{max}	taekwondo
Thursday	90 minutes	70% HR_{max}	taekwondo
Friday	90 minutes	60% HR_{max}	taekwondo
Saturday	60 minutes	50% HR_{max}	taekwondo
Sunday	60 minutes	50% HR_{max}	taekwondo
Monday	-	-	rest
Tuesday	30 minutes	-	stretching
Wednesday	30 minutes	-	stretching
Thursday	30 minutes	-	stretching
Friday		travel	
Saturday	day of competition		

If the athlete is subjected to intensive training bouts without adequate rest, he/she will eventually show signs of overtraining, which is also called staleness or burn-out. Overtraining is usually the result of a long-term process, but may also be realized on a short-term basis. In both cases, physiological and psychological symptoms will be evident and the result will always be a decrease in performance. The next section will discuss some of the physiological concomitants of overtraining, while a more detailed coverage from a psychological perspective will be presented in chapter VII.

Overtraining

Overtraining results from a disrupted work - rest interaction. In other words, if the athlete trains too hard for too long without taking adequate rest, the end product will be overtraining. Every workout is called a stressor: it puts stress on the individual, both in a physical and psychological sense. Psychological stress may also result from work, peers, relatives, friends, and so on. The total stress (physical and psychological) that the athlete has to endure will contribute to the athlete getting overtrained if no adequate recovery is adhered to. Although certain athletes seem to be more vulnerable to react to a stressor as described above than others, there are definite physiological and psychological signs that are indicative of overtraining or exhaustion. Some of these symptoms are listed in table II.4.

TABLE II.4 Selected Symptoms of Overtraining

A rise in the athlete's morning pulse (e.g., 8; 10)
Decreased performance (e.g., 7)
Reduced body weight (e.g., 7)
Emotional instability (e.g., 7; 8)
Sleep disturbance (e.g., 8; 10)
Depression (e.g., 10; 14)
Increased body temperature (e.g., 9)

To repeat, it should be understood here that overtraining is sometimes called staleness or burnout. All three terms will be used interchangeably in this book.

Although overtraining, as a result of training/competition and leading to a decrease in performance, is a familiar phenomenon to coaches, athletes and scientists alike, little objective data exist about it, especially in elite athletes (e.g., 12). One of the things that is known, however, is that there are two forms of overtraining: short-term and long-term overtraining. Short-term overtraining may be effectuated by (sudden) increases in training load, while long-term overtraining is the result of the cumulative effect of the athlete's training program. Although these two aspects of overtraining have a different physiological effect on the athlete that may also depend on the athlete's sport (4; 12), they both will result in decreased performance.

Dick Brown (3) has suggested that a rise of ten percent or more in the athlete's morning pulse may be an indication to reduce the next training load. Ten percent less sleep than normal may be another telltale sign to reduce the training load as are body weight oscillations of three percent. Therefore, it is recommended to weigh oneself every day at the same time to detect any changes in body weight. If the athlete was not able to finish the workout as planned, this may yet be another reason to cut back on the training load. The message again is to listen to the athlete's body and to plan both workload and recovery accordingly.

Although each athlete will react differently to the same training stimulus, as mentioned before, it may be helpful to use a five-point scale as suggested by Kuipers (11) to assess the athlete's reaction to the training load. A score of one or two may be used to continue to work out, whereas a score of three or higher should be an indication to modify the training load.

The scale is as follows:

1 = the athlete feels "strong"; everything seems to go easy and the athlete has the feeling that he/she can accomplish anything;

2 = although everything is going o.k., high intensity loads lead to slight fatigue; however, with a little extra willpower the athlete is still able to perform;

3 = the legs do not really feel well; low intensity workouts can be sustained, but high intensity bouts feel more strenuous than normal;

4 = the legs do not feel well: there does not seem to be any power in them and even low intensity workouts feel heavy;

5 = the legs do not feel well at all; they are tired, feel heavy and lack power; only very low intensity loads can be sustained.

This scale is a rough approximation of how athletes, on the average, may react to the training stimuli. It will aid the athlete to sort out his/her feelings regarding the workload, but should not be used as the only tool to indicate his/her response to training. Additional entries in the athlete's training log will definitely help both the athlete and coach in assessing and determining the appropriate work and recovery periods. In general, the athlete should make an attempt to describe how he/she feels before, during and after a workout, regardless of whether the scale above meets whatever it is that he/she has to report. If the scale meets how one feels, by all means, use it, but do not consider it something that has to be used at all cost.

Decreased performance is the one variable that is of the greatest concern to elite athletes in case they burn out. Although they may be able to sustain high intensity training loads for a long time, they will eventually suffer from the adverse effects of overstressing their body. Elite judo athletes, for instance, have been found to decrease in strength during an overtraining period, while it improved when their total training load was lowest (4). It should be remembered, however, that in a sport such as taekwondo, other symptoms of overtraining may be apparent than have been diagnosed for more aerobic oriented activities (see table II.4) (4). In addition, sport-specific performance, as is evident in a taekwondo bout or tournament, may be affected by overtraining without any physiological symptoms, such as a decrease in strength, endurance, or other factors. Strength may be affected in an overtraining situation, but this may not necessarily be the case for other variables and vice versa. Psychological factors, such as a low level of vigor and high levels of tension and fatigue in addition to a decrease in strength and other physiological components, may very well lead to a more noticeable decrease in taekwondo performance than any of the variables in themselves.

TABLE II.5
Selected Factors That May Facilitate Overtraining (Based on 6 and 11)

Coach-Related	**Athlete-Related**	**Environment-Related**
Overlooking rest periods	Insufficient hours of sleep	Overwhelming family-related responsibilities
Abrupt increases in training load after rest, illness, vacation, etc.	Excessive smoking, alcohol, etc. Poor diet	Frustration due to work, family, peers, husband, wife, etc.
Placing training demands on the athlete exceeding his/her capacity	Conflicts with peers, husband, friends, etc.	Fights with family, wife, husband, etc. regarding taekwondo
Monotony of training	Illness, high fever, allergies	Dissatisfaction with work, study

By way of summary, table II.5 displays some of the causes that may lead to overtraining. It is most likely that any one cause in itself may not be sufficient to lead to overtraining, but that a combination of these factors will most likely result in a state of burnout. Regardless of the cause, overtraining, again, will invariably lead to a decrease in performance and to injuries. Both the coach and athlete should remember that the stress put on the athlete in the form of weekly training loads are not the only stressors that the athlete has to deal with. A wise coach will make sure to inform him/herself of the other potential stressors that the athlete is faced with and to adjust his/her training schedule accordingly. The responsibility of the athlete, in turn, is to reduce those stressors that are under his/her control, such as getting sufficient sleep, taking care of injuries, avoiding excessive use of alcohol and other stimulants, and so on. A (sport) psychologist may be consulted to deal with more complicated problem areas, such as work-related stress, family conflicts, and so forth.

There is a number of options that the taekwondo coach and athlete have in dealing with factors that are related to burnout (1). Both may seek more knowledge about the training process, work-rest ratio and the phenomenon of overtraining. If the coach-related problems persist, the athlete may want to look for an-other coach. On the other hand, the coach may be honest to all concerned and advise the athlete to go to a better qualified coach. If the athlete- or environment-related problems persist, the athlete may want to redefine his/her goals in terms of training and competition. In all cases, both the coach and athlete may seek help from others, such as a physician or a (sport) psychologist.

References

1. Bompa, T. O. (1983), *Theory and Methodology of Training*, Dubuque, Iowa: Kendall/Hunt Publishing Company.
2. Brooks, G. A. and Fahey, T. D. (1985), *Exercise Physiology. Human Bioenergetics and Its Applications,* New York: MacMillan Publishing Company.
3. Brown, R. (1986), Stop signs. Stress-proof running by learning when to yield to four telltale signals, *Runner's World,* 21, 5: 72-73.
4. Callister, R., Callister, R. J., Fleck, S. J. and Dudley, G. A. (1990), Physiological and performance responses to overtraining in elite judo athletes, *Medicine and Science in Sport and Exercise*, 22, 6: 816 - 824.
5. Fox, E. and Mathews, D. (1981), *The Physiological Basis of Physical Education and Athletics,* Philadelphia: Saunders College Publishing.
6. Harre, D. (ed.) (1981), *Trainingslehre*, Berlin: Sportverlag.
7. Hollmann, W. and Hettinger, T. (1980), *Sportmedizin, Arbeits und Trainingsgrundlagen*, Stuttgart: F. K. Schattauer Verlag, pp. 549 - 552.
8. Israel, S. (1976), Problematik des Übertrainings aus internistischer und leistungsphysiologischer Sicht, *Medizin und Sport*, 16, 1: 1 - 12.
9. Kereszty, A. (1971), Overtraining, In: L. A. Larson (ed.), *Encyclopedia of Sport Sciences and Medicine,* New York: The MacMillan Co., pp. 218 - 222.
10. Kindermann, W. (1986), Das Übertraining - Ausdruck einer vegetativen Fehlsteuerung, *Deutsche Zeitschrift für Sportmedizin*, H8: 138 - 145.
11. Kuipers, H. (1991), *Melkzuur, Anaerobe Drempel, Tests, Optimalisering van Training*, Haarlem: De Vrieseborch.
12. Lehmann, M., Dickhuth, H. H., Gendrisch, G., Lazar, W., Thum, M., Kaminski, R., Aramendi, J. F., Peterke, E., Wieland, W. and Keul, J. (1991), Training - overtraining. A prospective, experimental study with experienced middle- and long-distance runners, *International Journal of Sports Medicine*, 12, 5: 444 - 452.
13. Martin, D. (1979), *Grundlagen der Trainingslehre. Teil 1: Die inhaltliche Struktur des Trainingsprozesses*, Schorndorf: K. Hofmann Verlag.

14. Morgan, W. P. (1985), Selected psychological factors limiting performance: a mental health model, In: D. H. Clarke and H. M. Eckert (eds.), *Limits of Human Performance.* The Academy Papers #18, Champaign, IL: Human Kinetics Publishers, pp. 70 - 80.
15. Noble, B. J. (1986), *Physiology of Exercise and Sport,* St. Louis, etc.: Times Mirror/Mosby College Publishing.
16. Vrijens, J. (1988), *Basis Voor Verantwoord Trainen*, Gent: W. Verbessem.
17. Wilmore, J. H. and Costill, D. L. (1988), *Training for Sport and Activity*, Dubuque, Iowa: Wm. C. Brown Publishers.

CHAPTER III

PERIODIZATION IN TAEKWONDO

Introduction

Periodization simply refers to dividing the season into periods. On the basis of suggestions by Matvejev (5), three periods are usually distinguished (2): the pre-season, in-season and off-season. During the pre-season, general and specific conditioning are emphasized as well as sport-specific, i.e., taekwondo-specific, requirements. The in-season is the time of competition where competition-specific drills and exercises are practiced. The off-season, finally, is the period to recuperate from the previous two parts of the total season in order to be refreshed for the next season. The goal, of course, is to peak at the right time, whether once or more times a year.

Peaking

Peaking is a training state in which physical, technical, tactical and psychological factors all "fall into place" to result in a performance that is the apex of the competition period. It is a moment where everything just "feels" right and the athlete is at the height of his/her present possibilities. As alluded to above, one may peak more than once a year. In taekwondo, one may want to peak between 2 - 3 times, depending on the competition calendar of that year. Typically, peaking is done for important tournaments, but the athlete may choose to participate in more test competitions than those for which he/she wants to peak. The athlete will need several of these less important competitions in order to fine-tune him/herself for his/her peak performance. Peaking is characterized by excellent health, absence of injuries and psychological readiness (highly motivated, focused, self-confident) as well as physical and physiological preparedness of the athlete (1).

Figure III.1 shows an example of the three periods that the entire season is divided into and, in this case, when the athlete wants to peak. Between peaks, the athlete should taper-off with reduced volume and intensity of training (see previous chapter). Too many peaks should be avoided as the athlete will run the risk of getting exhausted (burnt out). Taper-off periods prior to certain test tournaments may not be as important as those prior to the major competitions. For instance, if there is a dual meet between two schools, no tapering may be necessary. If there is a local tournament, tapering may be employed, while it is definitely indicated prior to team trials or national championships.

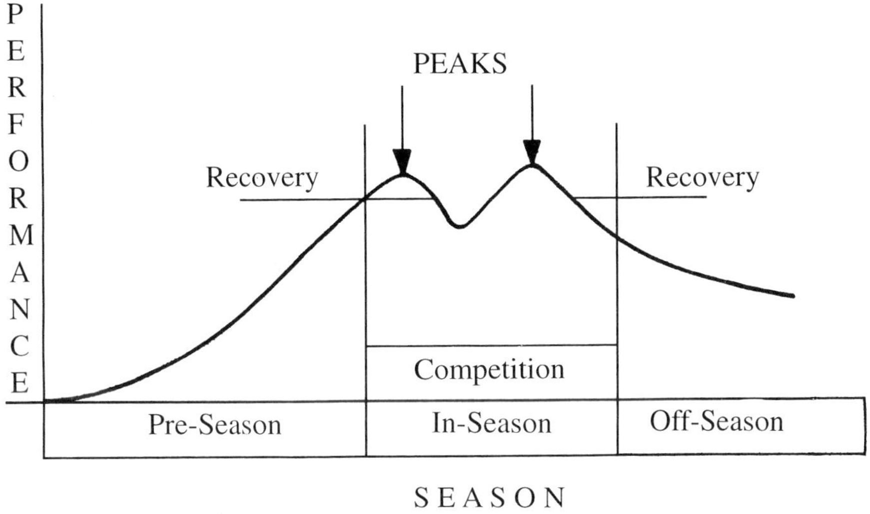

FIGURE III.1: Peaking During In-Season

According to Bompa (1), there are several factors that will enhance peaking. Peaking is the result of a complex interplay between these factors and they should not be considered in isolation as contributing to peaking. The following factors are identified:

The capacity to endure high intensity work and to recover quickly. If the athlete lacks the capacity to sustain high intensity training loads, chances are that he/she will not do as well during competition either. Competition, of course, is characterized by extremely high stress (physical, technical, tactical and psychological) put on the athlete. Similarly, the potential to recover from these very strenuous stimuli will influence the athlete's peaking ability.

Almost perfect neuro-muscular coordination. This refers to the capacity to perform almost flawlessly from a technical and tactical point of view. For instance, if the athlete lacks in the technically correct execution of the roundhouse or spinning back kicks in taekwondo, his/her chances of peaking will be reduced accordingly. By the same token, even if the skills were mastered to a high degree, the lack of similarly well-developed tactics will keep the athlete from peaking as well. When to use a roundhouse kick instead of another technique is as important as knowing how to execute it and vice versa.

Gaining training effects from one's preparation. Only by carefully planning the work and recovery periods will the athlete be able to get any training effects and, as a result, be able to peak for major competitions.

Tapering prior to (major) competitions and adequate rest intervals during high intensity workouts are main contributors to peaking. The interaction between volume of training (frequency and duration), which is characteristic of the *quantity of training*, and *intensity of training,* which is characteristic of the *quality of training*, is shown in figure III.2.

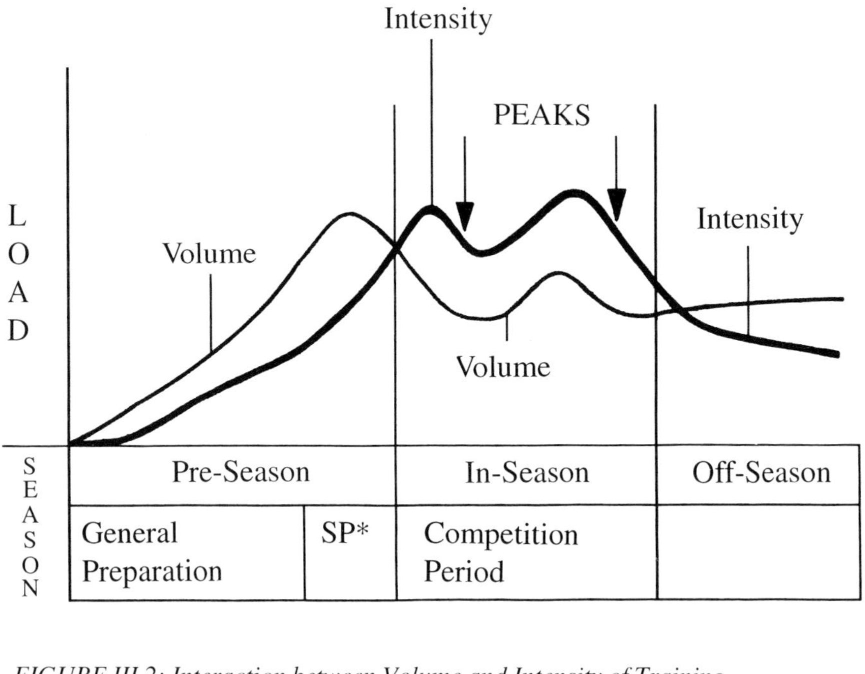

FIGURE III.2: Interaction between Volume and Intensity of Training
SP* = Specific preparation

As is evident from figure III.2, the volume of training gradually increases throughout the pre-season, while it diminishes during the in-season. The intensity of training, increases gradually during the pre-season as well, but not to the same extent as the volume of training. It increases more during the in-season, while the volume decreases. Prior to the peaks, both volume and intensity decrease: this is the taper-off period. In other words, volume and intensity never increase to the same extent at the same time: if the volume increases, the intensity decreases and vice versa.

The *psychological make-up* of the athlete is one of the determinants of peaking as well. The taekwondo competitor, who is ready to peak, is highly motivated, psychologically relaxed, focused and self-confident. The coach needs to create an atmosphere in which the athlete feels safe and confident. Psychological skills have been practiced and the competition has been "fought" in the athlete's mind several times over.

Trained and rested nervous system. As mentioned before, the nervous system plays a dominant role in the nearly flawless execution of techniques. Tactical plans can only succeed when technical and psychological preparations are optimal (see chapter VIII), which in turn will then facilitate peaking. Rest, again, depends on the recovery periods and the taper-off. It is self-explanatory that a fatigued nervous system will not be able to excite the muscles that are necessary for the execution of techniques. If the coach insists on loading the nervous system without adequate rest, even to the point of exhaustion, by exaggerated intensive training, the excitability of the nerves will diminish and, as a result, the athlete's performance will decrease. A disturbance of the delicate balance between training loads and recovery may either lead to peaking too early or too late. In both cases, the athlete will not peak during the main competition as planned and will not be able to live up to his/her potential.

Another factor that is related to peaking at the right time, is selection and number of competitions. Peaking, of course, can only be done a limited number of times. However, this does not mean that the athlete cannot compete in other tournaments. For convenience's sake, one may distinguish between test and main competitions.

A test competition is one where the coach and athlete have planned to practice certain aspects that have been worked on during training. For instance, during a dual meet, the coach may want to find out whether a certain combination of techniques will lead to the desired effect of scoring a point. The taekwondo coach may want to test the spinning back kick after a modified sequence of steps. In order to avoid injuries, if no padding for the instep of the foot will be allowed during the main competition, the coach may want to test the feasibility of a modified tactical plan to score points, and so on. Prior to test competitions, the athlete should also adhere to a taper-off period to get accustomed to it when used before the main competitions.

It is during the main competitions that the athlete wants to peak. The number and selection of test and main competitions should be carefully planned, since too many of them will off-set peaking at the right time. In a sport such as taekwondo, injuries play an important role in the decision as far as how many competitions to participate in. Both the coach and the tournament director need to be aware that everything possible should be done to ensure that the taekwondo athlete will not get injured. The use of protective padding is a necessity (see chapter X on injuries in taekwondo).

The last factor contributing to peaking at the proper time is the *number of peaks* per year. In taekwondo, two to three peaks per year are not impossible. Too many peaks, as too many competitions, may distract from peaking at the major competitions and lead to exhaustion. This implies that during a test match, victory should not be emphasized. Figure III.2 shows that after a peak, the training should decrease in both volume and intensity to give the athlete a chance to recuperate from the high physical and psychological stress of the main competition. In other words, not only is there a taper-off prior to main competitions, but there is also a period of reduced training after these contests. The rationale for the latter is related to the following:

- the taekwondo athlete needs time to recover physically from the main competition (e.g.,.fatigue, injuries);
- the athlete also needs time to recover psychologically (e.g., emotional recuperation, motivational);
- time is needed to evaluate the athlete's performance (e.g., anxiety level, technical, tactical, goals accomplished).

General Plan

Before devising a more detailed annual training plan, the taekwondo coach needs to develop a so-called general plan, which states the format within which the annual plan will be designed (6). The following components should be included in this general training plan (6):

1. general objectives;
2. athletic profile of the athlete(s);
3. components of training;
4. preparation period;
5. competition period.

The *general objectives* of training depend on the competition calendar. If major competitions, such as European or World Championships are on the agenda, smaller international meets will become secondary in importance. If the national championships and team trials are used as the decisive tournaments to select the national teams, Open Championships will become less important. In some cases, the national championships are not used to select the national team members, which implies that the athlete may not want to peak at those championships. In the general plan, a statement as to when peaking should occur will suffice. Expectations about the athlete's performance at those peaks will be detailed in the annual plan.

The *athletic profile* of the athlete will aid in identifying strong and weak points in the competitor's overall make-up. This athletic profile will give the coach information regarding the athlete's physical, technical, psychological and tactical development. Tests and measurements may be conducted to acquire these specifics. For instance, information regarding the athlete's strength and endurance levels as well as his/her motivational state will give the coach a tool in hand to improve those aspects that are felt to be deficient and to maintain or even further develop those that are already sufficiently trained. In addition, other athlete-related factors, such as lifestyle, family background, job-related requirements, and so on, are needed to give a more complete picture of the athlete as a unity of physical, psychological and social aspects.

Components of training refer to the physical, technical, psychological and tactical constituent parts. On the basis of the general objectives and the profile of the athlete, the coach will have to determine what each component will consist of. In other words, will there be more emphasis on anaerobic exercises this time or more aerobic? Does the athlete need more strength in his or her hamstrings and calfs or should the upper body get more attention? How about relaxation exercises? What will be done to improve the athlete's motivation? These and many more questions will have to be answered in order to achieve the agreed-upon objectives.

During the *preparation period* in the pre-season, the development of general and specific requirements for competition is emphasized. In other words, training is geared toward development of aerobic and anaerobic endurance, strength, technical skill, flexibility, mental preparedness, and so on. The gains from this preparation period will culminate in the competition period (i.e., the in-season), in which the athlete will have to peak. During both periods, the interaction between training load and recovery needs to be indicated, i.e., when will the training be, when the taper-off and when the recovery periods? Here again, the annual plan will detail the specifics. The competition period should also specify how many competitions will be attended and whether they are test or main contests.

There are several ways to construct a general plan. For instance, it is possible to just make a list of when certain components of the plan will have to be accomplished (see table III.1).

TABLE III.1 Example of General Plan for 1986 - 1987

Components	**Date**
General Objective:	
- peaking at Team Trials	July 1987
- peaking at World Championships	September 1987
Evaluation of Athletic Profile	November 1986
Start Pre-season	November 1986
Evaluation of Athletic Profile	December 1986
In-Season	March 1987 - September 1987
Off-season	October 1987
Annual Plan	
- Pre-Season	November 1986 - February 1987
- In-Season	March 1987 - September 1987
- Off-Season	October 1987

According to this plan, the season started in November 1986, after the transition period (off-season) of the previous season (1985 - 1986) in October 1986. At the beginning of this new season (1986 - 1987), the athletic profiles are assessed, as it will be again after the general preparation phase (pre-season) to see what the effects were of this conditioning period. As can be seen from table III.1, it is assumed that there are two peaks in the 1986 - 1987 season. It is also possible to be a little bit more specific and define the objectives for each period or for each component of training (physical, technical, psychological and tactical). For instance, for the technical component, the coach could state that the objectives are to be able to execute a certain kick in a number of different situations. Yet another option is to specify the various aspects of the athletic profile, such as aerobic endurance, kicking force, muscular strength, and so on and so forth. Table III.1 should suffice for now, however.

Annual Plan

As mentioned above, the annual plan is the specification of the general plan. In order to achieve this, the annual cycle is divided into three periods: the pre-season, in-season and off-season (1; 6). If the taekwondo coach is working with more than one athlete, the whole group will get a so-called group's annual plan. In addition, since each individual athlete is different from his/her colleague, there are also individual annual plans with specific remarks and suggestions for that particular athlete (6). According to Martin (4), these remarks and suggestions entail an evaluation of the past season: performance record, strong and weak points in the athlete's preparation and performance, motivation, social-psychological matters, and so on. In addition, there will be individually set goals for the present season, the steps to be taken to reach these goals, problem solving strategies, and so forth. Regardless of whether the annual plan is meant for a whole group or an individual athlete, it will cover all three periods of the entire year.

Pre-Season

On the average, the pre-season will consist of two phases: a general preparatory phase and a specific preparatory phase. The first phase is characterized by volume of training, while the intensity of training is very gradually increased in the second phase, which implies that the first phase is of necessity relatively long (3) (see also figure III.2). It appears that performance level at the end of the first phase is a relatively good indicator of the performance during the competitive in-season. A slow improvement in performance during the in-season was found to be related to a sudden increase in intensity during the second preparatory phase (6). In other words, the taekwondo coach is advised to make sure that the first preparatory phase is characterized by volume, which means that the athlete should be given the chance (i.e., time) to develop his or her general physical potential, such as endurance (chapter IV) and strength (chapter V). The more time the athlete has to develop his/her aerobic or anaerobic endurance, for instance, the better prepared he/she will be for the competitions and the smaller the chance for detraining effects to surface during the taper-off periods. During the specific preparatory phase, the taekwondo-specific training should gradually increase. In this stage, general aerobic endurance from running, for instance, is converted to specific taekwondo aerobic endurance by means of the various taekwondo skills. If the intensity in this specific preparation phase is suddenly increased, instead of doing it gradually, performance during the in-season will take longer to improve.

In-Season

The in-season may have a pre-competitive phase before the main competitions start. In this period, the specific training from the second phase in the pre-season will become even more specific. Actual competition skills are now practiced. For instance, suppose that steps and a variety of techniques have been practiced during the second preparatory phase. In the pre-competitive phase of the in-season, these steps and techniques are subsequently integrated and applied to a competitive situation with a training partner. Actual match conditions are simulated, including tactical and psychological skills. This pre-competitive phase may culminate in test competitions, which will typically be at the beginning of the in-season.

The coach may choose to have two or three peaks during the season. If the entire season would look as the one depicted in figure III.1, this would be called a bi-cycle season (1). Depending on how close together the two peaks are, a very short transition phase of reduced training will be used right after the first peak. This transition period may be as long as one week and probably not longer. After that, a short preparatory phase will lead into the second pre-competitive phase with its test competitions before the second peak (1).

In a bi-cycle plan, the second distinct peak should be higher than the first one (1). It is precisely during the second competitive phase that the truly major competitions take place. For instance, the first peak may be during international tournaments, so-called Open Championships. The second peak may relate to the Team

Trials and Continental (African, European, Pan-American, etc.) or World Championships with a transition competition before the off-season, such as the National Championships. It is understood that before these main competitions, there will be a taper-off period as discussed above. Regardless of the number of peaks, prior to peaking, tactical and psychological training become more important. This means that more training time is spent on tactical and psychological aspects. For instance, how to set up an attack with a step and a kick, or how to alternate offensive and defensive fighting will be emphasized more. Similarly, psychological skills such as relaxing prior to competition and using imagery to set up a tactical defensive maneuver are emphasized more. An example of an annual plan will be given below, after a discussion of macro- and micro-cycles of which the annual plan is composed.

Off-Season

The off-season is a period to recuperate from the physical and psychological stress from the pre- and in-seasons and should probably not last longer than five weeks (1). The best way to spend this time is to stay active in activities that are not related to taekwondo. It is suggested that an active recuperation period will off-set the detraining effects, so that gains from the pre- and in-seasons will not decline as much (6). In fact, it was demonstrated that athletes, who maintain their physical conditioning throughout the year, were more successful and continued their sport longer than those who did not (7).

The off-season should be a fun and enjoyable time. Preferably, the taekwondo athlete should engage in activities that are not part of his or her normal training routine. For instance, if one's aerobic endurance during the pre-season is trained by riding the bicycle, one could consider running in the off-season and vice versa. Ball games, racket sports and others are excellent ways to spend one's off-season. It is even advisable to engage in some competition during this time (7). If the athlete likes badminton, table tennis or sand volleyball, he/she could maintain his or her conditioning level and the motivation to compete in a rather relaxed atmosphere, i.e., away from taekwondo competition. Whatever is decided upon, it is advised to maintain the same physical conditioning aspects that are needed for tae-kwondo training and competition: aerobic and anaerobic endurance, strength, strength endurance and flexibility. Since reduced training has an adverse effect on body fat in that it tends to increase during periods of less strenuous activity, it is recommended that good nutritional advise be sought to ensure a minimal disruption in the athlete's body fat.

Macro-Cycle

A macro-cycle usually spans several weeks and sometimes even a few months, depending on the individual case. For the present purposes, it is not unreasonable to have macro-cycles of several weeks. A macro-cycle should not only be progressive (1; 6), but it also determines the proportional contribution of each component of training to the total training load (6). In other words, the macro-cycle specifies how long the taekwondo athlete will spend on each training component of physical, technical, psychological and tactical preparation. For instance, since technique training is crucial in taekwondo, its macro-cycles may span 12 weeks, while the macro-cycle for endurance, for instance, may last six weeks. During the in-season, (a series of) competitions are usually scheduled at the end of each macro-cycle to evaluate the effect of this macro-cycle. One may choose to have the athletes assessed at the end of the macro-cycles during the pre-season as well, which would basically be a check-up of (part of) the athletic profile that was assessed at the beginning of the pre-season.

The macro-cycle is composed of several micro-cycles in which the rest-recovery interaction plays a crucial role. It is recommended to increase the training load during the first few micro-cycles of the macro-cycle and to taper during the last micro-cycle, at the end of which the taekwondo athlete could have a competition. An example of a macro-cycle is shown in table III.2. In this case, it is one for endurance during the pre-season.

Table III.2 displays a rather advanced macro-cycle. If the athlete is in the developing stages of his/her career, a more basic program may be more beneficial with a much more gradual increase in intensity. In this case, the macro-cycle may last 12 weeks instead of six weeks. In a macro-cycle of six weeks, the intensity will necessarily be higher than in one of 12 weeks. Table III.3 shows a macro-cycle with a 12-week program.

There are several ways to manipulate the interaction between training load and recovery during one macro-cycle. One option is to increase the training load gradually to culminate in the highest load at the end of the cycle. Another one would be to increase the load in the beginning, decrease it slightly and then increase it again. Depending on the goals of the macro-cycles, the coach may choose to work with a variety of possibilities.

TABLE III.2 Example of Macro-Cycle for Endurance in Pre-Season

Activity	**Time**
Objectives	
- To improve general aerobic endurance	
- To improve general anaerobic endurance	
Aerobic Endurance	Week 1 - 3
• Distance run: 15 minutes	Week 1 + part Week 2
• Distance run: 20 minutes	part Week 2 + Week 3
Anaerobic Endurance	Week 4 - 6
• Interval training	
200 m (5x); 100 m (4x)	Week 4
300 m (4x); 200 m (2x)	Week 5
400 m (4x); 300 m (1x)	Week 6
Test of endurance	End of week 6
• Aerobic	One day
• Anaerobic	Next day

TABLE III.3
Example of Macro-Cycle for Endurance in Pre-Season: 12-Week Program

Activity	**Time**
Objectives	
- To improve general aerobic endurance	
- To improve general anaerobic endurance	
Aerobic Endurance	Week 1 - 6
• Distance run: 15 minutes	Week 1 and 2
• Distance run: 20 minutes	Week 3 and 4
• Distance run: 25 minutes	Week 5 and 6
Test of aerobic endurance	End of Week 6
Anaerobic Endurance	Week 7 - 12
• Interval training	
200 m (3x); 100 m (3x)	Week 7 and 8
300 m (3x); 200 m (2x)	Week 9 and 10
400 m (3x); 300 m (1x)	Week 11 and 12
Test of anaerobic endurance	End of week 12

Micro-Cycle

The micro-cycle is the smallest unit within the training plan. It usually lasts for one week, but may also be for a few days. A taper-off cycle, for instance, will typically be of a rather short duration, such as five to ten days. A technique micro-cycle, on the other hand, may be as long as ten days or even three weeks. Depending on the objectives, then, a micro-cycle may last anywhere from one to three weeks (2). Alternating work and recovery periods are especially important in micro-cycles. On the basis of the interaction between work and rest in the micro-cycle, the macro-cycle's training load is determined and, as a result, that of the annual plan.

Volume and intensity of training cannot be increased to the same extent and at the same time in one micro-cycle and over a number of micro-cycles. For instance, depending on the specific situation of the athlete, the coach may want to increase the volume of training to develop aerobic endurance. If the objective of training is to develop anaerobic endurance, for instance, the intensity of training may become more important with a concomitant decrease in volume.

Each training session within one micro-cycle has alternating workloads as well. A typical training session always begins and ends with a warm-up and cool-down, respectively. The main part of the training session is characterized by intensities varying from high (e.g., 90 - 100% of HR_{max}) to medium (80 - 90% of HR_{max}) to low (70 - 80% HR_{max}). It is not recommended, physiologically as well as psychologically, to prolong a high intensity bout, since the athlete will fatigue and, as a result, hardly any learning or training effect will be accomplished. In addition, from a psychological perspective, the athlete will also lose his/her concentration and motivation. Technique and speed training are always done at the beginning of the session, while more muscular endurance types of activities are scheduled after that. For instance, a notoriously intensive training session is one where the goal is to develop the athlete's anaerobic endurance by means of interval training. If the athlete is not allowed to get adequate rest, both within one session and in the course of several training sessions, burnout may soon follow.

As far as intensity is concerned, a micro-cycle may have one or two, and sometimes even three, peaks with lower intensity training days (1). Various possibilities exist, depending on the individual circumstances. Two examples are illustrated in figure III.3, with one peak, and III.4, with two peaks, respectively. If the individual's maximum capacity is taxed, not more than two peaks should be scheduled in one micro-cycle.

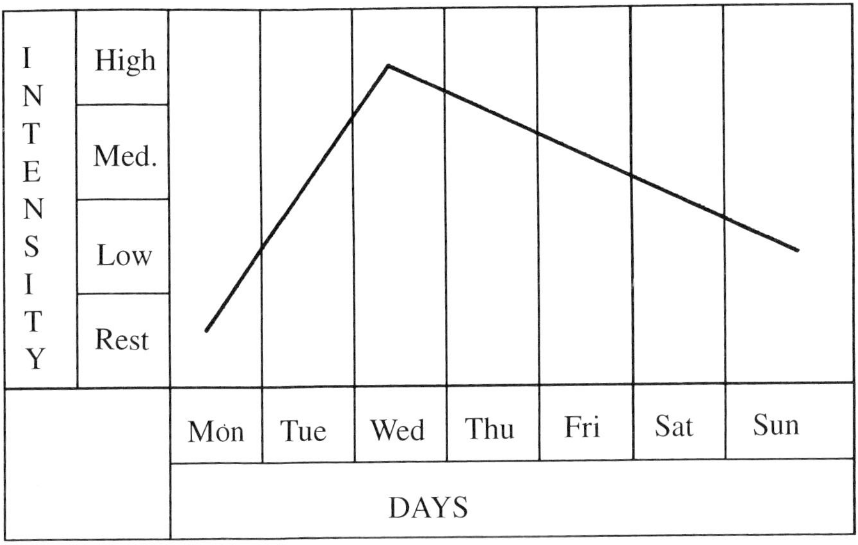

FIGURE III.3: Micro-Cycle with One Peak

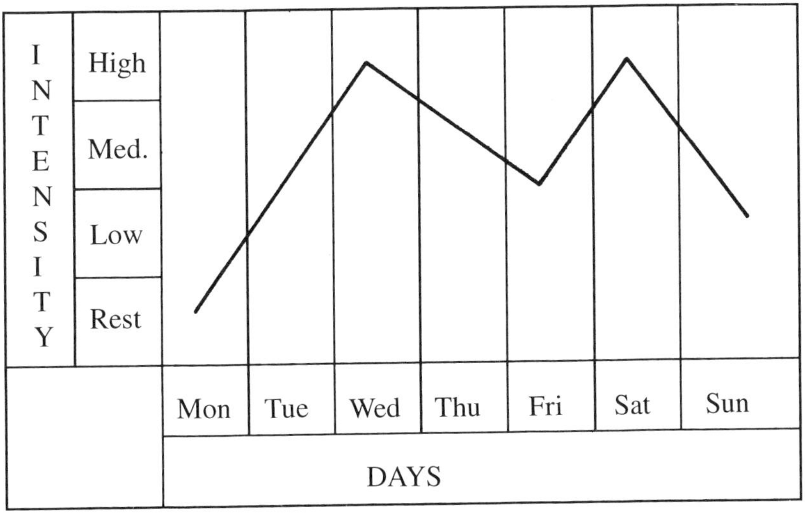

FIGURE III.4: Micro-Cycle with Two Peaks

Bompa (1) also observes that if the objective is to mimic the competition days, two peaks may be scheduled on two subsequent days in the micro-cycle. If this is not the case, then the coach may want to spread out the peaks to give the athlete adequate rest. In a taper-off micro-cycle, of course, the intensities will be much lower with more rest days. Since the individual circumstances may change relatively fast (e.g., due to injuries, sickness, etc.), it is advised to only plan two micro-cycles at the most ahead of time.

Table III.4 shows an example of a micro-cycle from the pre-season. In this case, the intensity is increased by increasing percentage HR_{max}. It is assumed that the athlete works out once a day. Naturally, it is quite possible to have more than one training session scheduled per day, depending on each individual case. If the taekwondo athlete has more than one training session per day, it is extremely important to alternate work and recovery periods. It is self-explanatory that the more sessions are scheduled, the greater the chances are to overtrain the athlete. In addition to scheduling the micro-cycle, the taekwondo coach should also plan each training session, an example of which is presented in table III.5. Before and after each micro-cycle, the coach may choose to meet with the athlete(s) to present the schedule and, at the end of the micro-cycle, to evaluate it to get feedback from the athletes themselves.

In table III.4, running at a higher intensity may also mean running faster or running at a higher % HR_{max}. The intensity of the strength component is manipulated by increasing the weights. Another way to increase the intensity in strength training is to shorten the rest periods (see chapter V).

Speed training, regardless of its intensity, is always done in such a way that maximal executions of techniques are interspersed with complete rest intervals. Speed training, whether general or taekwondo-specific speed, taxes the central nervous system (CNS) and without complete rest, the CNS will fatigue, thereby precluding optimal training effects. General speed refers to speed that is not dependent on taekwondo techniques, such as sprinting 20 m or 30 m. Taekwondo-specific speed refers to performing taekwondo techniques as fast as possible. Of course, speed training is also related to the athlete's physical preparation, such as endurance and strength. The stronger the athlete is or the better his/her endurance, the more speed work he/she will be able to do. As a result, the intensity of speed training will also be related to the athlete's physical preparation. For instance, the better the athlete's endurance, the shorter the rest intervals may become and the higher the resultant intensity of the speed workout will be.

TABLE III.4 Example of Micro-Cycle in Pre-Season

Objektives
- Work on general speed and anaerobic endurance.
- Improve side kick and punch.
- Peaks on Wednesday and Saturday.

Intensities
- Monday: Rest.
- Tuesday and Friday: Medium (80 - 90% HR_{max} for running).
- Wednesday and Saturday: Low (70 - 80% HR_{max} for technique).
- Thursday and Sunday: High (90 - 100% HR_{max} for running).

Tuesday and Friday	**Wednesday and Saturday**
Sprints: 5 x 20 m 3 x 30 m Interval: 5 x 100 m 5 x 200 m Strength: 3 sets/8 repetitions	Technique training: 1 hour Special attention to: - punch - side kick - concentration Basketball game: 30 minutes
Thursday and Sunday	**Monday**
Sprints: 5 x 20 m 3 x 30 m Interval: 5 x 100 m 5 x 200 m Strength: 3 sets/5 repetitions - higher weights	Rest

TABLE III.5 Example of Two Training Sessions in Micro-Cycle

Tuesday

Sprints - Medium intensity
Interval training - Medium intensity
Strength training - Medium intensity

Work interval for sprints: 85% of maximum speed

Rest interval between sprints:
at least five minutes for 20 m's or ten minutes for 30 m's.

Work interval during anaerobic training:
- for both 100 m and 200 m: 80% of maximum HR.

Rest interval between anaerobic work bouts:
- for 100 m's: 2 minutes
- for 200 m's: 3.5 minutes

Wednesday

Taekwondo technique training: Low Intensity
Problem areas:
- shoulder muscles during punch (too tense)
- upper body during punch
- path of punching arm
- support leg during side kick
- path of kicking leg
- upper body during side kick
- height of knee of kicking leg at the beginning

Techniques to be practiced:
- punch
- side kick
- defensive maneuvers with arms
- attacking with arms/hands
- all other kicks

For concentration:
- focus during technique training
- forms

Basketball game: 30 minutes

Designing an Annual Plan

Although the annual plan has been discussed above, designing such a plan was postponed until this point because several concepts needed to be covered first, such as periodization, macro-cycle and micro-cycle. Having done this, a detailed discussion of how to devise an annual plan is now possible.

Designing the annual plan is a reflection of the coach's knowledge of the training process in general, his/her creativeness, his/her experience as well as his/her knowledge of the specific sport, i.e., taekwondo. The intricate interaction between workload, recovery, components of training, training principles, determinants of success in taekwondo competition, and so on, all have to come into play when designing the annual plan. The annual plan will change over time, of course, since the coach will gain more experience in and knowledge about taekwondo as well as the scientific considerations regarding taekwondo. In fact, the more experience the coach has in taekwondo, the better his/her knowledge is of taekwondo and the scientific developments in this area, the more sophisticated the annual plan will be. Although each coach is free in devising the yearly cycle, a few guidelines may be of help. The following entries may be found in an annual plan (1).

Introduction. In this part, the coach should state the duration of the plan as well as some pertinent demographical information on the athlete, such as name (if one is coaching more than one athlete), sex, age, height, weight, body fat, marital status, education, parental status (children, no children), and so on.

Retrospective Analysis. This refers to the evaluation of the athlete's performance in the past season in terms of all components of training in view of the objectives stated for that season and, of course, in light of the objectives for the coming season. The basis for evaluation will be information gathered during various competitions as well as from specific tests administered in the past season. As far as the physical component is concerned, the coach should evaluate the athlete's endurance, strength, flexibility and coordination during the pre- and in-season. It is conceivable, for instance, that the athlete scored quite well on endurance during the pre-season, but fell short during the in-season. The analysis of the technical component of training will focus on the execution of various taekwondo skills as well as the appropriateness of using certain techniques during competition. The evaluation of the tactical training involves the utilization of tactical maneuvers during competition and their appropriateness as well as the mastery of them. Similarly, the coach should assess the athlete's psychological preparation in terms of its success during competition. On the basis of this evaluation, the coach will decide whether to continue or eliminate certain aspects of the athlete's training. Part of this retrospective analysis is any collaboration with other specialists, such as a sport psychologist, physician, nutritionist, and so on, with regard to past and future performance of the taekwondo athlete. This rather comprehensive evaluation will serve to define the objectives for the coming season and to make any predictions about future progress and performance.

Predicting Performance. One of the skills that a good taekwondo coach needs to have is the ability to predict his/her athlete's future performance and progress. This prediction will be based on information derived from a variety of sources: the coach's experience, his/her scientific knowledge, assessments of athletic profile, performance during competition and training, conversations with the athlete, and so on. Naturally, in a subjective sport such as taekwondo, it is very difficult to assess how the athlete will do in future competitions. However, a good coach will take all the unknowns into account. Predicting performance will aid the coach in designing the annual plan in a progressive manner. For instance, when the long-term goal is to win the World Championships, the coach needs to assess how long it will take to reach that goal. Based on the athlete's predicted performance each year, the coach will then be able to design a four-year plan or however long he/she thinks it will take to reach that goal.

Objectives. Relative to the retrospective analysis and the performance prediction, the coach will set realistic goals for the next season. In order to define these objectives, the coach will also consider the rate of improvement of the athlete in addition to the calendar of competitions for the upcoming year. The athlete's strengths and weaknesses relative to the various components of training will most certainly play a role when setting the objectives. For instance, an answer to the question: 'is the psychological or technical preparation of the athlete the limiting factor to improved performance?' will aid the coach in defining one of the goals of the annual plan.

Calendar of Competitions. Although the coach is the main person setting the calendar of competitions, it will facilitate the interaction between coach and athlete if they both have a say in it, especially if he/she is dealing with elite athletes. It is advisable to have the coach be the main decision maker if the athletes have only recently begun to compete. The coach should know when to plan the test and main competitions as well as how many the athlete will participate in. Based on the calendar of competitions, the periodization of the annual plan will be made, so that no changes in competitions may be allowed at a later date. The coach ought to be aware that no demanding competitions should be planned prior to the main competition, nor should the main competition be scheduled in a period when athletes, who are students, have their exams.

Testing/Evaluation. It is essential for the coach to know what the athletic status is of his/her competitors. This means that, at the beginning of the new pre-season or at the end of the previous off-season, an assessment needs to be made of the athlete prior to designing the annual plan. In the course of the new season, the coach should plan a number of additional tests to assess the effect of the training program. Preferably, these tests should be administered during the pre-season. An exception is made for psychological tests, such as assessments of anxiety or overtraining, which may be done until even one day before competition. Testing during the in-season will typically consist of the competitions the athlete will participate in. The results of the tests, whether laboratory tests, field tests or competitions, are indicative of how well the athlete adapted to the conditioning and training programs and whether any changes need to be made. Evaluating matches should always be done right after the competition is over. Evaluating and modifying goals, on the other hand, may be done at any time within the training program. Depending on the tests chosen, the coach may want to collaborate with sport scientists and other specialists to get the most out of the results. Table III.6 and figure III.5 display a hypothetical annual plan for a taekwondo athlete.

References

1. Bompa, T. O. (1983), *Theory and Methodology of Training*, Dubuque, Iowa: Kendall/Hunt Publishing Company.
2. Bosboom, H., Brouns, F., Heere, L. P., Keizer, H. A., Swinkels, J. and Verstappen, F. (1985), Algemene uitgangspunten, In: F. Verstappen (ed.), *Training, Prestatie en Gezondheid in de Sport,* Utrecht: Wetenschappelijke Uitgeverij Bunge.
3. Harre, D. (ed.) (1981), *Trainingslehre*, Berlin: Sportverlag.
4. Martin, D. (1980), Grundlagen der Trainingslehre. Teil 2: *Die Planung, Gestaltung, Steuerung des Trainings und das Kind- und Jugendtraining,* Schorndorf: K. Hofmann Verlag.
5. Matvejev, L. P. (1972), *Periodisierung des sportlichen Trainings*, Berlin: Bartels und Wernitz.
6. Vrijens, J. (1988), *Basis Voor Verantwoord Trainen*, Gent: W. Verbessem.
7. Wilmore, J. H. and Costill, D. L. (1988), *Training for Sport and Activity*, Dubuque, Iowa: Wm. C. Brown Publishers.

TABLE III.6 Example of Annual Plan for Taekwondo Athlete

Annual Plan for July 1, 1992 - June 13, 1993.

INTRODUCTION

Gender:	female	Age: 25 years
Height:	165 cm	Weight: 55 kg
Body fat:	38 mm (sum of six skinfolds)	
Marital status:	married, no children	
Parental status:	married	Occupation: High school teacher

RETROSPECTIVE ANALYSIS

Competition Performance	*Planned*	*Achieved*
- Main competition 1	3rd place	1st place
• Concentration	good	optimal
• Self-confidence	optimal	optimal
• Motivation	optimal	optimal
• Anxiety	optimal	optimal
- *Main competition 2*	3rd place	1st round loss
• Concentration	good	mediocre
• Self-confidence	optimal	low
• Motivation	optimal	optimal
• Anxiety	low	high

Tests

Endurance

Aerobic endurance:	50 ml/kg/min
Anaerobic endurance (peak power):	705 W
Anaerobic endurance (power decline):	25%

Strength

Hamstrings/quadriceps ratio (right leg):	80% (300°/sec)
Hamstrings/quadriceps ratio (left leg):	85% (300°/sec)

TABLE III.6 Example of Annual Plan for Taekwondo Athlete (Continued)

RETROSPECTIVE ANALYSIS (CONTINUED)
Tests (continued)

Psychological tests
Two of three tests administered are time-dependent tests, i.e., the results depend on the time that the tests are given. Consequently, only the result of one test will be reported here. The other two tests are administered on a periodic basis before the start of competition (one week, one day and one hour prior).

Competition trait anxiety: 27

Speed (meters/second)

Reverse punch	right: 9 m/s	left: 10 m/s
Side kick	right: 6 m/s	left: 8 m/s
Round kick	right: 12 m/s	left: 14 m/s
Spinning back kick	right: 7 m/s	left: 8 m/

Force (Newton)

Reverse punch	right: 1020 N	left: 1167 N
Side kick	right: 1186 N	left: 1298 N
Round kick	right: 1206 N	left: 1216 N
Spinning back kick	right: 1670 N	left: 1746 N

Physical Preparation
- Aerobic endurance: excellent.
- Hamstrings/quadriceps strength ratio: hamstrings need more strength.
- Anaerobic endurance: good.

Technical Preparation
- Round and spinning back kicks: excellent (both sides)
- Punches: excellent (both sides)
- Left side kick: good; needs work on timing
- Right side kick: good; needs work on timing, speed, force
- Axe kicks: good; needs work on speed, more relaxed
- Push and spinning hook kicks: excellent (both sides)
- Flexibility, balance and coordination: excellent
- Mobility: mediocre

TABLE III.6 Example of Annual Plan for Taekwondo Athlete (Continued)

Technical Preparation (continued)
- Spatial orientation: good; more fine tuning.
- Offensive: all techniques good.
- Defensive: needs work on side kick, push kick, blocks (both sides).

Tactical Preparation
- Offensive
  - Steps: excellent (both sides).
  - Kicks: side kick - faster; axe kick - faster; all other kicks excellent.
  - Punch: excellent (both sides).
- Defensive
  - Steps: excellent (both sides).
  - Kicks: side kick - weak; axe & push kicks - faster; others - excellent.
  - Punch: excellent (both sides).
- Alternating offense and defense: more fine tuning.
- Distancing: excellent (both sides).

Psychological Preparation
- Concentration: getting better.
- Self-confidence: still weak.
- Motivation: excellent.
- Support group: weak; big influence; needs much work.
- Anxiety: too high.

Nutritional Preparation: excellent.

Injuries: overtrained; long period of injuries.

OBJECTIVES

Competition Performance
- First Peak: October - December 1992
  - Tournament 1 (October): 3rd place. Probability: 80%
  - Tournament 2 (November): 1st place. Probability: 90%
  - Tournament 3 (December): 3rd place. Probability: 80%
- Second Peak: March - April 1993
  - Tournament 4 (March): 2nd place. Probability: 85%
  - Tournament 5 (April): 1st place. Probability: 85%

TABLE III.6 Example of Annual Plan for Taekwondo Athlete (Continued)

Physical Preparation
- Strength: improve hamstrings and hip flexor muscles.
- Speed: improve starting speed of kicks.
- Endurance: improve mean anaerobic power; reduce power decline.

Technical Preparation
- Mobility: all around improvement.
- Speed: improve starting speed of kicks.
- Spatial orientation: fine tuning.
- Kicks: improve weak points (see Retrospective Analysis).

Tactical Preparation
- Offensive: improve execution speed of kicks.
- Defensive: improve timing and speed of side, push and axe kicks.
- Alternating offense and defense: more fine tuning.

Psychological Preparation
- Fine tune psychological skills: visualization/relaxation.
- Support group: more counseling.

PERIODIZATION
- ***Testing:*** June 29 and 30, 1992.
- ***Pre-season:*** July 1 - September 12, 1992.
- ***In-season:*** September 14, 1992 - June 13, 1993.
  Second preparation phases indicated in figure III.5.
- ***Off-Season:*** June 14 - July 10, 1993.

(A more detailed periodization may be found in figure III.5.)

FIGURE III.5: Example of Periodization in Annual Plan

Dates	June		July	August			September					October			November				December				
	29	30	1	13	14	15	4	11	12	14	24	15	23	24	14	20	21	22	6	11	12	13	26
Testing	X	X		X	X																		
Pre-Season																							
General Preparation																							
Specific Preparation																							
In-Season																							
Off-Season																							
Test Competitions									X														
Main Competitions														X			X	X			X		
Psychological Testing							X	X	X			X	X	X	X	X	X		X	X	X		

FIGURE III.5: Example of Periodization in Annual Plan (Continued)

Dates	Dec.	January			February			March				April				May			June				
	28	24	30	31	6	12	13	6	12	13	14	17	23	24	25	15	21	22	6	11	12	13	14
Testing																							
Pre-Season																							
General Preparation																							
Specific Preparation	////	////																					
In-Season			////	////	////	////	////	////	////	////	////	////	////	////	////	////	////	////	////	////	////	////	
Off-Season																							////
Test Competitions				X			X											X				X	
Main Competitions										X	X			X	X								
Psychological Testing		X	X	X	X	X	X	X	X	X		X	X	X		X	X	X	X		X	X	

CHAPTER IV

TRAINING ENDURANCE IN TAEKWONDO

Introduction

As in other sports, endurance in taekwondo is very important in order to compete at the highest level. In some cases, endurance may make the difference between winning or losing. It will allow the athlete to continue a high level of performance during a bout for a longer period of time: the athlete will be able to execute his/her skills accurately and to keep up his/her concentration for as long as necessary. Endurance is also important relative to the prevention of injuries. The more tired the athlete gets, the easier mistakes will creep into the execution of techniques, which may lead to injuries such as muscle pulls, twisted ankles, hyperextension of the knee, or maybe even injuries as a result of failing defensive maneuvers.

This chapter will provide the reader with basic information on how to improve general aerobic, general anaerobic and taekwondo-specific endurance. Furthermore, tests for the assessment of the different kinds of endurance will be presented, which will enable the coach to gain better insight in and monitor the responses of the athlete to the conditioning and training programs.

Energy Deliverance to the Working Muscles

For every movement we make, energy is needed. The same is true for taekwondo: for every kick or punch we perform, energy is needed. Similar to gasoline in a car, the human body has its own source of energy, which is called ATP (adenosine triphosphate), a chemical substance. Whenever a kick, punch, block or form *(p'umse)* is performed, ATP is used as the source of energy. There also is another high energy bond present in the human body, CP or CPK (creatine phosphate or creatine phosphokinase). CP is not able to generate energy directly, but can do so via ATP, which then provides the energy needed. The amount of CP stored in the body will only last for a very short period of time during all-out actions, i.e., about ten seconds.

In order to continue executing taekwondo techniques, the body needs a constant supply of ATP. The food that is taken in, the carbohydrates and fats, is converted into the above mentioned high bonds of energy. The utilization of *glucose,* a form of sugar, to make ATP is called *glycolysis. Glucose* is stored in the liver and muscles as *glycogen.* The utilization of *glycogen* in the process of ATP-formation is called *glycogenolysis.*

In a steady state when there is a balance between the demand and supply of ATP, the ATP required is generated by the oxidation of fat and glucose. Oxidation refers to using fat and glucose with the help of oxygen. This way of energy utilization is called the aerobic pathway. For low, steady-state intensities, the main source of fuel used is fat. If the demand of energy is higher but still in a steady state mode, glucose will become more important as the source of energy. The athlete may keep up this intensity for several hours, such as in a marathon, triathlon or in the Tour de France.

In case the demand of ATP becomes more than its supply by the aerobic system, extra ATP may be generated by the so-called anaerobic pathway. ATP can be generated faster by breaking down glucose without the use of oxygen, hence the name anaerobic energy system, but it has lactic acid as its byproduct. Lactic acid accumulates in the working as well as in the non-working muscles, which causes them to fatigue. High-intensity activities, which mainly rely on the anaerobic pathway for their energy supply, can only last for two to three minutes after which the athlete will have to cease his/her activities. The buildup of lactic acid, then, is the limiting factor in the anaerobic pathway of energy deliverance. For example, when kicking against a heavy bag, a kind of stiffness or soreness is usually felt in the legs after some 15 or more continuous all-out kicks that makes the athlete unable to continue with the same speed and force. This kind of burning, aching, sensation is caused by the accumulation of lactic acid.

Anaerobic endurance may be divided into two phases: the alactic and lactic phases. In the alactic phase, usually the first ten to fifteen seconds into the activity, the energy deliverance is by means of stored CP. As mentioned above, CP is converted into ATP, which in turn provides the energy needed. This phase is called alactic because no lactic acid is formed during the conversion of CP into ATP. During the lactic phase of the anaerobic pathway, typically after the first ten to fifteen seconds after starting the activity, lactic acid is formed by the glycolysis of glucose to generate the ATP needed. Figure IV.1 shows the interplay between the anaerobic and aerobic systems relative to the contributions of each system to the total energy production.

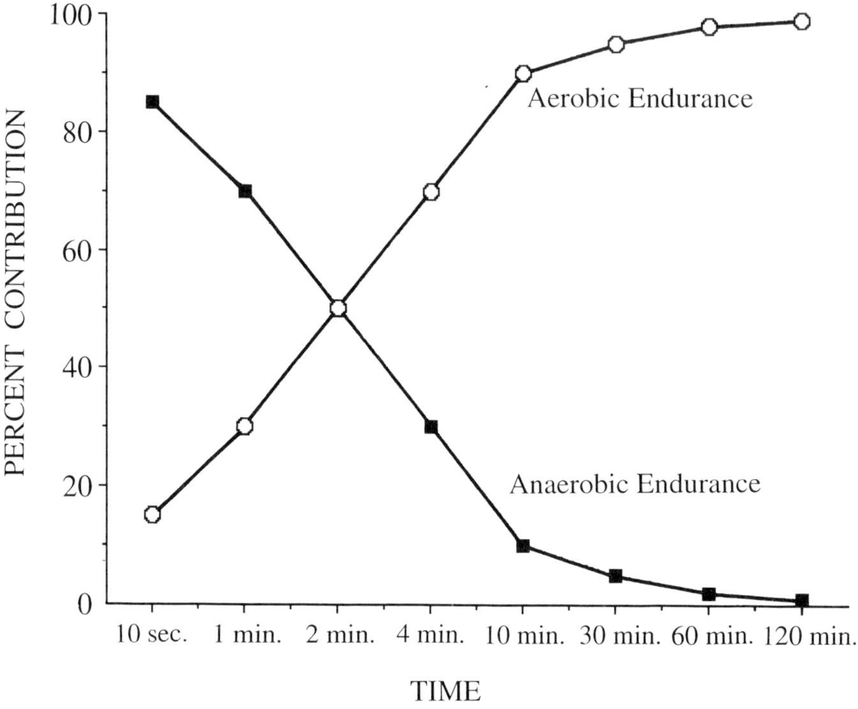

Figure IV.1 Relative Contribution of the Anaerobic and Aerobic Systems to Total Energy Production (Based on 1)

As is clear from figure IV.1, the longer the activity, the more the aerobic pathway has to come into play to provide the energy and conversely, the shorter the activity, the more the athlete has to rely on the anaerobic pathway as a source of energy. In taekwondo competition, there are either three rounds of two minutes each with a 30-second break in between rounds, or three rounds of three minutes with a one-minute break. From figure IV.1 it can be seen that the taekwondo athlete will have to possess a relatively high level of aerobic endurance as well as anaerobic endurance. Based on results from the OTRP, it is now possible to better define the relative proportional contribution of both types of endurance for taekwondo competition (see section on Pre-Season).

To assess components of the athletic profile of an individual, several laboratory tests may be performed. One such component is the physiological dimension.

Another is the psychological profile, and so on. Within the physiological dimension, which is the topic of this chapter, one may distinguish aerobic endurance, anaerobic endurance and strength. Strength and assessing strength will be covered in the next chapter. Here, testing of aerobic and anaerobic endurance will be discussed. Testing of endurance, or any other physiological variable of interest, serves several purposes (9). Initially, it will give the coach as well as the athlete baseline information about the latter's strengths and weaknesses in any of the variables assessed upon which the conditioning and training programs may be based.

Secondly, testing will provide feedback. It will make comparisons possible with previous or future test results. If the athlete is injured, the results of the last testing session will provide a guideline regarding the level of performance that he/she will have to return to (see also chapter X). Regularly monitoring the physiological variables of interest, such as aerobic/anaerobic endurance and strength, will allow the coach to adjust the goals of the conditioning or training program. Thirdly, testing will also provide information regarding the health status of the athlete. Training and competing at the elite level require a delicate balance of physical and psychological stress and recovery. The human body is taxed to its limits by the high demands of modern competition, which may cause health problems. Finally, testing is an educational process. Both the coach and athlete alike will gain a better understanding of the demands of their particular sport in relation to the physical (and psychological) make-up of the athlete.

In addition to laboratory tests, there are also so-called field tests. A field test is a test that is conducted while the athlete is actually performing in the pool, on the track, in the ice rink, and so on. For instance, testing the aerobic endurance of a cyclist on a stationary bike in the laboratory would be a laboratory test. Testing his/her aerobic endurance on the bike while riding in a criterion would be a field test. Field tests are not as reliable as laboratory tests, but they are certainly more valid because of their specificity (9). The reason a field test is not as reliable has to do with the factors that the researcher cannot control, such as weather, surface conditions, and so forth. An example of a laboratory test in taekwondo would be to test aerobic endurance on a treadmill. A field test to assess the same component would be to test the athlete while competing or working out. However, as of this writing (1995) and to the best of the present authors' knowledge, there are no field tests available yet to assess aerobic or anaerobic endurance in taekwondo. Field tests and laboratory tests should, wherever possible and applicable, be used in conjunction with each other: they should provide complementary information. On the other hand, they should not be viewed as a substitute for each other either (9).

A word of caution seems to be in order at this point. Testing in general, whether administered in the laboratory or in the field setting, should not be considered as a magic potion that will lead the athlete to the highest performance level possible. Instead, it should be viewed as an educational tool that will aid the coach and athlete in structuring the athlete's training in a more systematic way. One only has to remember that it is not always feasible to simulate actual competition conditions in the laboratory to appreciate this cautionary word. In addition, as has been mentioned before, (high-level) performance is the result of a multitude of factors that cannot be adequately assessed in the laboratory where only one component is usually isolated and tested.

Knowing how endurance was assessed will help both the coach and the taekwondo athlete to better understand the results of the physiological component of the Oregon Taekwondo Research Project as well as gain insight into some of the weaknesses of physiological testing in the laboratory setting. It will also contribute to a better appreciation of the implications of the recommendations based on these results. Although aerobic and anaerobic endurance may be assessed in various ways, the two most common methods to do so will be covered in the next section.

Testing Endurance

Aerobic endurance is represented by what is termed maximal oxygen uptake. Maximal oxygen uptake or consumption (maxO_2) refers to the maximum amount of oxygen that an individual is able to take up in a given period of time (usually per minute) and can use in his/her body. Since body weight is related to the amount of oxygen taken up and consumed (the heavier one is, the more oxygen one will need), maximum oxygen uptake is usually expressed in terms of body weight. The standard method to report aerobic endurance is to represent it in terms of milliliters of oxygen per kilogram of body weight per minute (ml/kg/min or ml. $kg^{-1}.min^{-1}$). If it is reported in absolute terms, aerobic endurance is expressed in liters per minute (l/min).

Aerobic endurance, as part of the physiological component of the Oregon Taekwondo Research Project (OTRP), was estimated by using a modified Åstrand protocol recommended for athletes (6). A protocol is a schedule, a step-by-step program, that the researcher uses to assess a certain variable. In the present case, the athletes performed a graded treadmill test to elicit their maximal effort. The test was set up in such a way that the athlete would run for at least ten minutes before it had to be terminated. The subject's heart rate was continuously monitored throughout the test for safety purposes. As can be seen from figure IV.1, ten minutes of activity will ensure a major contribution of the aerobic pathway as the main source of energy.

Anaerobic endurance is typically divided into anaerobic peak power and anaerobic average power. Anaerobic peak power refers to the maximum amount of work that can be done without a significant contribution of oxygen. Anaerobic average power refers to the ability of the individual to persist this maximum effort without a significant contribution of oxygen (7). Anaerobic peak power and average power were determined by the so-called Wingate Anaerobic Cycling Test (7). The subjects were asked to ride a stationary bike for 30 seconds in an all-out effort. A warm-up of 2 - 4 minutes with an intensity sufficient to raise the athlete's heart rate to 150 - 160 beats per minute (bpm) preceded the test. Both the warm-up and the cool-down were on the bicycle. During the actual test, the subject pedaled as fast as possible while the resistance was increased to a predetermined load based on the subject's body weight within 2 - 4 seconds by the first observer. As soon as this load was reached, the pedal revolutions were registered for 30 seconds by a second observer with the help of a computer connected to the bike.

Peak anaerobic power, average anaerobic power and power decline were calculated by the computer from the changing number of pedal revolutions each five seconds of the test. Peak anaerobic power usually will occur during the first five to ten seconds (see figure IV.1) of the test. The energy comes from the splitting of CP and ATP. Average power is simply the average of all power readings over the 30 seconds of the test and is supposed to be representative of the breakdown of CP, ATP and glycogen. Both peak and average anaerobic power are expressed in Watts (W). The difference between the highest and lowest power is indicative of power decline and can be used as a measure of fatigue (7). Power decline is expressed in a percentage: the higher the value, the more fatigued the athlete became during the course of the test. Fatigue rate is especially relevant for the taekwondo athlete, as lactic acid will play a role in the second half of the test. The better the athlete is able to resist fatigue, the better he/she will be able to execute kicks in the last round of a match when lactic acid will have had a chance to accumulate.

Pre-Season

Aerobic Endurance

In the pre-season, conditioning of the taekwondo athlete should be emphasized as mentioned in the previous chapter. Aerobic and anaerobic endurance as well as strength constitute the main part of the conditioning program of the taekwondo athlete in the general preparation phase of the pre-season. In order to get a better impression of the relative importance of both aerobic and anaerobic endurance, the results from the physiological component of the OTRP will be presented first. Based on these results, training guidelines will be formulated and exercises suggested to train both types of endurance.

Taaffe and Pieter (13) investigated the anaerobic and aerobic endurance of adult American elite male and female taekwondo athletes. The mean age of these athletes was 24.3 years for the men and 25.6 years for the women. The athletes' height was 1.79 m for the men and 1.72 m for the women, respectively, with a weight of 72.5 kg for the men and 61.4 kg for the women, respectively. Table IV.1 shows the results for aerobic endurance of American adult elite taekwondo athletes. The discussion of the anaerobic endurance of these athletes will follow below. As far as aerobic endurance is concerned, that of adult elite male taekwondo athletes is comparable to American and Canadian elite male judo athletes and elite Canadian wrestlers, but higher than taekwondo club athletes and Canadian Greco-Roman wrestlers (see table IV.2).

Only a few studies were found containing comparable data for female combative athletes. Little (8) assessed aerobic power of young female (14 - 17 years) and male (17 - 20 years) as well as adult female (18+ years) and male (21+ years) judo athletes, who belonged to the 1989 Alberta provincial judo team. Compared to the Alberta adult female judo athletes, the adult female taekwondo athletes scored higher on aerobic endurance relative to body weight (10), but lower than American elite female judo athletes (5). The elite female taekwondo athletes scored slightly higher than female martial sport athletes from various styles (3). In general, the adult female taekwondo athletes recorded a similar value to other intermittent-activity female athletes when aerobic endurance is expressed in terms of body weight (13). See table IV.2 for a comparison of the results.

TABLE IV.1
Means of Aerobic Endurance of Elite Taekwondo Athletes (From: 13).

	Men	Women
$O_{2\,max}$ (l/min)	4.02	2.82
$O_{2\,max}$ (ml/kg/min)	55.79	46.95

TABLE IV.2 Means of Aerobic Endurance (in ml/kg/min) of Elite Combative and Other Athletes

	Men	Women
Canadian judo athletes (14)	57.67	
Canadian wrestlers (2)	57.67	
Canadian Greco-Roman wrestlers (15)	50.40	
Taekwondo club athletes (16)	44.00	
Martial sport athletes from different styles (3)	54.20	44.90
American elite judo athletes (5)	55.60	52.00
Alberta judo athletes (8)	53.75	43.72
American volleyball athletes (11)		50.60
American basketball athletes (17)		49.60

On the basis of these data, it is recommended that the taekwondo athlete trains his/her aerobic endurance similar to athletes in other intermittent-activities, since training more than this does not seem logical nor necessary. Training aerobic endurance beyond this point will result in the body adapting too much to the demands put upon it by the aerobic exercise, which means preparing for aerobic endurance over and above what is required for taekwondo competition. Consequently, the athlete's explosiveness as needed in taekwondo competition will deteriorate, since training for aerobic endurance typically involves steady state, low-intensity work (see previous section), whereas anaerobic exercise is characterized by (supra-)maximal, high-intensity work loads as found in taekwondo competition. It is nevertheless important to train aerobic endurance, since a well-developed anaerobic endurance can only be based on good aerobic endurance. Besides, the nature of taekwondo competition – (supra-)maximal activity interspersed with submaximal work during a single bout and the capacity to last for a whole tournament - requires aerobic endurance.

Training Guidelines for Aerobic Endurance

The training principles discussed in chapter II may be applied to improve aerobic endurance. An example of how this may be done follows.

Frequency of training. As mentioned in the preceding chapter, a minimum of three days a week should be adhered to. Assuming that the athlete works out four to six days a week, aerobic endurance may be trained on alternating days: Tuesday, Thursday and Saturday.

Duration of training. Excluding the warm-up and cool-down, the duration of training for aerobic endurance should be at least ten minutes, but does not have to exceed 30 minutes per training session. Refer to figure IV.1 to appreciate the rationale for a minimum duration of ten minutes.

Intensity of training. The intensity should be increased progressively. As alluded to before, after the off-season, it is wise to start at a low percentage of maximum heart rate. Using the Karvonen formula, a possible range may be from 65 - 85%. For example, if one's heart rate at rest is 54 bpm and one's estimated maximum heart rate is 200 bpm (220 minus age of the athlete), then one's target heart rate will be:

$$HR_{ex} = HR_{rest} + 0.70\ (HR_{max} - HR_{rest})$$
$$HR_{ex} = 54 + 0.70\ (200 - 54) = 156 \text{ bpm.}$$

Of course, depending on the training status of the individual, this percentage may be higher initially. If the training is to be progressive, it will have to be increased in the course of the pre-season. Another way of increasing the intensity is by increasing the distance or the duration. For example, one could start out with a duration of ten minutes and increase this to 15 minutes.

Mode of training. The preferred mode of training is one of a cyclical nature involving large muscle groups. Although riding the bike and swimming meet these requirements, running to improve the athlete's aerobic endurance is recommended. One reason for this choice is related to the time element. Riding the bike or swimming will have to be done for a longer period of time in order to gain the same training effects as running (e.g., 18). If one's time to work out is limited, a more efficient method of using it will be an advantage. Another reason is related to specificity of training. Running uses some of the leg muscles similarly to the way they are used in taekwondo. The same muscle groups are employed slightly differently in swimming as opposed to running, which would make the former less suitable to improve the taekwondo athlete's aerobic endurance. In addition, bicycling may have deleterious effects on the athlete's flexibility, which is a very important component for success in taekwondo competition.

Training Program for Aerobic Endurance

With the aforementioned training guidelines in mind, a program may be devised to improve general and specific aerobic endurance during the pre-season. Although such a program will vary according to personal preference and circumstances, the one presented here will serve its purpose as an example of how it could be done (see table IV.3).

TABLE IV.3 Program to Improve Aerobic Endurance in Pre-Season: General Preparation Phase

	Week 1 - 3		
Frequency	**Duration**	**Intensity**	**Mode**
Tuesday	15 minutes	75% HR_{max}	running
Thursday	15 minutes	75% HR_{max}	running
Saturday	15 minutes	75% HR_{max}	running
	Week 4 - 6		
Frequency	**Duration**	**Intensity**	**Mode**
Tuesday	20 minutes	75% HR_{max}	running
Thursday	20 minutes	75% HR_{max}	running
Saturday	20 minutes	75% HR_{max}	running

In order to develop a program to improve aerobic endurance, it is necessary to make a few basic assumptions. First of all, it is assumed that aerobic endurance and anaerobic endurance are trained separately. A more advanced program would allow to train both types of endurance at the same time. Secondly, it is also assumed that the program will last for six weeks, which is arbitrarily chosen as the minimum period of time to get a training effect. Thirdly, in the program, the intensity of training will only be varied by manipulating the time factor. In other words, to accommodate for the athlete's improved endurance level after administering the training stimulus, i.e., running, the intensity will be increased by having the athlete run longer. It is also possible, of course, to increase the intensity by manipulating the percentage HR_{max} with which the athlete runs, or by manipulating both time and percentage of HR_{max} (see chapter II). For convenience's sake, the program is also divided into two parts, each three weeks long. Another option would be to have three parts, each of two weeks. Again, this is only an example. The coach has the freedom to devise a program that is tailored to the individual's needs.

Since the taekwondo athlete's training program does not only consist of its conditioning component, taekwondo-specific training will also take place. An example of what such a program would look like is depicted in table IV.4. For now, only the aerobic portion and taekwondo training have been entered. Later, anaerobic endurance and strength training will have to be integrated into the program. A more complete program will be shown in the next chapter and will include, for the pre-season, both types of endurance as well as the strength component. The rationale for incorporating taekwondo workouts in the pre-season program is related to the transfer of training effects from the conditioning program, i.e., running and strength training, to the taekwondo techniques. In other words, the improved endurance from running or the improved strength from resistance training, should translate into improved taekwondo endurance and more powerful executions of taekwondo techniques. Stretching for flexibility should always be part of the athlete's training. It will off-set any decrements in flexibility from running and strength training, but it is also essential for the execution of taekwondo techniques. In addition, it will serve as a preventive measure for the occurrence of potential injuries.

As far as the taekwondo training is concerned, in the pre-season, the emphasis should be on technique training. Although technique training should be part of the entire training program all season long, it is during the pre-season that it will be emphasized. This implies that the overall intensity will of necessity be low, because technique training taxes the central nervous system to its fullest. Therefore, complete rest periods should be interspersed, while the various techniques should be executed at maximal speed and force.

In addition to technique training, the taekwondo component in the pre-season program may also include aerobic and anaerobic taekwondo workouts. As far as the aerobic taekwondo training is concerned, similar to the general aerobic training for which running was selected as the mode of training, the taekwondo

TABLE IV.4 Program That Includes Both Taekwondo and Aerobic Endurance Training in Pre-Season
** technique/aerobic (technique plus aerobic taekwondo training)*

Week 1 - 3

Day	**Training**	**Mode**	**Duration**
Monday	rest	-	-
Tuesday	aerobic	running	15 minutes
Wednesday	taekwondo	techique/aerobic*	2 hours
Thursday	aerobic	running	15 minutes
Friday	taekwondo	techique/aerobic	2 hours
Saturday	aerobic	running	15 minutes
Sunday	taekwondo	techique/aerobic	2 hours

Week 4 - 6

Day	**Training**	**Mode**	**Duration**
Monday	rest	-	-
Tuesday	aerobic	running	20 minutes
Wednesday	taekwondo	techique/aerobic	2 hours
Thursday	aerobic	running	20 minutes
Friday	taekwondo	techique/aerobic	2 hours
Saturday	aerobic	running	20 minutes
Sunday	taekwondo	techique/aerobic	2 hours

techniques need to be done continuously. As before, the various techniques should always be performed in an all-out fashion. However, as mentioned in chapter II, the rest between techniques may be incomplete and should be of an active nature, i.e., one should keep moving between single techniques or combinations of them. The overall intensity is in steady state and the skills should be performed for at least ten minutes before taking a break. As in running, the coach could manipulate the intensity by increasing the time that the athlete is executing the techniques, or by having these techniques performed in such a way that the athlete's exercise heart rate will go up.

For instance, suppose that the athlete is working out in blocks of ten minutes at submaximal pace for total intensity. Remember that this is an aerobic taekwondo workout. After every ten minutes, the athlete or the coach should take the former's heart rate to see whether the intensity was as planned. If so, then the second block of ten minutes could continue in the same way as the first. If the heart rate was too high, the techniques should be performed at an overall slower pace by lengthening the rest periods, for instance, and if the heart rate was too low, the pace should be sped up.

To summarize, the taekwondo training in the pre-season could consist of technique and aerobic components. Make sure to always do the technique training before doing the aerobic taekwondo training. As alluded to above, technique training taxes the central nervous system (CNS) and if the aerobic taekwondo training were to be done first, the CNS would be too fatigued to handle the technique training. This means that any training effect as a result of technique training will be lost. As for the aerobic taekwondo training, similar to the general aerobic training (i.e., running), the coach could manipulate the intensity by modifying the time and/or the exercise heart rate (as a percentage of HR_{max}) of the athlete. By incorporating the taekwondo workouts in the pre-season program, the gains from the general conditioning part of the program, i.e., aerobic/anaerobic endurance and strength, will be transferred to the taekwondo skills. This will also allow the motor programs in the athlete's brain to adjust themselves, so that aerobic training effects from running will translate into an improved aerobic endurance in taekwondo, or in terms of strength, the bench press will result in more powerful punches.

Anaerobic Endurance

Table IV.5 shows the means for anaerobic endurance of elite male and female taekwondo athletes as found in the OTRP. There is a paucity of comparable data on anaerobic endurance for combative athletes. Table IV.6 displays data on peak power relative to body weight, while table IV.7 shows power decline of selected other athletes. Elite male taekwondo athletes have been found to score higher on anaerobic peak power in both absolute terms and relative to body weight than Australian judo athletes, but much lower than Canadian elite judo athletes (10). The female elite taekwondo athletes scored higher on peak power per kilogram body weight, but also fatigued faster (the taekwondo athletes had a higher power decline) than the female speedskaters. In terms of power decline, the male elite taekwondo athletes recorded a value in between speedskaters and wrestlers. As far as the authors know, no values are available for power decline in other combative male or female athletes.

TABLE IV.5 Means of Anaerobic Endurance of Elite Taekwondo Athletes (From: 13).

	Men	Women
Peak Power (Watts)	864.6	621.4
Peak Power (Watts/kg)	11.8	10.2
Mean Power (Watts)	671.2	481.9
Mean Power (Watts/kg)	9.2	7.9
Power Decline (%)	37.9	37.7

TABLE IV.6
Means of Anaerobic Peak Power Relative to Body Weight of Other Athletes

	Men	Women
Speed skaters (12)	10.6	8.6
Wrestlers (4)	12.0	
Canadian elite judo athletes (14)	13.7	

TABLE IV.7 Means of Power Decline (in %) of Other Athletes

	Men	Women
Speed skaters (12)	25	30
Wrestlers (4)	43	

Training Guidelines for Anaerobic Endurance

Frequency of training. Three days a week should be reserved again to train anaerobic endurance. As mentioned before, anaerobic endurance could be trained after the first six weeks in the pre-season; in other words, after the aerobic part. So, Tuesday, Thursday and Saturday will now become "anaerobic" days.

Duration of training. The duration of each exercise is very short, since the anaerobic pathway will only be able to supply sufficient energy for a couple of minutes (see section on Energy Deliverance above). Depending on the specific phase of the anaerobic endurance practiced, the duration of each exercise may vary from about five seconds to a maximum of two minutes. Exercises that last more than two minutes will not tax the anaerobic pathway anymore, but will become more aerobic in nature (see figure IV.1).

Intensity of training. Anaerobic training bouts are maximal or supra-maximal workloads. This implies that the intensity, as reflected by the Karvonen formula, will be around 95% or higher of max HR. For a 20-year old taekwondo athlete with a resting heart rate of 60 bpm, the following exercise heart rate may be applicable:

$$HR_{ex} = HR_{rest} + 0.95\ (HR_{max} - HR_{rest})$$
$$HR_{ex} = 60 + 0.95\ (200 - 60) = 193 \text{ bpm.}$$

Remember that for a 20-year old athlete, the estimated HR_{max} equals 220 minus his/her age: 220 - 20 = 200 bpm. Another way of modifying the intensity of the anaerobic workouts is by manipulating the work and recovery intervals (see mode of training) or the distance run.

Mode of training. Running, again, is the preferred mode of training. The best way to train anaerobic endurance is by means of interval training. Interval training consists of alternating work and recovery periods. Depending on intensity and duration, the recovery intervals may vary from a few seconds to several minutes. A rule of thumb is to advise the athlete to listen to his/her own body. Another rule of thumb is to employ a recovery heart rate of 120 bpm before the next work interval is started. No hard scientific evidence exists, however, why a recovery heart rate of 120 bpm should be used. As before, it all depends on the individual athlete: his/her training status, genetic endowment, health status, and so forth.

One may choose to use combinations of interval training formats within one training session or practice them separately. For instance, one interval training format could look like this: ten times 100 m, or eight times 200 m, and so on. One could choose to do the 100 m dashes in only one training session for a certain period of time: two weeks, for instance. In the third and fourth week, one could choose to do 200 m sprints, and so on and so forth. A combination would look something like this: five times 100 m and four times 200 m in one training session. Depending on the training status of the athlete, the number of repetitions could be increased. In table IV.8, separate interval formats are chosen for each session per two weeks (see next section).

The recovery intervals are periods of *active* rest, which means that the athlete should not stand still or sit down. Instead, the athlete should walk or jog at a very low intensity level to recover from the last exercise bout. The rationale for active rest is related to the training effect on the heart as a result of the training stimulus. The training stimulus refers to the exercise during the work interval. As the heart rate goes down, the contractility of the heart muscle increases. Increased contractility means that more blood is pumped through the body at a lower heart rate, which is exactly what the training effect is all about: to increase the efficiency of the body's functions.

Active rest periods will enhance the removal from the body of any waste products, such as lactic acid, that will otherwise get a chance to accumulate. It will also prevent the blood from pooling. During exercise, the blood vessels of the working muscles are open to provide a constant supply of oxygen and nutrients and to remove waste products. The contraction of the working muscles is the main system by which the blood, coming out of these muscles, is returned to the heart. The contracting muscles "squeeze" the blood vessels and, as a result, push the blood back to the heart, which is called the pumping mechanism of the muscles. If the athlete were to cease exercising abruptly, this mechanism will stop working and will result in the blood remaining in the muscles, which is called pooling of the blood. This may cause the athlete to faint because of a temporary lack of blood supply to the brain. An accumulation of blood will also prevent further removal of waste products and therefore a delay in the recovery process.

A very rough guideline to devise a program for anaerobic endurance training is presented in table IV.8 (see section below: Training Program for Anaerobic Endurance). Here again, the coach ought to remember that the program should be tailored to the individual athlete's unique needs.

Training Program for Anaerobic Endurance

The same assumptions that were mentioned under Training Program for Aerobic Endurance (see above) apply here (see table IV.8). As for the taekwondo portion of this part of the pre-season in which anaerobic endurance is emphasized, similar to the aerobic taekwondo training, an anaerobic taekwondo workout may be scheduled in addition to taekwondo technique training. This means that the same principles of training, such as frequency, intensity, duration and mode may be applied.

As far as frequency is concerned, three days a week seem appropriate. The intensity may be varied by means of exercise heart rates, duration of work and recovery intervals, number of kicks executed during the work interval or combinations thereof. The mode, of course, refers to taekwondo techniques. An example of an integrated program, i.e., general anaerobic endurance and taekwondo anaerobic endurance, is shown in table IV.9. It goes without saying that technique training is still very much part of the taekwondo workouts at this point in the pre-season. As before, taekwondo technique and anaerobic training may be done in one session with technique training always preceding the anaerobic part.

TABLE IV.8
Conditioning Program to Improve Anaerobic Endurance in Pre-Season

		Week 1 - 2	
Frequency	**Duration**	**Intensity**	**Mode**
Tuesday	varies	95 - 100% HR_{max}	5 x 100 m/4 x 200 m
Thursday	varies	95 - 100% HR_{max}	5 x 100 m/4 x 200 m
Saturday	varies	95 - 100% HR_{max}	5 x 100 m/4 x 200 m
		Week 3 - 4	
Frequency	**Duration**	**Intensity**	**Mode**
Tuesday	varies	95 - 100% HR_{max}	4 x 200 m/2 x 300 m
Thursday	varies	95 - 100% HR_{max}	4 x 200 m/2 x 300 m
Saturday	varies	95 - 100% HR_{max}	4 x 200 m/2 x 300 m
		Week 5 - 6	
Frequency	**Duration**	**Intensity**	**Mode**
Tuesday	varies	95 - 100% HR_{max}	2 x 300 m/3 x 400 m
Thursday	varies	95 - 100% HR_{max}	2 x 300 m/3 x 400 m
Saturday	varies	95 - 100% HR_{max}	2 x 300 m/3 x 400 m

TABLE IV.9
Program That Includes Both Taekwondo and Anaerobic Endurance Training
** technique/anaerobic (technique plus anaerobic taekwondo training)*

Week 1 - 2

Day	**Training**	**Mode**	**Duration**
Monday	rest	---	---
Tuesday	anaerobic	10 x 100 m	varies
Wednesday	taekwondo	techique/anaerobic*	2 hours
Thursday	anaerobic	10 x 100 m	varies
Friday	taekwondo	techique/anaerobic	2 hours
Saturday	anaerobic	10 x 100 m	varies
Sunday	taekwondo	techique/anaerobic	2 hours

Week 3 - 4

Day	**Training**	**Mode**	**Duration**
Monday	rest	---	---
Tuesday	anaerobic	6 x 200 m	varies
Wednesday	taekwondo	techique/anaerobic	2 hours
Thursday	anaerobic	6 x 200 m	varies
Friday	taekwondo	techique/anaerobic	2 hours
Saturday	anaerobic	6 x 200 m	varies
Sunday	taekwondo	techique/anaerobic	2 hours

Week 5 - 6

Day	**Training**	**Mode**	**Duration**
Monday	rest	--	--
Tuesday	anaerobic	5 x 300 m	varies
Wednesday	taekwondo	techique/anaerobic	2 hours
Thursday	anaerobic	5 x 300 m	varies
Friday	taekwondo	techique/anaerobic	2 hours
Saturday	anaerobic	5 x 300 m	varies
Sunday	taekwondo	techique/anaerobic	2 hours

In-Season

Specific Taekwondo Competition Endurance

Specific taekwondo competition endurance is a combination of aerobic and anaerobic endurance. According to what is presently known about taekwondo, the emphasis in taekwondo competition will probably be on the anaerobic energy pathway. Additional research, however, is indicated before more definitive conclusions can be reached. Observing taekwondo athletes during a competition bout reveals that they alternate attacks with feints, blocks, moving around, and so on. Expressing the actions of the athletes in terms of intensity, a typical taekwondo match will look something like this: low intensity, maximal intensity, submaximal intensity, maximal intensity, low intensity, and so forth. If these intensities were related to the athlete's heart rates during a bout, it would resemble the heart rates as depicted in figure IV.2.

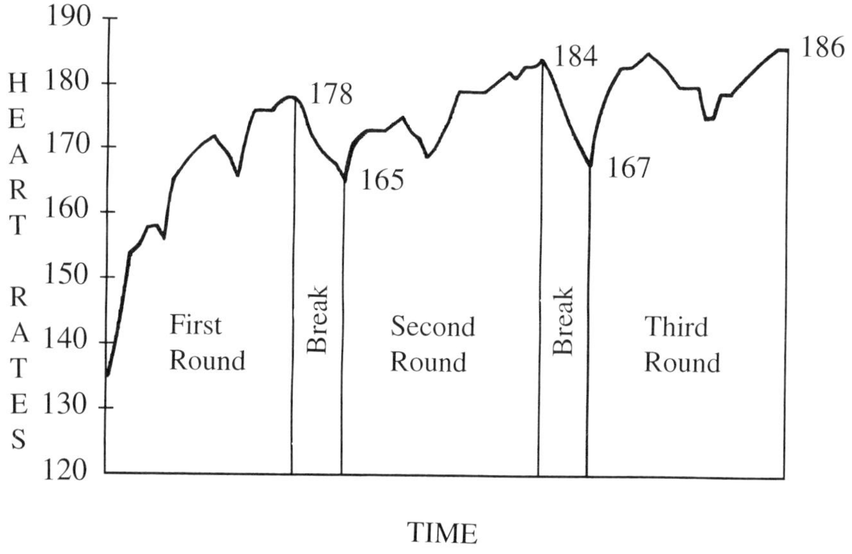

FIGURE IV.2 Typical Heart Rate Pattern in Taekwondo Match

The high heart rate values (178, 184 and 186 bpm) are the heart rates at the end of the first, second and third rounds of the bout, respectively, while the two low values (165 and 167 bpm) are the heart rates at the end of the first and second break, respectively. Consequently, the program for training the specific free-fighting endurance of taekwondo athletes would consist of actual free-fighting bouts. As usual, individual training goals will dictate the exact format and contents of the athlete's program.

The training program for the in-season consists of taekwondo workouts exclusively. Although the length may vary, a minimum of eight weeks for the in-season program is not unusual. It all depends on when the athlete has to peak and how much he/she needs in the way of specific competition training. If the athlete is relatively inexperienced, twelve weeks for the in-season program before the first peak may be needed. Each session may be divided into two or more blocks in which attention is paid to any weaknesses, strengths, or special exercises. For instance, one may choose to work on attacking with a maximum break of ten seconds in between attacks and do this in the first block of two weeks. The next block of two weeks may be devoted to sparring six rounds of three minutes and repeat this for an X number of times during the workout. Subsequent blocks may be planned and are left to the discretion of the coach. A possible program for the in-season is displayed in table IV.10.

This program should only be considered a very tentative one. There ought to be room for flexibility in any program, which means that the coach should be prepared to modify it when necessary. Since rest periods are crucial to achieve training effects, the coach should allow for more than one rest day per week. A rule of thumb would be to allow for a maximum of four days of rest per week, depending on how the athlete feels. Anything more will not be conducive to the athlete's optimal preparation for competition. No rest days at all, will definitely be detrimental to performance (see chapter II). After an intensive week with two peaks, such as in week 2 in table IV.10, the next week should only have one, such as in week 1 in the table.

Sample of Exercises for Specific Taekwondo Training

Some examples of taekwondo techniques that may be used to work on the athlete's specific taekwondo endurance are the following:

1. Fighting combinations against an imaginary opponent.
2. Fighting combinations against a pad.
3. Fighting combinations against a kicking bag.
4. Fighting combinations with an opponent.

TABLE IV.10
In-Season Program to Improve Taekwondo Specific Endurance

Week 1

Frequency	**Duration**	**Intensity**	**Mode**
Monday	-	-	rest
Tuesday	2 hours	70 - 75% HR_{max}	taekwondo
Wednesday	2 hours	75 - 85% HR_{max}	taekwondo
Thursday	2 hours	80 - 85% HR_{max}	taekwondo
Friday	2 hours	75 - 80% HR_{max}	taekwondo
Saturday	2 hours	85 - 90% HR_{max}	taekwondo
Sunday	2 hours	95 - 100% HR_{max}	taekwondo

Week 2

Frequency	**Duration**	**Intensity**	**Mode**
Monday	-	-	rest
Tuesday	2 hours	70 - 75% HR_{max}	taekwondo
Wednesday	2 hours	70 - 75% HR_{max}	taekwondo
Thursday	2 hours	95 - 100% HR_{max}	taekwondo
Friday	2 hours	75 - 80% HR_{max}	taekwondo
Saturday	2 hours	85 - 90% HR_{max}	taekwondo
Sunday	2 hours	95 - 100% HR_{max}	taekwondo

Against an Imaginary Opponent
- Preset fighting combinations that may be used in real competition against an imaginary opponent. Practice at least two techniques in a row.
- Fighting combinations moving forward and backward, at random.
- Fighting combinations at random called by the coach.

Against a Pad
- Fighting combinations against a stationary pad.
- Preset fighting combinations against a moving pad.
- Fighting combinations with the last technique hitting a pad.
- Fighting combinations at random called by the coach against a pad.

Against a Kicking Bag
- Fighting combinations against a stationary kicking bag.
- Fighting combinations with the last technique hitting the bag.
- Fighting combinations against a swinging bag.

With an Opponent
- Preset fighting combinations with a moving opponent.
- At random fighting combinations with a moving opponent.
- Fighting combinations with different opponents.
- Fighting combinations standing in the middle of a circle with opponents standing around the athlete. The opponents attack one by one, preset or at random.

Examples of Fighting Combinations

- Low roundhouse kick, spinning back kick and punch.
- Low roundhouse kick, low roundhouse kick opposite leg, spinning back kick.
- Twice low roundhouse kick with the same leg, spinning back kick with opposite leg.
- Low roundhouse kick, opposite leg high roundhouse kick, spinning back kick.
- Low roundhouse kick, same leg high roundhouse kick, spinning back kick.
- Low roundhouse kick, opposite leg forward pushing kick, same leg axe kick.
- Low roundhouse kick, spinning back kick, low roundhouse kick.
- Side kick, spinning back kick, low roundhouse kick.
- Down block, punch, low roundhouse kick, spinning back kick.

FIGURE IV.3: Fighting Combinations I

Right Reverse Punch

Right Middle Round Kick

Right Axe Kick

FIGURE IV.4: Fighting Combinations II

Right Middle Round Kick

Left High Round Kick

Right Middle Spinning Back Kick

Off-Season

As discussed in chapter II, the off-season will consist of active rest. Depending on the athlete's competition schedule and long-term plans, the off-season may last anywhere from two to four weeks. Active rest may be composed of other activities than taekwondo, such as swimming or ball games. Care should be taken not to incur any injuries that may interfere with the athlete's training goals. A possible scenario may look like the one shown in table IV.11. The coach and athlete are free to choose any number of activities the athlete will engage in. Tennis and frisbee, for instance, are activities the athlete may want to do in week 2 in the off-season instead of swimming and basketball.

TABLE IV.11 Off-Season Program For One Week

Frequency	**Duration**	**Intensity**	**Mode**
Monday	rest	-	-
Tuesday	2 hours	50 - 60% HR_{max}	swimming
Wednesday	2 hours	70 - 80% HR_{max}	swimming
Thursday	2 hours	65 - 70% HR_{max}	basketball
Friday	rest	-	-
Saturday	2 hours	70 - 80% HR_{max}	basketball
Sunday	2 hours	65 - 70% HR_{max}	swimming

References

1. Åstrand, P. O. and K. Rodahl (1986), *Textbook of Work Physiology,* New York, etc.: McGraw-Hill Book Company.
2. Bell, R. D., Faulkner, R. A., Goldade, R. and Laxdal, V. A. (1989), Performance characteristics of elite Canadian wrestlers, *Journal of Physical Education and Sport Sciences,* 1, 1: 33 - 37.
3. Birrer, R. B., Stein, R., Kalman, F., McGloin, E. and Chesler, R. (1988), The fitness profile of the black belt martial arts athlete, In: C. O. Dotson and J. H. Humphrey (eds.), *Exercise Physiology. Current Selected Research,* New York: AMS Press, Inc., pp. 133 - 140.
4. Bouchard, C., Taylor, A. W., Simoneau, J.-A. and Dulac, S. (1991), Testing anaerobic power and capacity, In: J. D. MacDougall, H. A. Wenger and H. J.

Green (eds.), *Physiological Testing of the High-Performance Athlete,* Champaign, IL: Human Kinetics Books, pp. 175 - 221.

5. Callister, R., Callister, R. J., Staron, R. S., Fleck, S., Tesch, P. and Dudley, G. A. (1991), Physiological characteristics of elite judo athletes, *International Journal of Sports Medicine*, 12, 2: 196 - 203.
6. Heyward, V. (1984), *Designs for Fitness,* Minneapolis: Burgess Publishing Company.
7. Lamb, D. (1984), *Physiology of Exercise. Responses and Adaptations*, New York: MacMillan Publishing Company.
8. Little, N. G. (1991), Physical performance attributes of junior and senior women, juvenile, junior, and senior men judokas, *Journal of Sports Medicine and Physical Fitness,* 31, 4: 510 - 520.
9. MacDougall, J. D. and Wenger, H. A. (1991), The purpose of physiological testing, In: J. D. MacDougall, H. A. Wenger and H. J. Green (eds.), *Physiological Testing of the High-Performance Athlete*, Champaign, IL: Human Kinetics Books, pp. 1 - 5.
10. Pieter, W. (1991), Performance characteristics of elite taekwondo athletes, *Korean Journal of Sport Science,* 3: 94 - 117.
11. Puhl, J., Case, S., Fleck, S. and Van Handel, P. (1982), Physical and physiological characteristics of elite volleyball players, *Research Quarterly,* 53, 3: 257 - 262.
12. Seresse, O., Simoneau, J.-A., Lortie, G., Bouchard, C. and Boulay, M. R. (1989), unpublished raw data.
13. Taaffe, D. and Pieter, W. (1990), Physical and physiological characteristics of elite taekwondo athletes, In: *Commonwealth and International Conference Proceedings. Volume 3. Sport Science Part 1, Auckland*, New Zealand: NZAHPER, pp. 80 - 88.
14. Taylor, A. W. and Brassard, L. (1981), A physiological profile of the Canadian judo team, *Journal of Sports Medicine and Physical Fitness*, 21, 2: 160 - 164.
15. Taylor, A. W., Brassard, L., Proteau, L. and Robin, D. (1979), A physiological profile of Canadian Greco-Roman wrestlers, *Canadian Journal of Applied Sports Science,* 4, 2: 131 - 134.
16. Thompson, W. R. and Vinueza, C. (1991), Physiologic profile of tae kwon do black belts, *Sports Medicine, Training and Rehabilitation*, 3, 1: 49 - 53.
17. Vaccaro, P., Clarke, D. H. and Wrenn, J. P. (1979), Physiological profiles of elite women basketball players, *Journal of Sports Medicine*, 19, 1: 45 - 54.
18. Wilmore, J. H. and Costill, D. L. (1988), *Training for Sport and Activity*, Dubuque, Iowa: Wm. C. Brown Publishers.

CHAPTER V

TRAINING STRENGTH IN TAEKWONDO

Introduction

Movement in taekwondo, as in daily life, takes place by means of muscular strength. Contrary to some sports where strength may be more dominant than endurance, e.g., shot put, javelin, and contrary to sports where endurance may be more dominant than strength, e.g., marathon, 10K, strength and endurance in taekwondo may be considered equally important. It is important in relation to kicking and punching, but also in relation to the prevention of injuries. For example, depending on how strength is measured, it seems to be associated with how fast the body or body parts can be moved (23). Research has shown that strength assessed on an isokinetic machine (see below for isokinetic strength) was positively related to kicking speed in taekwondo (6). It was also found that there was a relationship between strength and kicking force. As for strength and its role in the occurrence of injuries, it is suggested that strength may have a preventive effect (4; 10; 12). This means that the stronger certain areas of the body are, e.g., thigh and calf muscles, the less likely it will be that they and their surrounding structures, e.g., the knee, will get injured.

Incorporating a strength program in the athlete's preparation for taekwondo competition is a relatively new phenomenon. There are still many coaches and athletes who think that strength training might be detrimental to taekwondo performance. Part of this believe may be based on hearsay, tradition, a lack of information about the positive effects of strength training, or a combination of these and other factors. Similar to boxing (7), the following reasons to include a strength program in the taekwondo athlete's total training program may be advanced: injury prevention, increased muscular endurance, increased muscle contraction speed, increased force and increased power.

One of the misconceptions regarding the effect of strength training on taekwondo performance is, that strength training will have a negative effect on speed, flexibility and coordination. Granted, one may have seen isolated cases of people who did lose any or all of the previously mentioned variables. More than likely, these people have not adhered to proper strength training principles and/or failed to practice already acquired skills, such as flexibility or coordination. The following suggestions to combat any deleterious effects of strength training on speed, flexibility or coordination are based on Lombardi (14).

When strength training, be sure to always warm-up and cool down. Use both general warm-up as well as specific warm-up exercises (see training guidelines below), which will minimize the occurrence of sore muscles. Include a stretching and flexibility program in your strength routine to off-set any potential losses in flexibility and to help prevent injuries. Very important: practice your taekwondo skills in addition to strength training. If you do not practice your taekwondo techniques, they are bound to deteriorate, regardless of whether you strength train or not. Make sure to do all exercises in your strength program through the full range of motion (see training guidelines below), which will aid in maintaining your flexibility.

Another misconception that seems to exist is that strength training will cause the taekwondo athlete to "bulk up". Gaining excessive muscle mass is related to the format that one uses in strength training. If one lifts heavy weights with one to three repetitions and long breaks in between lifts, one will definitely acquire muscle mass. However, this kind of strength, called maximal strength, such as needed in the shot put and javelin throw, is not necessary for taekwondo competition. Instead, low weights and many repetitions are indicated for taekwondo (see below), which will merely "tone" the muscles.

However, a word of caution is nevertheless in order. There is a chance that strength training will lead to slight weight gains due to some increase in muscle weight. This is especially true for those, who have a "natural" weight right above a lighter weight division and who usually have to lose the extra kilos to compete in this lighter weight category (16). In addition, if this athlete does not have much fat to lose and may even be "naturally" muscular, problems may arise when strength training. For instance, if the cut-off point for the women's bantam weight division is 55 kg, the competitor who weighs around 57 kg may want to try to lose the weight. If this person happens to be one with a low fat content to begin with, even the slightest muscle gains through strength training will pose a serious problem. In such cases, it is advised to consult with a sports nutritionist and a strength training specialist.

This chapter will deal with muscle strength and strength training for taekwondo competition. It will cover the ways muscles can contract and the various types of strength training. It will also discuss how strength may be tested, while the results of the strength component of the OTRP will be presented as well. Training guidelines and principles will be offered in addition to a possible program for the pre-season and in-season.

Muscular Contractions

When muscles contract, they will cause movement. In general, the following types of contractions are distinguished:

- static contractions
- dynamic contractions
  - concentric
  - eccentric.

Static contractions. These contractions are also called isometric contractions. Isometric literally means equal length, i.e., the contracting muscles do not visibly change their length nor does the angle of the joint that they span change appreciably (14). In taekwondo, this type of contraction can be seen when doing a straight punch without retrieving the arm or when kicking without pulling the leg back. The time during which the arm or the leg is kept extended, the muscle are contracting isometrically. Another example of isometric contractions in taekwondo would be the actions of the muscles during a block at the end of the movement. For instance, when doing the down block *(arae makki),* the muscles of the arm will contract isometrically at the end of the block when the forearm is above the thigh.

Dynamic contractions. These contractions are also known as *isotonic* contractions. During isotonic contractions, the length of the muscles visibly change (14). Although the word isotonic means "equal tension", it is actually a misnomer, because the tension of the muscles do change (13; 14). What does not change is the external load that these muscles are working against. For instance, when doing a biceps curl with a 30 kg dumbbell, the tension in the biceps will change, depending on the angle that the joint is going through, while the external load of 30 kg will not change. When the biceps during this curl *shorten* (during the upswing), the muscles are said to contract *concentrically*. During the downswing of the curl, the muscles are *lengthening* and they are said to contract *eccentrically*. In taekwondo, the front thigh muscles (quadriceps) are shortening during the extension phase of the round kick, for instance: the muscles contract concentrically. During the same kick, the back thigh muscles (hamstrings) are contracting eccentrically during the same phase.

Another type of contraction that the taekwondo athlete may encounter when strength training depends on rather sophisticated equipment and does not have its counterpart in taekwondo. It is called *isokinetic* and refers to muscles contracting at an equal speed that is set by the machine. It is a form of muscle contraction under ideal circumstances, in the sense that this type of contraction can only be elicited with a so-called isokinetic dynamometer. Isokinetic exercises are characterized by movements with a constant speed, while the muscles are contracting maximally or almost maximally through the whole range of motion (14). The speed of the machine is preset and the more recently developed isokinetic machines will allow both concentric and eccentric contractions of the muscles.

To summarize, there are basically three types of contractions that the taekwondo athlete will encounter in strength training. During isometric contractions, the length of the muscles do not visibly change. Keeping the arm extended during a punch would be an example of isometrically contracting muscles. During dynamic contractions, the length of the muscles changes. When the muscles are shortening, this is called concentric contraction and when the muscles are lengthening, it is called eccentric contraction. An example of both types of contractions would be the actions of the quadriceps during the extension phase of the round kick (concentric contraction) and that of the hamstrings (eccentric contraction). The last type of contraction that may be found in strength training is dependent on a special machine, the so-called isokinetic machine. During both concentric and eccentric contractions, the muscles have maximal or near maximal tension throughout the whole range of motion at a preset speed of the device. Based on these types of contractions, the following types of strength training may be distinguished.

Types of Strength Training

Isometric Training

Isometric training may be done with or without weights. An example of isometric training without weights would be using the wall or another immovable object to push against with one's arms in a certain angle. Strength gains as a result of isometric training are angle-specific (e.g., 3; 8). This would make isometric training inferior to other forms of strength training when strength is sought through the full range of motion. However, in combination with dynamic strength training, isometric training may prove quite valuable. It is often used to overcome so-called sticking points in a range of motion during a dynamic exercise (8; 14). A sticking point is that point in a range of motion where the athlete has more problems lifting the weight than in any other angle. By exercising isometrically in this specific angle, the individual will increase his/her strength at this angle and, as a result, will be able to carry the weight during a dynamic exercise through this point. Although isometric training is angle-specific, one may choose to exercise at various angles to improve strength over a wider range of motion.

Constant Load Dynamic Strength Training

Constant load dynamic strength training refers to dynamic exercises with a *constant* external load, such as a 60 kg barbell. Typically, this type of strength training uses such equipment as barbells, dumbbells or multi-purpose machines such as the universal gym apparatus with which a variety of exercises can be done. Both concentric and eccentric contractions are possible during constant load dynamic strength training. Strength is gained through the full range of motion, as opposed to isometric training. Research seems to suggest that a combination of both concentric and eccentric contractions will lead to optimal gains in strength (8). One way to do this is to lower the weight slowly after having lifted it concentrically. For instance, when doing the biceps curl, one would contract the biceps concentrically during the upswing and when lowering the weight slowly, the biceps would be contracting eccentrically thereby leading to the optimal strength desired when training effects occur. A word of caution is warranted when using eccentric strength training, however. Muscle soreness as a result of this type of training occurs rather frequently, but will diminish eventually (8; 14). In addition, be sure to have a spotter for safety purposes when using free weights. Constant load dynamic strength training is the typical mode of training for many athletes.

One type of strength training that is entirely based on eccentric contractions is called plyometric training (3; 14). During plyometric training [sometimes called implosion training or explosive power training (14)], the muscles are forcefully stretched before contraction. Exercise done during plyometric training include hops, jumps, or leaps (22). An example of plyometric training is shown in figure V.1. The athlete jumps off the bench and keeps her knees bent before jumping up in the air. The quadriceps, in this case, are forcefully stretched (they are contracting eccentrically) when she lands on the floor after jumping off the bench and then contract concentrically to jump in the air. Plyometric training was used successfully by the authors to improve jumping power in taekwondo athletes.

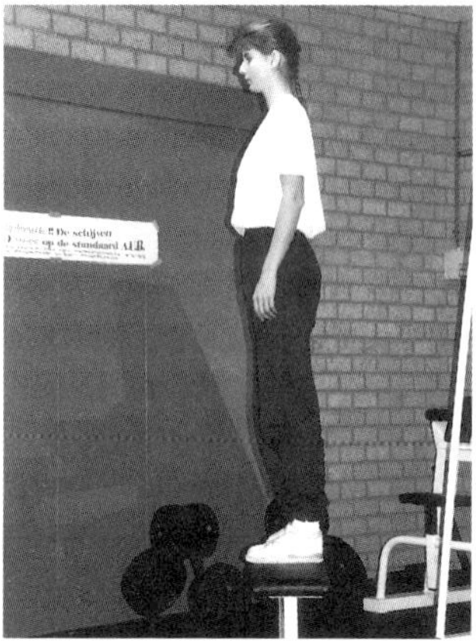

Start on the Bench

Jump off the Bench

Jump in the Air

FIGURE V.1: Example of Plyometric Training: Depth Jump

Variable Resistance Dynamic Training

As the name implies, in variable resistance dynamic strength training, the resistance of the external load varies through the range of motion to accommodate weaker and stronger angles in this range of motion. The sticking point phenomenon mentioned above, is characteristic of constant load dynamic strength training. By using special machines equipped with cams or pulleys (8), the resistance of the weights is varied to accommodate the strength of the athlete thereby truly leading to strength gains through the full range of motion. Although the principle of using accommodating resistance makes sense from an anatomical/biomechanical point of view, it is not possible to build machines to meet each individual's difference in body build and the resultant difference in limb length and other variations in anatomical structure (8). Nevertheless, improvements in strength with variable resistance machines will definitely occur. If there is an opportunity to combine constant load and variable resistance training, the taekwondo athlete would have a tool in hand to make his/her strength training program more enjoyable.

Isokinetic Training

As mentioned above, special apparatus is needed to strength train isokinetically. The major advantage of using isokinetic equipment is that resistance is proportional to the strength of the individual at all angles through the range of motion. One serious disadvantage is that at high speeds, such as 300°/sec or even higher, the movement will only be truly isokinetic over a very short range of motion. The limb needs time to adjust to the speed of the machine, which means that it will have traveled through part of the range of motion already before it can catch up. Consequently, only through part of the range of motion will the muscles show strength gains as a result of isokinetic training. At the lower speeds, such as 30°, 60° or 90°/sec, strength will be gained over the full range of motion. Strength gains by means of isokinetic training is speed-specific. When training at 30°/sec, for instance, strength will improve at that speed only, but not necessarily at lower or higher speeds (e.g., 8). Research seems to suggest that optimal speeds for isokinetic training may be between about 95° and 110°/sec to cover strength gains at both lower and higher speeds (8).

Testing Strength

Assessing muscular strength of the taekwondo competitor will give more information about the strength profile of the individual. The results may serve as baseline data to be used during the rehabilitation period if the athlete sustains an injury. In this way, it will be possible to compare the strength of the injured limb with that of the uninvolved limb. Assessing strength will also aid in monitoring training progress of the athlete. For instance, after the pre-season, the coach may want to evaluate his/her training program and administer a battery of tests to assess, among other things, muscular strength. Changes may be made depending on the results of the tests.

Although several methods exist to assess strength, the athletes who volunteered for the OTRP were tested isokinetically. To this end, a so-called Cybex machine was used that was linked to a computer. The athletes were tested at four different speeds: 120°, 180°, 240° and 300°/sec during leg extension and flexion. Time constraints prevented testing of arm strength and more testing of hip strength, so that incomplete data are available for hip strength and no data at all for arm strength. Arm strength, of course, is relevant for punching, while hip strength is important for kicking. The rationale for testing leg extension and flexion is related to the use of the quadriceps and hamstrings during kicking. In the OTRP, only concentric contractions of the quadriceps and hamstrings were tested. The main focus was to determine the ratio between hamstrings strength and that of the quadriceps. The lower the relative strength of the hamstrings (relative compared to the quadriceps), the higher the chances are that they may get injured. Research has shown that the hamstrings are very susceptible to injuries in taekwondo (25). During the execution of the axe and round kicks, the stress on the hamstrings is especially high.

During the test, the athletes were seated on the isokinetic machine with their upper body and leg to be tested fastened with Velcro straps to preclude any additional movements that may interfere with an objective assessment of the strength of the quadriceps and hamstrings. The athletes were allowed a general warm-up and a specific warm-up on the machine to get used to the testing procedure. The specific warm-up consisted of extensions and flexions on the isokinetic apparatus. They would be allowed three trials for each speed tested during the actual test. A rest period of about one minute was allowed in between speeds. Peak torque, the highest force recorded, was used regardless of the angle it occurred at.

Results from Taekwondo Research

Table V.1 shows the means of the hamstrings to quadriceps ratios, also called H/Q ratios, of elite male and female taekwondo athletes at the four speeds tested (19).

TABLE V.1 Means of H/Q Ratios (in %) of Elite Taekwondo Athletes (Based on 19)

Speed	Females	Males
120°	65	69
180°	69	73
240°	72	75
300°	75	76

With increasing speed, the H/Q ratios tend to increase as well. It is suggested that at the highest speeds tested, 240° and 300°/sec, the H/Q ratios should be around 80 - 90+% (19; 21). It is recognized that H/Q ratios are not only dependent on the speed that the isokinetic machine is set at, but that "ideal" H/Q ratios are sport-dependent. In other words, optimal H/Q ratios may also be dependent on the sport of the athletes tested. Research (25) and anecdotal evidence suggest, however, that the hamstrings are very susceptible to injuries during taekwondo kicking, which makes having strong hamstrings all the more important.

In view of the occurrence of potential injuries and having baseline data available to compare the injured limb with, information on H/Q ratios of the left and right legs are necessary. Table V.2 displays the means of the H/Q ratios of both legs for elite male and female taekwondo athletes who were tested at three speeds (20).

TABLE V.2 Means of H/Q Ratios (in %) of Elite Taekwondo Athletes: Left - Right Comparisons (Based on 20)

	Females		**Males**	
Speed	**Right**	**Left**	**Right**	**Left**
180°	70	72	72	75
240°	74	73	75	75
300°	75	78	73	79

As can be clearly seen, there is a difference between the right and left legs in H/Q ratios. Research has suggested that a difference between the right and left legs of about 10 - 20% in strength is predictive of the onset of injuries (e.g., 9; 18). In other words, if the left hamstrings, of instance, were to be between 10 - 20% weaker than the right hamstrings, they would stand a greater chance of getting injured than the right hamstrings. It was shown that a comparison between the left and right legs was within 7% (the left hamstrings were only 7% weaker, at the most, than the right) and in some cases, the left hamstrings were even stronger than the right hamstrings (20). However, in more practical terms, conversations with the athletes revealed that some of them were suffering from hamstrings injuries. In other words, although the difference between the right and left legs was within the range suggested in the literature, the difference between the hamstrings and the quadriceps was apparently too large, as expressed by the relatively low H/Q ratios, which caused the hamstrings to get injured. It is recommended, therefore, to make the hamstrings as strong as possible.

Comparisons with other combative athletes are difficult to make. As usual, there are hardly any data available to make comparisons. Secondly, depending on how the athletes were tested, comparisons may not be warranted. Very tentatively, the H/Q ratio of Canadian elite male judo athletes at 120°/sec was found to be around 72.5% (24). A better comparison with athletes who were tested the same way the American elite taekwondo athletes were, may be derived from as yet unpublished data. Elite Belgian taekwondo, judo and karate athletes were tested on leg extension and flexion at 240°/sec (5). Based on a study to be published, in which comparisons are made between these athletes and taekwondo athletes tested in the OTRP, it was observed that both the American male and female taekwondo athletes scored higher H/Q ratios at 240°/sec than their Belgian counterparts. The Belgians scored in the low 50% (males) or high 50% (females). The difference in H/Q ratios between the American and Belgian athletes is believed to be related to the relatively weak hamstrings of the latter.

Strength Training Principles

Although there are general training principles as described in chapter II, each component of conditioning training, i.e., endurance and strength, has its own principles that the taekwondo athlete should adhere to. Specific training principles for aerobic and anaerobic endurance have already been discussed in the previous chapter. In this section, specific strength training principles will be covered. The information is based on texts by Brooks and Fahey (3), Fleck and Kraemer (8), Lamb (13) and Lombardi (14). The following principles will be dealt with:

- Overload and specificity
- Full range of motion
- Large muscles/small muscles
- Front/back and upper/lower balance
- Recovery
- Training velocity.

Overload and Specificity. If the strength program is to lead to improved taekwondo performance, it should provide for overloading the specific muscle groups that are important to taekwondo skills. This overload should be in a progressive manner to avoid the occurrence of muscle soreness. It makes logical sense to strengthen those muscles that are specific to taekwondo techniques to enhance performance in competition. Which muscles are involved in taekwondo skills may be determined by a so-called Needs Analysis (see next section).

Specificity also refers to specificity of movement, in addition to training the specific muscles that are involved in the technique. Specificity of movement would be best trained by executing taekwondo skills. This does not mean that one should wear weighted belts around one's knees or wrists when kicking or punching. Doing this would disrupt the motor programs of those techniques and hence their actual performance and may even lead to injuries. It also does not imply that one should use strength training equipment to execute kicks and punches if such were possible. What it does mean, however, is that one should isolate the muscles that are used in taekwondo skills and try to include exercises in one's program that are related to taekwondo techniques, such as the bench press, leg extensions and leg curls (see Needs Analysis and Pre-Season).

Full Range of Motion. Strength is only gained at the specific angles trained. Since taekwondo techniques are always executed through the full range of motion, strength exercises should also move through the full range of motion (FROM) as well. As mentioned above, the major disadvantage of isometric strength training is that it will only lead to strength gains in specific angles. It is possible to complement dynamic strength training with isometrics to overcome sticking points. In such cases, limited joint range of motion may be done, but never to the exclusion of FROM exercises.

Large Muscles/Small Muscles. When muscles fatigue, training will become less effective. Usually, movements become fatiguing because smaller muscle groups that are involved in those movements become fatigued. For instance, if one were to do wrist curls and extensions first, the forearms may become tired, so that bench presses or biceps curls would become more difficult than necessary. Instead, one should do the bench press first, then the biceps curls and elbow extensions and finally the wrist curls and extensions.

Front/Back and Upper/Lower Balance. It is essential to balance opposing muscle groups. The most important reason for doing this is related to the prevention of injuries (e.g., 4). As alluded to above, if the hamstrings are relatively too weak compared to the quadriceps muscles, chances will be greater that they will get injured during kicking. How much the difference should be between two opposing muscle groups is not easy to answer. For taekwondo, a range of 85 - 90+% is suggested at a testing speed of about 240° - 300°/sec on an isokinetic machine. A rule of thumb would be to exercise front/back and upper/lower body muscles with an eye on making the opposing muscles as strong as possible. Another reason to strive for a balanced development of one's muscles has to do with the potential negative effect on flexibility, in that flexibility may be reduced. Obviously, reduced flexibility will be detrimental to taekwondo performance. Reduced flexibility may also lead to injuries, which brings us back to the first reason for a balanced muscle development.

Recovery. As has been repeatedly stressed throughout this book, it is of the utmost importance to allow for adequate rest periods. In other words, make sure to have at least one day between strength training sessions. As with training for endurance, strength training three days a week on alternating days is sufficient for the competitive taekwondo athlete. As mentioned in previous chapters, if no adequate rest is taken, overtraining may result.

Training Velocity. Training velocity refers to the velocity with which the athlete lifts weights in isotonic strength training or at which speed he/she moves the arm on an isokinetic device. Based on the literature, it is probably best to adhere to a moderate speed. Moving the weights as fast as possible will result in adequate resistance for only a very brief period of time. On an isokinetic machine, as mentioned above, speeds between 95° and 110°/sec are considered optimal velocities to gain strength. Higher speeds, as in isotonic exercise, will only train the muscles in a short portion of the range of motion. To train muscular endurance (see below) on an isokinetic dynamometer, a speed of about 180°/sec has been suggested with repetitions until exhaustion in three sets (17).

Needs Analysis

The coach will have to analyze the type of strength that is needed for taekwondo competition as well as which muscles play a role when performing techniques. For instance, power athletes such as shot putters or javelin throwers, will need maximal strength, while marathoners will fare better with aerobic strength endurance. Taekwondo athletes, on the other hand, will need anaerobic strength endurance. An example of which muscles are involved in a round kick in karate and how to strength train them may be found in the article by Hobusch and McClellan (11).

Maximal strength is the maximal amount of force that an athlete can exert at one time as reflected in the highest load that this athlete can lift. In addition to maximal strength, power athletes also need what has been called absolute strength (2), which is the maximal strength exerted regardless of body weight. As was the case with endurance (both aerobic and anaerobic), body weight also plays a role in strength: the heavier one is, the higher one's maximal or absolute strength. Relative strength, on the other hand, would be strength divided by one's body weight, in this case, and is very important in weight-categorized sports, such as taekwondo, where the athlete has to propel him/herself through space. In other words, the higher the athlete's relative strength, the better it will contribute to improved performance.

Aerobic strength endurance (also called aerobic muscular endurance) refers to the endurance of the muscles. In the previous chapter, where aerobic and anaerobic endurance were discussed, the word "endurance" referred to the endurance of the heart (14). When speaking of aerobic strength endurance, the term „endurance“ now refers to endurance of the muscles (14). Aerobic muscular endurance training is characterized by high repetitions (more than 20) and low weights (2; 8).

Anaerobic strength endurance, which is needed in taekwondo, would be characterized by high intensity muscular endurance and can be trained by relatively high repetitions (10 - 20) using low weights (2; 8). Anaerobic strength endurance will help the taekwondo athlete to improve his/her lactic acid tolerance level. This means that the athlete will be better able to withstand the accumulation of lactic acid, especially in the last round of a match. Lactic acid tolerance may be trained by using short rest periods between strength exercises (shorter than one minute), which will cause lactic acid concentrations in the body to increase.

Having established the kind of strength needed for taekwondo competition, the coach subsequently needs to identify the specific muscle groups that are dominant in executing taekwondo techniques [refer to the article by Hobusch and McClellan (11) for an example in karate]. This will require a basic knowledge of anatomy and biomechanics. To help the coach who lacks this information, a suggested program consisting of exercises that will strengthen the muscles used in kicking and punching has been included below (see Pre-Season). For more information about which muscles to strengthen for taekwondo competition, the coach and athlete alike are referred to a strength specialist or an exercise physiologist to help design the athlete's strength program. Generally speaking, it is always recommended to consult with a professional, because the chances of getting injured are very real and will interfere with the athlete's taekwondo career.

A final consideration in a Needs Analysis is related to individuality (8). The coach may develop a program that is suited for the whole group that he or she is responsible for, but there should be room for an individual approach. For instance, if one athlete lacks strength in the hamstrings, additional exercises may be developed to strengthen these muscles. It would also be possible to have this athlete do an additional set of leg curls, for instance.

Pre-Season

The pre-season is the time to spend on general as opposed to specific strength. This may be done by isotonic or isokinetic equipment. Isometric exercises may also be done on both isotonic and isokinetic devices. With isokinetic machines, isometric exercises can be realized by setting the speed to zero degrees per second. During the specific preparation period of the pre-season, specific strength should be trained. The athlete may utilize isotonic or isokinetic equipment again, but will switch to a heavy bag later during this specific preparation period. The heavy bag will also be used during the in-season. It will serve two purposes. First of all, the athlete will be able to use taekwondo techniques on the bag, thereby kicking and punching as hard as possible, which will exercise taekwondo-specific strength. Secondly, it will also be possible to practice lactic anaerobic endurance (see chapter IV).

If the athlete is a novice at strength training or if the overall strength level of the athlete is low, his/her maximal strength should be developed first. The general preparation period of the pre-season is used to develop maximal strength and will comprise a variety of exercises. A list of potential exercises is shown in table V.3. It is assumed that the coach and athlete have chosen to use isotonic strength training. The exercises in table V.3 are not in any particular order. It is just a listing of exercises, not a program with the training principle in mind regarding large/small muscles. The number of repetitions to develop maximal strength will be low (3 - 5) with relatively heavy loads and three sets per exercise. Anaerobic strength endurance will be done during the specific preparation period in the pre-season. As mentioned above, the load will be relatively low with high repetitions (10 - 20). Another example of a strength training program for taekwondo was presented by Lowell (15), although no mention was made relative to the season it should be used in.

TABLE V.3 A Sample of Exercises to Develop Maximal Strength

Upper Body	Lower Body
Bench press	Squat
Lat pull	Leg press
Seated military press	Leg extension
Bent-over row	Leg curl
Inclined chest fly	Heel raise
Deltoid fly	Thigh abduction
Biceps curl	Thigh adduction
Triceps extension	Hip flexion
Shoulder shrug	Lunge
Wrist extension	Depth jump
Wrist flexion	
Sit-ups	
Back extension	
Pull-up	
Upright row	

Before presenting the training guidelines, it will be instructive to define a number of strength training terms. *Repetition* refers to how many times a certain load is lifted. The highest load that can only be lifted once and not more than once is called *repetition maximum* (RM). One exercise, which may consist of one or more RM, is called one *set*. For instance, doing the bench press with 10 RM once, would be one set, while doing it twice with 10 RM would be doing two sets, and so on. Ten RM refers to the ability of the athlete to lift a certain weight ten times, while the 11th time would result in failure to lift the load with good technique.

Training Guidelines

As written before, during the general preparation period of the pre-season, maximal strength and strength endurance are emphasized. The following guidelines would be in effect in that case.

Frequency. For taekwondo athletes, three times per week to devote to strength training is sufficient. It may be best to schedule the strength sessions on a different day from the aerobic and anaerobic endurance sessions, since it has been suggested that simultaneous training for strength and endurance may interfere with strength development (3). This may only be true for developing maximal strength, which means that muscular endurance sessions may be done on the same days that aerobic or anaerobic endurance sessions are scheduled. There is not enough research available on the topic yet, so much is still unknown. It may very well be possible, for instance, that if the athlete were to schedule two training sessions per day, once for endurance and the second time for strength, that no interference may take place. Therefore, it is left to the discretion of the coach how to schedule the endurance and strength sessions of his/her athletes.

Duration. The length of the strength sessions, of course, varies per individual. It depends on such factors as number of exercises chosen, rest between exercises, rest between sets, number of repetitions and number of sets. Working on maximal strength may take longer than working on strength endurance, because there are more exercises and longer rest periods between exercises and between sets. The total duration of the strength training program may be set to 12 weeks for developing maximal strength and 6 weeks to develop strength endurance.

Intensity. Instead of heart rates, which were used as indicators of intensity for endurance training (see chapter IV), load may be used to determine intensity of strength training sessions. It is also possible, of course, to vary the frequency of training and manipulate the rest intervals to change the intensity of the workouts. For the time being, the frequency will stay the same throughout the entire strength program, i.e., three days per week. The rest intervals between exercises and between sets for maximal strength will be set to two minutes. The rest periods between exercises and sets for muscular endurance will be set to one minute. This means that only the number of repetitions will be manipulated in addition to the load lifted to vary intensity. As the athlete improves in strength, the load will have to be increased to cause any training effects. To develop maximal strength, 3 - 5 RM will be used and to develop strength endurance, 10 - 20 RM. In tables V.4 and V.5, only the number of repetitions is indicated to denote the intensity. An exception is made for sit-ups and back extensions: the athlete could use as many repetitions as desired. Increasing the number of repetitions may be done at any time the athlete feels he/she can handle it.

Mode. The mode of training refers to the type of strength training that the athlete will use, which, among other things, depends on the facilities that are available. For convenience's sake, it will be assumed that isotonic constant load strength training will be employed. A visual representation of some exercises is shown in figure V.2 - V.12.

TABLE V.4 Program to Improve Maximal Strength in Pre-Season

	Week 1 - 4		
Frequency	**Duration**	**Intensity**	**Mode**
Tuesday	varies	3 RM	isotonic
Thursday	varies	3 RM	isotonic
Saturday	varies	3 RM	isotonic
	Week 5 - 8		
Frequency	**Duration**	**Intensity**	**Mode**
Tuesday	varies	4 RM	isotonic
Thursday	varies	4 RM	isotonic
Saturday	varies	4 RM	isotonic
	Week 9 - 12		
Frequency	**Duration**	**Intensity**	**Mode**
Tuesday	varies	5 RM	isotonic
Thursday	varies	5 RM	isotonic
Saturday	varies	5 RM	isotonic

It is assumed that strength training will take place on the same day that the athlete will work on his/her endurance. One could choose to do a morning session to work on endurance and an afternoon or evening session to strength train. Naturally, the coach is free to devise a different plan.

A list of exercises to develop maximal strength was already depicted in table V.3. Table V.6 shows a list of the exercises that the athlete may want to do to develop strength endurance. When training to develop maximal strength and muscular endurance, it is important to alternate muscle groups exercised. In addition to exercising opposing muscle groups (see Strength Training Principles), the athlete should also alternate between upper body and lower body exercises. A detailed description of how to execute the various exercises and the exact muscle groups they work falls beyond the scope of this book. The coach and athlete are advised to consult a strength training specialist.

TABLE V.5 Program to Improve Strength Endurance in Pre-Season

Week 1 - 3			
Frequency	**Duration**	**Intensity**	**Mode**
Tuesday	varies	10 RM	isotonic
Thursday	varies	10 RM	isotonic
Saturday	varies	10 RM	isotonic
Week 4 - 6			
Frequency	**Duration**	**Intensity**	**Mode**
Tuesday	varies	15 RM	isotonic
Thursday	varies	15 RM	isotonic
Saturday	varies	15 RM	isotonic

TABLE V.6 A Sample of Exercises to Develop Strength Endurance

Upper Body	Lower Body
Bench press	Squat
Lat pull	Leg extension
Bent-over row	Leg curl
Biceps curl	Depth jump
Triceps extension	Hip flexion
Sit-ups	Heel raise
Back extension	

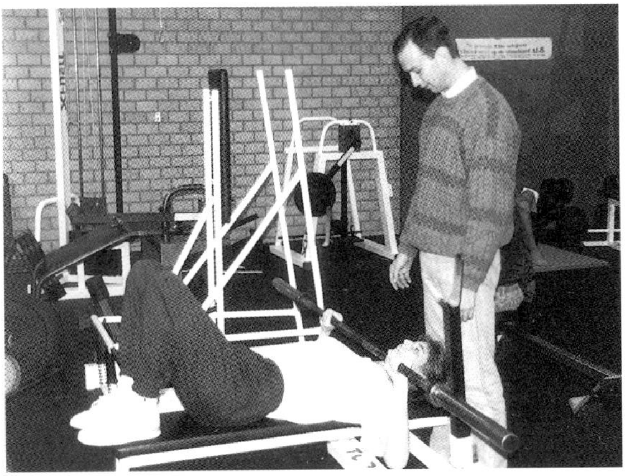

Start

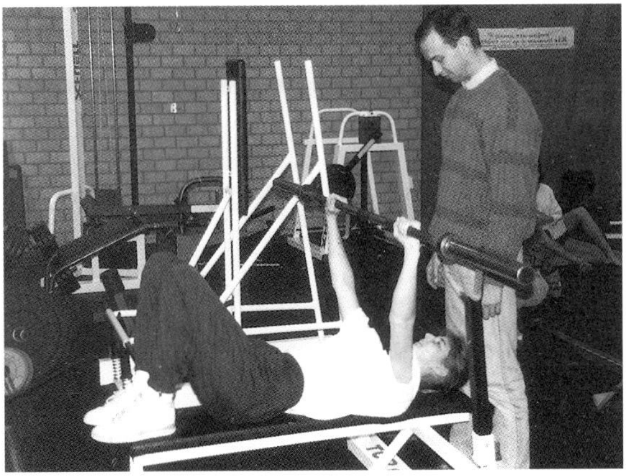

End

FIGURE V.2: Bench Press

FIGURE V.3: Lat Pull *Start* *End*

FIGURE V.4: Bent-Over Row *Start* *End*

FIGURE V.5: Biceps Curl *Start* *End*

FIGURE V.6: Triceps Extension *Start* *End*

FIGURE V.7: Sit-Ups *Start* *End*

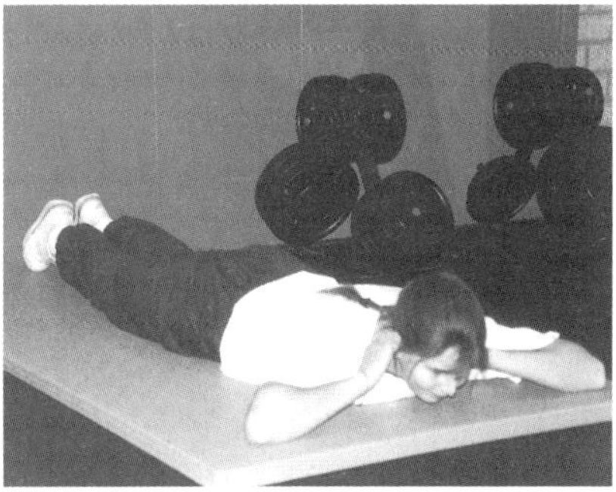

Start

FIGURE V.8: Back Extension End

Start

FIGURE V.9: Leg Press

End

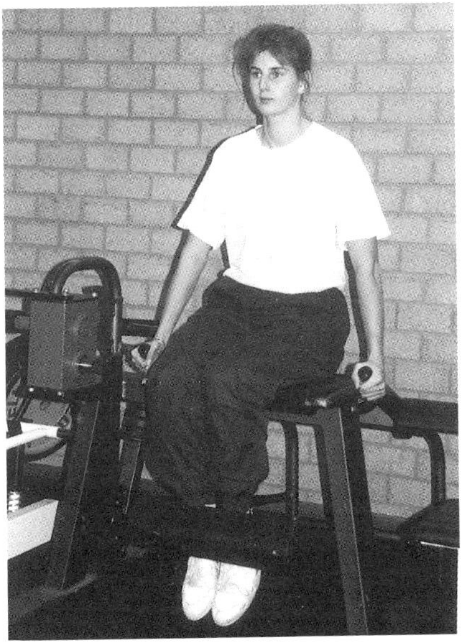

FIGURE V.10: Leg Extension *Start*

End

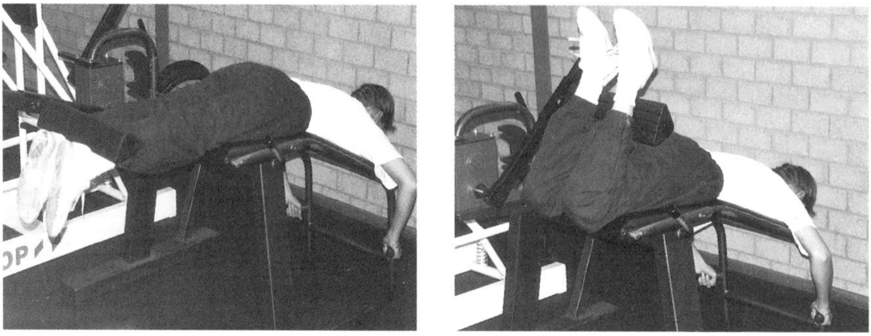

FIGURE V.11: Leg Curl *Start* *End*

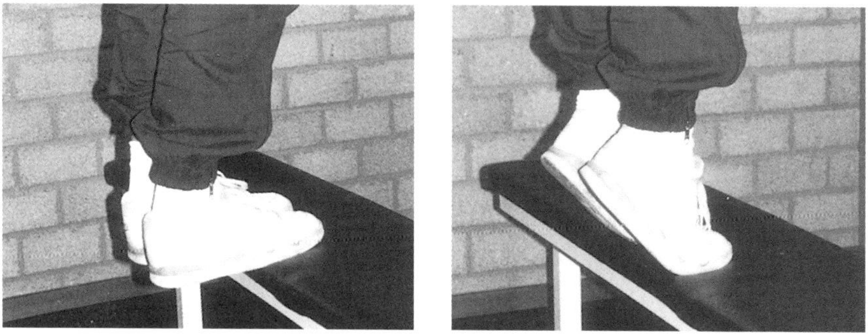

FIGURE V.12: Heel Raise *Start* *End*

A possible program that includes both endurance, strength and taekwondo training in the pre-season is shown in table V.7. Depending on the phase that the athlete is in, strength training may be maximal or strength endurance training, while endurance training may be of an aerobic or anaerobic nature. The same line of reasoning is true for taekwondo training. If the athlete is practicing aerobic endurance, for instance, the taekwondo training may consist of technique training and aerobic taekwondo training. The intensity, not shown in table V.7, varies depending on the goals of training (see this chapter and the previous one).

TABLE V.7 Program that Includes Endurance, Strength and Taekwondo Training in Pre-season

* endurance/strength = endurance and strength training
technique/endurance = technique and taekwondo endurance (aerobic or anaerobic) training
runing/isotonic = running and isotonic strength training

Week 1 - 6			
Day	**Training**	**Mode**	**Duration**
Monday	rest	---	---
Tuesday	taekwondo	technique/endurance*	2 hours
Wednesday	endurance/strength*	running/isotonic*	varies
Thursday	taekwondo	technique/endurance	2 hours
Friday	endurance/strength	running/isotonic	varies
Saturday	taekwondo	technique/endurance	2 hours
Sunday	endurance/strength	running/isotonic	varies

In-Season

As mentioned above, the latter part of the specific preparation period during the pre-season may be devoted to kicking the heavy bag to convert the strength developed through strength training to taekwondo-specific strength. This taekwondo-specific strength straining should continue in the in-season. An example of a possible program for the in-season is shown in table V.8. It is up to the coach how much time will be devoted to bag training during one training session, but the total bag training should probably not exceed three days per week to give the body sufficient time to recuperate. The major advantage of kicking the heavy bag is that both muscular endurance and anaerobic endurance are worked at the same time. By manipulating the rest periods between exercise bouts, the coach may want to emphasize one over the other. For instance, when recovery periods of between one and four minutes are used, the anaerobic lactic system will come into play (1). Using rest periods of one minute or less, will work anaerobic muscular endurance (8). The work intervals, of course, will have to be adjusted accordingly. For instance, when using the longer rest periods, the work interval may last as long as one minute. When using the shorter rest periods, the work intervals may last from about five seconds to about ten seconds. The number of repetitions in this case may be around 10 or 20. When using the longer work and rest intervals, the number of repetitions may have to be reduced till about five or six, depending on the individual athlete.

TABLE V.8 Example of Program that Includes Bag Training in In-Season
** technique/tactical= technique and tactical training*

Week 1 - 6			
Day	**Training**	**Mode**	**Duration**
Monday	rest	--	---
Tuesday	taekwondo	technique/tactical*	2 hours
Wednesday	taekwondo	technique/bag/tactical	2 hours
Thursday	taekwondo	technique/tactical	2 hours
Friday	taekwondo	technique/bag/tactical	2 hours
Saturday	taekwondo	technique/tactical	2 hours
Sunday	taekwondo	technique/bag/tactical	2 hours

In addition to the taekwondo-specific strength training on the heavy bag, the athlete should also have a maintenance strength program working with weights or other resistance apparati. Assuming that the athlete is again using isotonic constant load strength training, the maintenance program may be carried out once a week. The number of exercises could be reduced to a few essential ones. An example is provided in table V.9. A brief description of the training guidelines for the in-season follows.

TABLE V.9 A Sample of Exercises for the Athlete's Maintenance Program During the In-Season

Upper Body	**Lower Body**
Bench press	Leg extension
Lat pull	Leg curl
Sit-ups	Hip flexion
Back extension	

Training Guidelines

Frequency. To maintain one's strength, one training session per week is sufficient. As discussed in chapter II, the loss of strength after cessation of training is less dramatic than flexibility and can be easily maintained by one session per week. Research seems to indicate that 45% of maximal strength is retained after one year without strength training, while 70% of muscular endurance was retained after 12 weeks of detraining (17). Although it is not precisely known what the exact loading, frequency or type of strength training should be to maintain strength levels during the in-season (8), it is probably best to continue the load the same way it was during the specific preparation period in the pre-season.

Intensity. The intensity, then, would be three sets of 15 repetitions each per exercise, except for sit-ups and back extensions, which may be done for as many times as the athlete can handle.

Duration. Since the number of exercises has been reduced, the total duration of each training session will be much shorter than the one during the pre-season. Bompa (2) has suggested to continue this maintenance program until the taper-off period prior to competition, but this may not be true for taekwondo training. The present authors recommend to stop the maintenance program about four weeks prior to the taper-off period.

Mode. As before, the mode of training will be isotonic constant load strength training. This is not to say, of course, that the athlete will not use isometric or isokinetic methods. In fact, it is probably a good idea to try to combine isotonic and isometric training. Isokinetic machines are very expensive and usually not readily available. If they are, however, the coach certainly has the option of incorporating them in the athlete's program.

Off-Season

The off-season, as the reader should know by now, is a time to recuperate from the training in the pre- and in-seasons. The same rationale holds that was presented in the previous chapter to which the reader is referred. Depending on the length of the off-season, the coach may choose to have a short one day a week strength session, which would basically be a maintenance program with the same format as the one used during the in-season: a few exercises, low weights and 10 - 20 repetitions. A possible scenario may look like the one displayed in table V.10.

TABLE V.10 Off-Season Program

Frequency	Duration	Intensity	Mode
Monday	rest	-	-
Tuesday	2 hours	70 - 80% HR_{max}	swimming
Wednesday	2 hours	65 - 70% HR_{max}	basketball
Thursday	2 hours	50 - 60% HR_{max}	swimming
Friday	2 hours	70 - 80% HR_{max}	basketball
Saturday	2 hours	65 - 70% HR_{max}	swimming
Sunday	2 hours	10 RM	strength

References

1. Åstrand, P. O. and K. Rodahl (1986), *Textbook of Work Physiology*, New York, etc.: McGraw-Hill Book Company.
2. Bompa, T. O. (1983), *Theory and Methodology of Training,* Dubuque, Iowa: Kendall/Hunt Publishing Company.
3. Brooks, G. A. and Fahey, T. D. (1985), *Exercise Physiology. Human Bioenergetics and Its Applications,* New York, etc.: John Wiley & Sons.
4. Burkett, L. N. (1970), Causative factors in hamstring strains, *Medicine and Science in Sport,* 2, 1: 39 - 42.
5. Claes, L., Claes, D., Holemans, S. and Verhoeven, M. (1990), Isometrische en isokinetische krachttest van de kniestrekkers en kniebuigers bij goed getrainde atleten, *Sportmedische Tijdingen*, 11, 44: 394 - 415.
6. Conkel, B., Braucht, J., Wilson, W., Pieter, W., Taaffe, D., Fleck, S. and Kearney, J.T. (1988), Isokinetic torque, kick velocity and force in taekwondo, *Medicine and Science in Sports and Exercise*, 20, 2 (Supplement): S5.
7. Cordes, K. (1991), Reasons to strength train for amateur boxing, *National Strength and Conditioning Association Journal*, 13, 5: 18 - 21.
8. Fleck, S. J. and Kraemer, W. J. (1987), *Designing Resistance Training Programs,* Champaign, IL: Human Kinetics Books.
9. Grace, T. G. (1985), Muscle imbalance and extremity injury. A perplexing relationship, *Sports Medicine,* 2, 2: 77 - 82.
10. Grace, T. G., Sweetser, E. R., Nelson, M. A., Ydens, L. R. and Skipper, B. J. (1984), Isokinetic imbalance and knee-joint injuries, *Journal of Bone and Joint Surgery,* 66A, 5: 734 - 740.

11. Hobusch, F. L. and McClellan, T. (1990), The karate roundhouse kick, *National Strength and Conditioning Association Journal*, 12, 6: 6 - 9, 84 - 89.
12. Knapik, J. J., Bauman, C. L., Jones, B. H., Harris, J. M. and Vaughan, L. (1991), Preseason strength and flexibility imbalances associated with athletic injuries in female collegiate athletes, *American Journal of Sports Medicine,* 19, 1: 76 - 81.
13. Lamb, D. (1984), *Physiology of Exercise. Responses and Adaptations,* New York: MacMillan Publishing Company.
14. Lombardi, V. P. (1989), *Beginning Weight Training*, Dubuque, IA: Wm. C. Brown Publishers.
15. Lowell, L. (1990), Resistance training for taekwondo, *Sports Medicine Update*, 5, 4: 20 - 21.
16. Lamers, J. W. J. and Van der Molen, P. (1988), Gewichtsproblemen bij gewichtsklassesporters, In: W. H. M. Saris and M. Stasse-Wolthuis (eds.), *Sport en Voeding*, pp. 84 - 96, Alpen a/d Rijn: Samsom Stafleu.
17. Moffatt, R. J. (1988), Strength and flexibility considerations for exercise prescription, In: S. N. Blair, P. Painter, R. R. Pate, L. K. Smith and C. B. Taylor (eds.), *Resource Manual for Guidelines for Exercise Testing and Prescription*, pp. 263 - 270, Philadelphia: Lea & Febiger.
18. Osternig, L. R. (1986), Isokinetic dynamometry: implications for muscle testing and rehabilitation, In: K. B. Pandolf (ed.), *Exercise and Sport Sciences Reviews. Volume 14,* pp. 45 - 80, New York: MacMillan Publishing Co.
19. Pieter, W. and Heijmans, J. (1989), Hamstrings / quadriceps ratios en piek vermogen bij toptaekwondoka, *Nederlands Tijdschrift voor Fysiotherapie*, 99, 10: 283 - 286.
20. Pieter, W. and Taaffe, D. (1990), Peak torque and strength ratios of elite taekwondo athletes, In: *Conference Proceedings, Commonwealth and International Conference on Physical Education, Sport, Health, Dance, Recreation and Leisure, Volume 3, Part I,* pp. 67 - 79, Auckland: The New Zealand Association of Health, Physical Education and Recreation, Inc.
21. Pieter, W., Taaffe, D., Troxel, R. and Heijmans, J. (1992), Quadriceps / hamstrings ratios of taekwondo club athletes and beginning tennis players, *Journal of Physical Education and Sport Sciences,* IV, 1: 31 - 39.
22 Radcliffe, J. C. and Farentinos, R. C. (1985), *Plyometrics: Explosive Power Training,* 2nd. ed., Champaign, IL: Human Kinetics Publishers.
23. Sale, D. G. (1991), Testing strength and power, In: J. D. MacDougall, H. A. Wenger and H. J. Green (eds.), *Physiological Testing of the High-Performance Athlete,* Champaign, IL: Human Kinetics Books, pp. 21 - 106.

24. Taylor, A. W. and Brassard, L. (1981), A physiological profile of the Canadian judo team, *Journal of Sports Medicine and Physical Fitness,* 21, 2: 160 - 164.
25. Zandbergen, A. (no date), Taekwondo Blessures en Fysiotherapie, Unpublished Thesis, Twentse Akademie voor Fysiotherapie, Enschede.

CHAPTER VI

TECHNIQUE TRAINING FOR TAEKWONDO COMPETITION

Introduction

Technique training in taekwondo is essential, as it is in many other sports. The more complex the movements in a sport, the more important technique training becomes (5). Technique may be defined as the specific way a certain movement is executed. Often, all things being equal, winning or losing is related to mastery of technique. Good technique may be characterized by the most rational performance of the skill as well as the most efficient way of performing it (5). In this case, most rational refers to the biomechanically sound (see below) execution of a particular technique, while most efficient refers to the physiological component of the technique. An efficient technique is one where only those muscle groups are activated that are necessary to complete the movement without wasting energy by contracting other muscles.

Unfortunately, taekwondo does not have generally accepted rules for executing techniques that could serve as a model for coaches and athletes. According to Bompa (5), "the technique of a champion rarely should be regarded as a model, since it does not always meet [the] conditions [of being biomechanically sound and physiologically efficient]" (p. 41). The reason that there are no accepted rules for performing taekwondo techniques is related to a lack of scientific research, which should not come as a surprise since taekwondo is a relatively young combative sport.

The technical execution of taekwondo skills should not be confused with one's style of performing them. Technique is dependent on biomechanical and physiological concerns, while style is the individual interpretation of performing the skill. For instance, the round kick has to meet certain criteria, such as leg lift, hip rotation, leg flexion, position of support foot, and so on, to call it a good technique from a biomechanical perspective. The individual interpretation of these criteria makes it an athlete's style, which is related to the athlete's temperament, flexibility, body build, coordination, and so forth.

Technique is also dependent on the athlete's physical and psychological preparation (5). If the athlete is tired, he or she will most likely have problems executing the movements effectively. In other words, the better conditioned the athlete is in terms of endurance, strength and flexibility, the better he/she will be able to perform the skills. Similarly, the athlete's psychological make-up is related to her/his technique. If the athlete is not focused, lacks self-confidence, is not motivated, and so on, his/her technique will suffer.

Technique should not be regarded as a rigid component. On the contrary, it is almost constantly in evolution and related to the requirements of competition, the coach's assessments, scientific research, or other sources of change (5). It is well known, for instance, that there is a number of ways to execute a certain technique, depending on the situation in competition. Not too long ago, for instance, the round kick was performed in a more roundabout way, travelling a full circle. Changing conditions during competition, however, have resulted in a more half-moon like execution. Although requirements of competition were at the basis of a modified round kick, it is also possible to come up with a biomechanical explanation of why the present kick would be more effective in competition. The traditional kick, by virtue of its more circular path, needed more time to be completed as opposed to the present variation of the kick with a shorter time of execution. In other words, from a biomechanical point of view, the new kick can be performed faster. Several other examples will undoubtedly come to the reader's mind. Since the biomechanical aspect of performing a taekwondo technique is one of the pillars of good technical preparation, basic principles from this scientific field will be dealt with below. First, however, a brief discussion will follow of how taekwondo techniques are acquired.

Learning Taekwondo Techniques

To be able to teach taekwondo athletes new techniques or to be able to correct mistakes, the coach needs to have a good understanding of basic biomechanical principles (see next section) as well as basic knowledge of how skills are learned by the athlete. Knowing how skills are learned will allow the coach to adequately guide the competitor through the process of mastering taekwondo techniques. The coach will also be able to find out where in the learning process errors may have crept in that have prevented the athlete from fully mastering the skill.

Research has suggested that learning of techniques takes place in three phases (19):

1.) a cognitive phase,
2.) an associative phase and
3.) an automation phase.

Cognitive Phase. In the cognitive phase, athletes become aware of what the basic elements are of the technique that they are presently learning (1). They only perceive the global picture of the entire skill. Providing the athlete with visual information at the beginning of this stage is important if learning is to occur. This means that the coach ought to show the athlete how the technique should be executed, while at the same time limiting verbal explanations to a minimum.

For instance, when teaching the side kick, the most essential point of the kick is the movement to the side with the kicking leg. This is the global picture that the athlete should be presented with. No extensive information should be shared yet with the athlete about the position of the upper body, the support leg, the foot of the support leg, the angle of the support leg with the floor, the foot of the kicking leg, and so on.

Throughout the entire cognitive phase, performance should not be emphasized. Instead, ample time should be given to practice with a model (the coach) as a visual aid, but only in the beginning. It is suggested that learning in the cognitive phase is directly proportional to the amount of practice that the athlete is allowed and inversely related to the amount of verbal explanations (1). In other words, the more verbal information given by the coach, the longer it will take to learn the skill, while the more practice the athlete gets, the faster learning will take place. The end of the cognitive phase is characterized by the athlete being able to perform the skill and at the same time being able to pay attention to a part of the skill. For example, during the execution of the side kick, the athlete will be at the end of the cognitive phase when he/she is able to concentrate on his/her arms while performing the kick, which was not possible at the beginning of this phase.

Associative Phase. While it was not required of the athlete to meet certain criteria of good performance in the cognitive phase, in the associative phase the athlete will have to learn to execute the skill better and more efficiently. Form and precision are important criteria that the athlete should be able to meet in the associative phase (1). Although visual information is still important, verbal directions will become more effective in this stage. Sufficient time should still be devoted to practicing the skill as it was during the preceding phase. Before continuing with an example of what to do in the associative phase, it is necessary to make a distinction between open and closed skills.

Closed skills are characterized by a stable environment in which the conditions do not change. Bowling, for example, is a closed skill. The pins are always positioned the same way and at the same distance from each other. In open skills, the environment changes almost continuously. Tennis, for instance, is an open skill. The opponent on the other side of the net will sometimes do a slice serve or a topspin serve. He/she will do drop shots, topspin shots, drop volleys, shots down the line, and so on. In taekwondo, an example of a closed skill would be the forms *(p'umse)*. An example of an open skill would be a match at a tournament.

When learning the side kick, an athlete in the associative phase may now be told to watch the support leg and the position of the support foot. Practicing the kick without a moving partner will make this technique a closed skill. As soon as a fellow athlete comes into the picture, the side kick becomes an open skill. In that case, the coach needs to give the athlete time to get used to a moving fellow athlete. This may be done by asking the partner to move back in a certain way without kicking him/herself or by asking the partner to move laterally and back to present the learner with a variety of practice conditions, which will enhance learning. In the associative phase, the athlete will still have to make a conscious effort to perform the kick, however. He/she will have to learn to focus on all details of the skill to improve his or her performance of the movement.

Automation Phase. In this phase, the athlete does not have to make a conscious effort to execute the technique anymore: it has become automated (1). Instead of focusing on the parts of the movement, it is essential to present the athlete with a whole array of conditions to practice the technique. For instance, the athlete could do the technique while going forward, backward, with a kicking pad, alternating left and right, with a moving partner, and so on. The more varied these conditions are, the better the technique will become and the better it will be stored in (long-term) memory. The correct execution of the movement is emphasized in the automation phase.

In the preceding paragraphs, learning of taekwondo skills has been discussed while assuming that the entire skill had to be taught. Obviously, for a coach who is preparing his/her athletes for competition, some of the examples used will not have been relevant, because the athletes will already know how to execute a side kick, for instance. Yet, technique training will still take place. For competitive taekwondo athletes, details of techniques become far more important than they are for non-competitors because, at the elite level, competition is fierce and the differences between competitors small. Optimal technical performance may give the athlete the decisive edge. An example of how attention to details may be incorporated in the competitor's technique training will be presented next.

Let us assume that the athlete is working on the reverse punch, without a block preceding it. The punch is executed from the fighting stance. In order to increase the force of the punch even more, details of the technique have to be emphasized. One detail would be to tell the athlete to pay attention to the rotation of the hips before performing the punch. Another detail would be the position of the shoulders before the punch, during the punch and after the punch. Yet another detail would be the movement of the arm in relation to the shoulders during the entire technique. Other details would include the position of the opposite arm, the position of the punching fist, the position of the legs, and so forth. Clearly, these examples are of a different magnitude than those given earlier for someone learning a technique for the first time.

For the coach to be able to adequately optimize the athlete's technical performance, basic biomechanical principles need to be understood. These principles will allow the coach to focus on details that will facilitate the athlete's competitive performance at the elite level (7). The next section will deal with basic biomechanical principles that will allow the coach to monitor his/her athlete's techniques more adequately.

Mechanical Principles

The science of biomechanics aims at studying the internal as well external forces that influence the human body in motion and the effects of these forces (8). Knowledge of biomechanics will enable the coach to determine the contributing factors for the optimal execution of a specific taekwondo technique in order to improve performance. Furthermore, the coach will be able to identify errors in the execution of a taekwondo technique, so that steps may be taken to correct them.

The word biomechanics consists of two parts: *bio* and *mechanics* (2; 3). *Bio*, of course, refers to the human body as a biological system. *Mechanics* refers to the application of mechanical laws to the locomotor system of the human body. In other words, taekwondo techniques are studied in terms of speed, force, kinetic energy, momentum, acceleration, and so on.

One of the functions of the science of biomechanics is the analysis of a movement by means of mechanical principles and the development of a mechanical model according to which this movement can be executed as efficiently as possible. Although a particular technique may have an optimal execution from a mechanical point of view, the human biological system may not be able to follow suit. It is feasible, for instance, that an optimal biomechanical execution of a particular skill would exert extreme forces on the unit of muscles and skeleton to where this system may get injured. In such cases, a compromise needs to be found between the mechanical principles involved in a certain movement (biomechanical theory) and the possibilities of the human locomotor system (taekwondo practice). A selection of biomechanical principles that are known to be important to technique training in taekwondo will follow next.

Force

"A push (or pull) that alters, or tends to alter, the state of motion of a body is called a *force*" (9, p. 153). In taekwondo, an *external force*, such as a roundhouse kick against the head of the opponent, will tend to change the head's state of motion. The force with which the brain will move within the skull as a result of this roundhouse kick, is called the *internal force*. This particular internal force could lead to a brain concussion and although vitally important, this kind of force will not be dealt with here. The remainder of the discussion will focus on external forces only or more specifically, on how to analyze and possibly optimize external forces of taekwondo techniques.

A force is the product of mass and acceleration. Expressed in a formula: F (force) = m (mass) x a (acceleration). The international unit of measurement of force is Newton (N). One Newton is "that force that will produce an acceleration of 1 m/s^2 in a body of 1 kg mass" (9, p. 156): 1 N = 1 kg x 1 m/s^2. Acceleration is defined as the difference in velocity of a body over time (9). In other words, acceleration equals the change in velocity of a body divided by the time it took for this change to take place. Thus

Acceleration = (Final velocity - Initial velocity) / Time.

To summarize, force (F) is the product of mass (m) and acceleration (a): F = m x a. An increase in force may be accomplished by either an increase in mass, in acceleration, or in both. Increasing the force of one's techniques, then, may be done by using more of one's body weight. It is also possible to accelerate faster from the starting position.

To apply the above principle in another way, if two taekwondo athletes kick with the same acceleration, the one with the greater mass (= body weight) will kick with more force than the one with the smaller mass. Conversely, if one of two taekwondo athletes with the same mass wants to kick with more force he/she should try to accelerate faster.

A force may be represented by a so-called *vector*. A vector is a symbol, usually in the form of an arrow, to denote *magnitude* and *direction* of a force. The length of the arrow symbolizes the magnitude of the force, while the arrow head signifies the direction. An example of two forces of different magnitude and direction is shown in Figure VI.1.

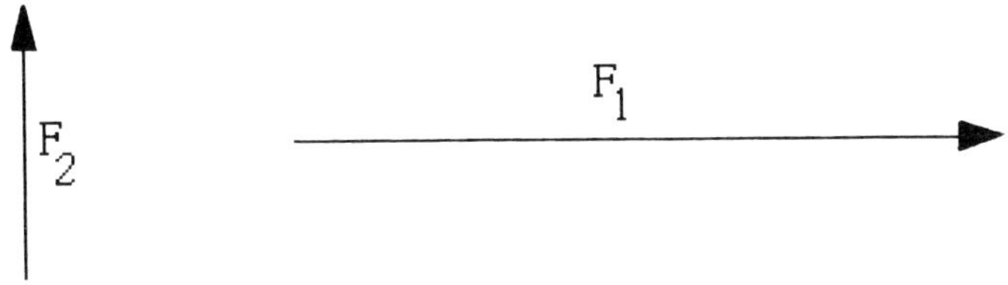

Figure VI.1: Vectors Representing Two Forces:
F_1 is greater than F_2 and in a different direction

Resolution of Forces

A force can be resolved into components that act in different directions. The most effective force with which to hit a target runs parallel to the floor and perpendicular to the target. Figure VI.2 shows the most effective way to execute a technique (VI.2B) and one that is less effective (VI.2A).

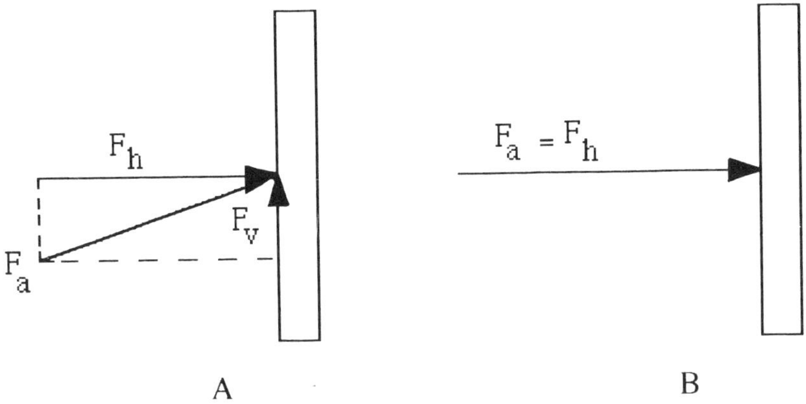

Figure VI.2: Two Possible Ways to Execute a Technique

Figure VI.3A: Low Side Kick

Figure VI.3B: Middle Side Kick: Most Powerful

Figure VI.3C: High Side Kick

For instance, let us assume that the technique used is a side kick. The force of this kick has a trajectory that coincides with the kicking leg. F_h is the horizontal force parallel to the floor and is known as the effective force with which the athlete kicks. The vertical force F_v is used to lift off the target or the athlete being kicked and is an example of a non-effective force. F_a is the applied force of the kick. If the side kick were used in competition, the most powerful side kick would be the one as shown in Figure VI.3B, because no force is lost as in Figure VI.3A and VI.3C.

Linear and Rotational Movements

Taekwondo techniques may be divided into linear and rotational or angular movements. A linear movement in taekwondo, for instance, would be a side kick or a punch. An angular skill would be a roundhouse kick or a block such as *mom-t'ong an makki* (inward middle block). Linear kicks, such as the side and front kicks are also referred to as thrusts kicks or, in case of a roundhouse kick, swing kicks (18). The force on impact in a linear movement lies in the extension of the movement, so to speak. The impact force during a rotational movement, however, does not follow the circular motion of the skill. Instead, it is the tangential force perpendicular to the radius of the circle (12). Figure VI.4 shows two linear movements in taekwondo: a punch (VI.4A) and a front kick (VI.4B).

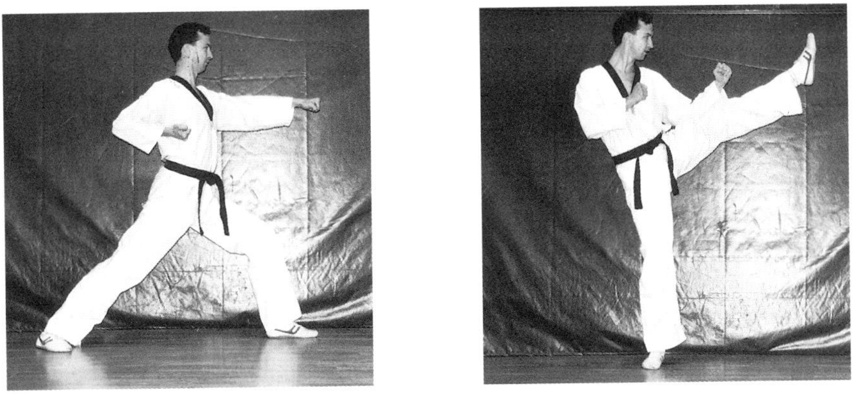

A *B*

Figure VI.4: Linear Movements in Taekwondo

Figure VI.5 shows the force of an angular technique, such as the roundhouse kick as it is normally performed (not one that is adapted for competition) in graphical form. The movement of the kick describes the path of the circle, while the force on impact is perpendicular to the radius of this circular motion.

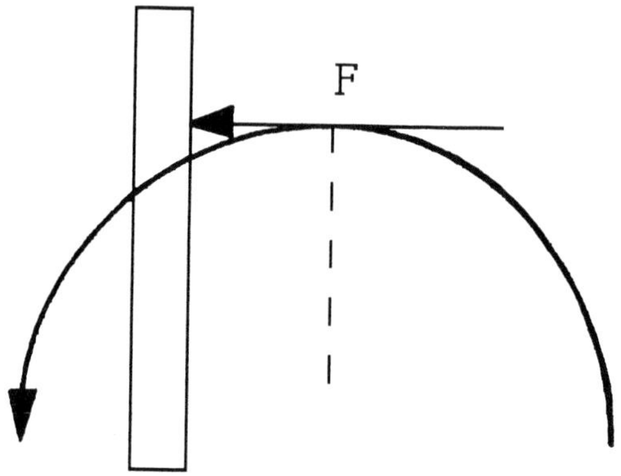

Figure VI.5: Impact Force During Rotational Movement

Factors Contributing to Total Force

The total force of any technique in taekwondo is a combination of various factors. Three of these factors will be covered here.

Summation of Forces. A larger force may be generated by the summation of several smaller forces. An example of this would be the forward backfist strike *(dung jumok ap'e ch'igi)*, where the legs, hip, shoulder, and arms all contribute to the resultant force of the striking forearm (16). Another example would be the *momt'ong an makki* (middle inward block) as shown in Figure VI.6A through VI.6E.

The total force of the block is a combination of movements and includes the hip (VI.6A) in the direction of the block; the rotation of the trunk (VI.6B), followed by the rotation of the shoulder (VI.6C), rotation of the arm (VI.6D) and finally, the rotation of the forearm (VI.6E). Not shown is the force generated from assuming the *ap kubi* (front stance) from the starting position.

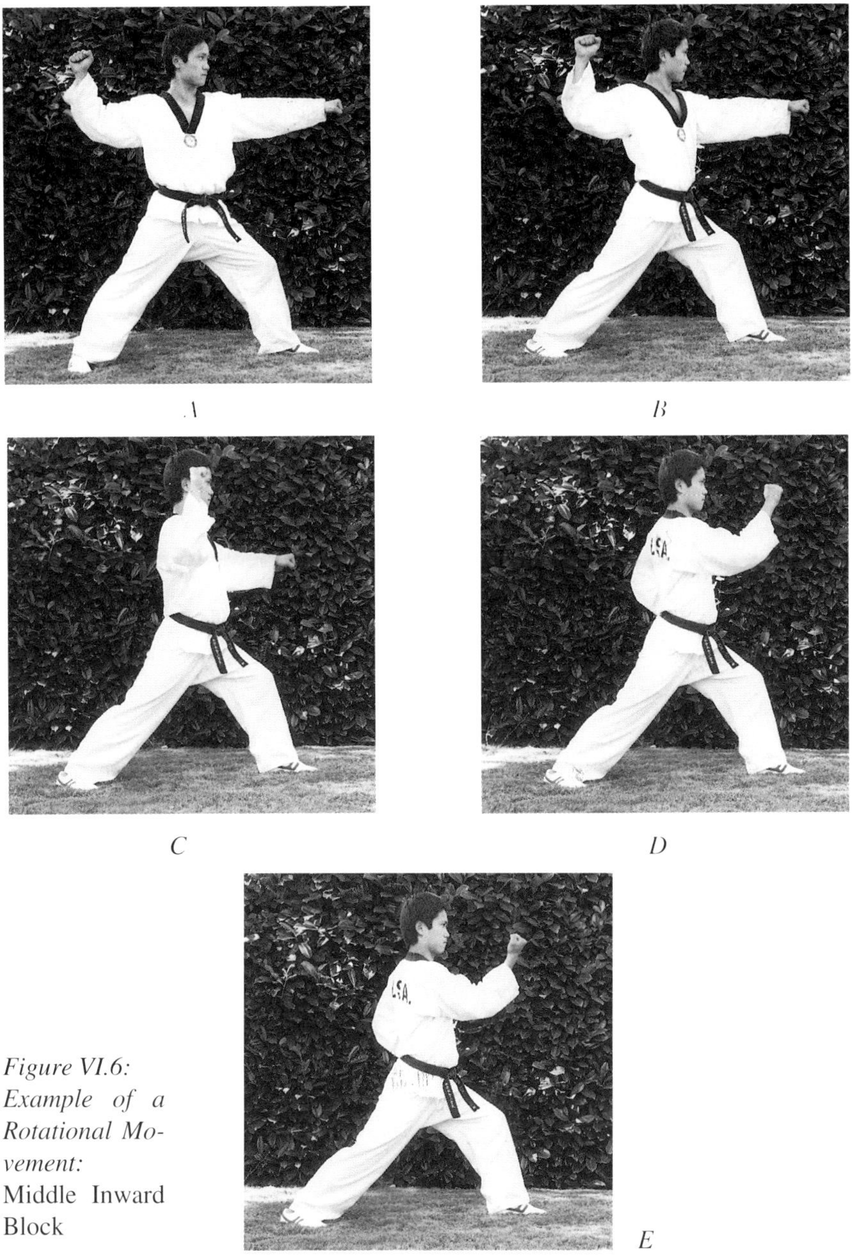

A *B* *C* *D* *E*

Figure VI.6: Example of a Rotational Movement: Middle Inward Block

For the summation of forces to be effective, the following two conditions need to be met (17):

1.) "for each successive joint action to make its maximal contribution, the joints below it must be firmly stabilized so that no backsliding results from the reaction component of force;
2.) "the forces of each successive joint action must be precisely timed" (p. 440).

These two conditions imply that, in order to get the optimal effect out of the execution of taekwondo techniques, all potentially contributing joints should be mobilized. In terms of kicking, this usually refers to using one's body weight, or as many coaches would say: "use your hips", as much as possible. It is also important to optimize the contribution of the kicking leg (thigh and lower leg) by lifting and flexing it properly. Using one's weight will increase the striking mass of the kick, which will subsequently contribute to the total force as was mentioned above (remember the formula: F = m x a).

Action - Reaction. As in many other activities in our daily lives or in the sport setting, this principle plays a major role in our movements. For instance, when kicking a heavy bag in taekwondo, the athlete executes an action onto the bag with the kick, while the bag, in turn, executes a reaction onto the athlete that is equal in magnitude but in the opposite direction. If the athlete's action is greater than the bag's reaction, the bag will be pushed away. If the reaction of the bag is greater than the athlete's action, he or she will lose his or her balance or may even fall over.

The same line of reasoning also holds for kicking the adversary during competition or breaking a board. It will be to the athlete's advantage to generate a greater action than the opponent's or the board's reaction (13). Increasing the magnitude of the action may be done by using one's body weight when kicking or optimizing the interplay between successive joints in their contribution to the total force of the kick.

Transfer of Forces. The most effective way to transfer forces is along a straight line. Transferring a force during a kick, for instance, takes place by extending the kicking leg at the moment of impact, so that the reaction forces may be distributed throughout the body by way of the hips (14). If the kicking leg or the support leg is not extended, forces may be wasted resulting in a less optimal kick. This principle will be illustrated by analyzing the support leg during the side kick (10).

When performing the side kick, action and reaction forces are transformed through the kicking leg, hips and support leg. According to Choi (6) and Ingber

(11), the support leg in taekwondo (Choi) and karate (Ingber) is bent during the side kick. However, this way of kicking may result in forces that the knee and ankle joints will have to mobilize in order to correct for any forces that will diminish the total force of the kick. The knee joint is a hinge joint (see chapter IX), which will be able to transmit forces better if it is extended instead of in a bent position (see figure VI.7). Consequently, it will be more advantageous to keep the support leg extended (not hyperextended or locked!), which will also save muscular energy that would be needed to keep the athlete in balance if it were bent.

Support Leg Extended

Support Leg Bent

FIGURE VI.7: Side Kick with Extended and Bent Support Leg

Therefore, it is recommended to attempt to extend the support leg during such techniques as the side and roundhouse kicks. Biological constraints may interfere with this theoretical recommendation, however. For instance, for most athletes, the support leg during the axe kick will be bent, because of a lack of flexibility. It should be remembered that the leg is extended, but not locked, so that no injuries will occur as a result.

Results from Taekwondo Research

It would make sense to assume that being able to kick and punch with both the left and right limbs equally as fast and as hard would be an advantage in competition. After all, the athlete could get into a situation in which he or she would be better off kicking or punching with the non-dominant side in order to score a point. Having a deficient extremity in either speed or force could mean the difference between winning or losing a bout.

One of the goals of the biomechanical component of the Oregon Taekwondo Research Project was to compare the right and left sides during the execution of selected techniques in adult elite taekwondo athletes relative to speed and force on impact. Speed was tested by means of two light beams. The beams were set a known distance apart from each other and connected to a computer. The athletes were asked to kick or punch through both light beams at the level of their midsection. The speed with which the foot or fist would go through the beams was then registered by the computer and expressed in meters per second (m/s). Hitting both light beams required more skillful execution of the technique than some athletes were used to. Other researchers (20) also met with this problem.

Force was assessed by means of a water-filled bag with a built-in force sensor unit, which was also connected to a computer. The bag could be adjusted to the athlete's height. The athletes wore so-called taekwondo shoes during all kicks. The raw scores that the computer registered were later converted to a force reading in Newtons (N).

The following techniques were tested in the OTRP: the round kick *(ap tollyo ch'agi)*, side kick *(yop ch'agi)*, spinning back kick *(twit ch'agi)* and reverse punch *(chirugi)*. No scientifically significant differences were found between the right and left side in terms of speed. However, differences in force were apparent between the right and left side (15). In other words, kicking or punching with the left side was not as forceful as with the right side. The athletes tested were dominant with the right limb. Therefore, it was recommended to practice the left side more often.

Table VI.1 shows the average speed of the various techniques tested in the biomechanical component of the OTRP, while table VI.2 depicts the average force of the same techniques.The data represented in table VI.1 are a good illustration of the genetic basis of speed. Although resistance training and special exercises may contribute to slight improvements, speed is largely determined by heredity (see chapter V on strength training). The margin for improvement by training is much smaller when it comes to speed as opposed to aerobic endurance or strength (23). Consequently, it is not surprising that there were no scientific differences in speed between the right and left side.

TABLE VI.1 Average Speed of Selected Taekwondo Techniques (in m/s)

	MEN		WOMEN	
Technique	**Right**	**Left**	**Right**	**Left**
Tollyo ch'agi	15.51	16.26	13.49	13.10
Yop ch'agi	6.87	6.32	6.00	5.21
Twit ch'agi	9.14	8.73	7.56	6.62
Chirugi	11.38	10.05	8.97	8.41

TABLE VI.2 Average Force of Selected Taekwondo Techniques (in N)

	MEN		WOMEN	
Technique	**Right**	**Left**	**Right**	**Left**
Tollyo ch'agi	518.74	510.51	406.97	404.11
Yop ch'agi	461.78	456.72	408.39	390.66
Twit ch'agi	606.92	661.86	584.22	500.89
Chirugi	560.48	457.37	391.65	341.77

Table VI.2 shows an interesting pattern. The extreme high force value for the right punch for the men is probably an aberration and most likely due to testing. However, for both men and women, there is a tendency for relatively more forceful punches than side kicks, which may also be related to the testing procedure. From a theoretical perspective, this phenomenon warrants some discussion. Even though a higher speed may be realized by the punch, more mass can be involved during the execution of the side kick, which led the researchers to expect that the side kick would be more forceful than the punch.

Apparently, the side kick is hardly used in competition. One could argue that the side kick is too slow a kick to be effective in competition, which usually leads to less time spent on practicing the skill during training, which subsequently leads to even slower executions of the side kick during a match, and so on. As alluded to above, training does result in some improvements in speed, albeit less than in endurance or strength. It is therefore advisable to pay more attention to the side kick.

One last observation about the information contained in table VI.1 and VI.2. The difference in speed between the right and left fist of the male taekwondo athletes tested in the OTRP may not be scientifically significant, but in competition, the right fist will strike its target much faster than the left. Although the rather high force values recorded for the punch are probably due to testing idiosyncrasies, the practical difference in speed is also poignantly illustrated by the difference in force between both limbs (the high force values per se are not relevant but instead, the discrepancy between the left and right). In this case, the difference has also become scientifically significant. As a consequence, the recommendation to practice the left punch more often should be taken quite seriously.

Comparison with Other Athletes

Comparing the results of the biomechanical component of the OTRP with those of other studies is difficult because of differences in methods used to measure speed and force. It is nevertheless instructive to contrast the results of the present study with those found in a study on Korean male elite taekwondo athletes to get an impression of some general trends as far as speed is concerned. Force is especially dependent on the method used to assess it. As a result, no comparisons will be made with the Korean study.

For instance, there is the expected difference between the various techniques in terms of speed. The highest speed, for both American men and women, was recorded during the roundhouse kick, and not during the reverse punch as one would have anticipated. Sung et al. (20) also found that the roundhouse kick to the mid-section was fastest.

Sung and co-workers (20), investigated the speed on impact of selected kicking techniques, among other things, of four male taekwondo athletes, who were all members of the 1986 Korean national taekwondo team participating in the Asian Games. The authors used high speed film and video cameras to measure speed. Impact speed of the Korean athletes was much higher than that of their American male colleagues: side kick, 10.3 m/s; roundhouse kick, 19.2 m/s; and back kick, 10.4 m/s. This disparity may be due to the difference in assessing speed in both studies.

Guidelines for Technique Training

To help the coach optimize his/her technique training for competition, the following guidelines may prove useful. Unless otherwise stated, they are based on suggestions by Weineck (22).

When teaching a new technique, it is essential to strive for an optimal performance of the skill from a biomechanical perspective to prevent "reprogramming" the athlete later to correct errors that have been automated. For instance, it is far more difficult to teach the athlete to extend his or her support leg when executing the side kick after he/she has automated the kick with a bent support leg than doing so in the cognitive phase of learning the technique.

Participating in competition at a time that taekwondo skills have not yet been fully automated will interfere with the learning process of these techniques. The pressure of competition will facilitate errors to creep into the movement pattern and delay progress in learning the technique. For instance, in a match, it is feasible that the kicking leg during the execution of the round kick may not be entirely extended as it should be from a theoretical perspective. Although specific conditions during competition warrant the performance of a modified round kick, optimal force can only be generated when the leg is almost extended on impact. On the other hand, when the correct execution of the kick has been properly learned, performing the modified round kick will still yield enough force to score a point.

Technique training taxes the athlete's concentration. This implies that technique training should only be done when the athlete is not yet fatigued. In other words, it is better to schedule technique training at the beginning of the training session. If the athlete is tired, errors will easily occur and the training effect may be minimal.

As has been mentioned throughout this book, technique training is related to endurance and strength. If the athlete is too weak and tires quickly, it will become increasingly difficult to improve his/her techniques. For instance, if the hamstrings are too weak relative to the quadriceps, it will not be possible to extend the kicking leg at full speed with optimal force. At the end of the extension phase of the kicking leg, the hamstrings will have to break the action of the quadriceps to prevent hyperextension of the knee. If the hamstrings are not strong enough, they may either break the movement too early, resulting in a less forceful and fast kick, or too late, which will result in hyperextension of the knee and most likely pulled hamstrings as well. A lack of endurance, of course, will prevent the athlete from devoting sufficient time to practice the skills. As alluded to earlier, the more practice the athlete gets, the better his/her skill acquisition.

Progress may not only be inhibited by lack of endurance or strength, but may also be a result of other factors. One factor would be overload in information processing on the learner's part. For instance, if the coach is too much in a hurry to spend sufficient time with the athlete to acquire the skill, learning may level off. In other words, if the athlete has to learn a technique without adequate time to practice it, he/she will have to deal with more information than he/she is capable of handling at that time. To use the example of the punch again, having to deal with details pertaining to the punching arm, the opposite arm, the trunk, the shoulders, the thighs, the lower legs and the feet all at the same time, will most likely overload the athlete's processing capabilities and interfere with his/her learning process.

A lack of information or misinformation provided by the coach is another factor that will be detrimental to the athlete's technique acquisition. Lack of information or misinformation is related to the knowledge base of the coach and should be remedied as soon as possible. For example, if the coach were not aware of the biomechanical principle of summation of forces, he/she will never be able to tell the athletes how to generate enough force while kicking and punching.

Other factors that will inhibit learning of taekwondo skills are lack of attention, motivation, self-confidence or concentration on the athlete's part. If the athlete is easily distracted, it will be quite difficult to focus on a specific technique as a whole, let alone any details of it. Motivation may decrease as a result, which will complicate matters even further.

Optimal technique training is only possible if the training sessions are not spread out too much. It would be quite useless to spend one day a week on technique training. A minimum of three days is preferred, depending on the season and each individual circumstance. Technique training, as mentioned in previous chapters, is characterized by complete recovery periods and should not take too long. Two hours of technique training would be an exaggeration. Depending on the athlete's endurance, strength, concentration, motivation, and so on, technique training may last from about fifteen minutes to one hour. The coach should also take the season into account (see next section).

When correcting an error, the coach should focus on the main errors first and should deal with them one at a time (21). More detailed errors may be covered after the main errors have been corrected. For instance, when dealing with the punch for a competitive taekwondo athlete, the two major errors may be the lack of rotation of the trunk and the position of the shoulder of the punching arm at the end of the punch: the shoulder is elevated too much at the end of the punch. The coach should first correct these two errors (one at a time), before going to a smaller error like the position of the striking fist, for instance.

The coach should avoid emphasizing the errors (21), which would be negative reinforcement. Instead, he/she should try to approach the athlete from a more positive perspective. This will enhance the athlete's motivation and his/her feelings of success. Telling the athlete that he/she did a good job will do wonders in terms of learning and motivation.

The coach is advised to use different methods to get his/her message across (21). In addition to verbal information, the coach may use pictures, drawings, graphs, video and so forth. Video is an especially potent learning tool and should be part of the coach's equipment. Whatever means is chosen, be sure to provide immediate feedback. If the video or picture is shown a few days after the training session to correct errors, the athlete will have forgotten what he/she did at that time.

Periodization of Technique Training

Although technique training will take place throughout the entire year, the time devoted to it as part of the total training program will vary depending on the season. As before, scheduling the athlete's technique training depends on individual circumstances. If the athlete needs much work on his/her techniques, the coach may want to define the objectives of his/her annual plan accordingly. A possible program is shown in table VI.3.

TABLE VI.3 Program for Technique Training in Pre-Season

	Week 1 - 2		
Frequency	**Duration**	**Intensity**	**Mode**
Wednesday	30 minutes	50% HR_{max}	taekwondo
Friday	30 minutes	50% HR_{max}	taekwondo
Sunday	30 minutes	50% HR_{max}	taekwondo

Week 3 - 4

Frequency	Duration	Intensity	Mode
Wednesday	45 minutes	50% HR_{max}	taekwondo
Friday	45 minutes	50% HR_{max}	taekwondo
Sunday	45 minutes	50% HR_{max}	taekwondo

Week 3 - 4

Frequency	Duration	Intensity	Mode
Wednesday	60 minutes	50% HR_{max}	taekwondo
Friday	60 minutes	50% HR_{max}	taekwondo
Sunday	60 minutes	50% HR_{max}	taekwondo

It is assumed that the general preparation period of the pre-season is six weeks long. It goes without saying that there is a number of ways to manipulate the duration and total intensity to increase the total load in technique training. As endurance and strength improve, for instance, it will take more work to reach 50% of HR_{max}. In table VI.3, it was decided to increase the duration after each set of two weeks, but it would also have been possible to increase the intensity, while keeping the duration at 30 minutes, or any other combination thereof.

During the specific preparation period in the pre-season, taekwondo training will be increased to six days a week (see also chapter III). Technique training may be spread out over those six days, but it will be of a shorter duration because other training components become more important. General strength and endurance will be converted to taekwondo strength and endurance, while time spent on psychological and tactical training will also increase gradually. For the specific preparation phase in the pre-season, then, the coach may choose a schedule such as the one displayed in table VI.4.

The remainder of the specific preparation phase will show a further decrease in time spent on technique training to about 20 minutes on all six days and will remain that way through the in-season as well. Remember that the schedule for technique training varies per individual. In general, however, time spent on technique training decreases until the second half of the specific preparation period and stays the same from there on through the in-season. It will always be a part of the athlete's total training program, though, including the off-season. A possible schedule for the off-season is presented in table VI.5. In the off-season, three days per week is quite sufficient to spend on technique training. The duration will of necessity be short to still give the athlete adequate time away from taekwondo to recuperate from the training loads in the pre- and in-seasons.

Technique training may be done before engaging in an off-season activity, e.g., swimming or tennis. In that case, based on table VI.5, swimming, tennis or another activity will follow taekwondo technique training on Tuesday, Thursday and Saturday. To avoid undue fatigue, it is recommended to schedule technique training before any off-season activity. The duration of technique training during the off-season should not be increased and the total intensity should stay low.

TABLE VI.4 Program for Technique Training During Specific Preparation Phase in Pre-Season

Week 1 - 3			
Frequency	**Duration**	**Intensity**	**Mode**
Monday	-	-	rest
Tuesday	30 minutes	50% HR_{max}	taekwondo
Wednesday	30 minutes	50% HR_{max}	taekwondo
Thursday	30 minutes	50% HR_{max}	taekwondo
Friday	30 minutes	50% HR_{max}	taekwondo
Saturday	30 minutes	50% HR_{max}	taekwondo
Sunday	30 minutes	50% HR_{max}	taekwondo

TABLE VI.5 Off-Season Program for Technique Training

Frequency	**Duration**	**Intensity**	**Mode**
Monday	-	-	rest
Tuesday	30 minutes	45% HR_{max}	technique
Wednesday	2 hours	65 - 70% HR_{max}	basketball
Thursday	30 minutes	45% HR_{max}	technique
Friday	2 hours	70 - 80% HR_{max}	basketball
Saturday	30 minutes	45% HR_{max}	technique
Sunday	varies	10 RM	strength

Offense and Defense

In chapter II, figure II.1, a distinction was made in technique training in terms of defense and offense. As far as the preceding biomechanical principles are concerned, as well as the training guidelines and the three phases of the learning process, whether techniques are used offensively or defensively is irrelevant. The biomechanical principles hold for both offensive and defensive techniques, as do the learning phases and training guidelines. It is conceivable, however, to emphasize certain biomechanical variables over others depending on whether one is dealing with offensive or defensive skills.

For instance, when learning defensive techniques by the athlete, the coach may want to concentrate on minimizing the energy absorption of the defensive techniques by rotational actions (4) (see Linear and Rotational Movements above). On the other hand, when learning offensive techniques by the competitor, the coach could emphasize minimizing the execution time by focusing on the straight path of the kick or punch (4) (horizontal force parallel to the floor; see Resolution of Forces and Transfer of Forces, above).

References

1. Adler, J. (1981), Stages of skill acquisition: a guide for teachers, *Motor Skills: Theory Into Practice,* 5, 2: 75 - 80.
2. Ariel, G. (1984a), The bio, *Track and Field Quarterly Review*, 82, 1: 55 - 61.
3. Ariel, G. (1984b), The mechanics, *Track and Field Quarterly Review*, 82, 4: 57 - 62.
4. Bauer, W. L. and Von Oehsen, E. (1988), Discovering common biomechanical factors of different karate techniques, In: G. de Groot, A. P. Hollander, P. A. Huijing and G. J. v. Ingen Schenau (eds.), *Biomechanics XI-B*, ISB, Volume 7-B, Amsterdam: Free University Press, pp. 920 - 924.
5. Bompa, T. O. (1983), *Theory and Methodology of Training*, Dubuque, Iowa: Kendall/Hunt Publishing Company.
6. Choi, H. H. (1972), *Taekwondo. The Korean Art of Self-Defence*, Toronto: International Taekwondo Federation.
7. Dillman, C. (1989), Improving elite performance through precise biomechanical analysis, In: J. S. Skinner, C. B. Corbin, D. M. Landers, P. E. Martin and C. L. Wells (eds.), *Future Directions in Exercise and Sport Science Research,* Champaign, IL: Human Kinetics Books, pp. 91 - 95.

8. Hay, J. G. (1985), *The Biomechanics of Sports Techniques*, Englewood Cliffs, NJ: Prentice Hall, Inc.
9. Hay, J. G. and Reid, J. G. (1982), *The Anatomical and Mechanical Bases of Human Motion,* Englewood Cliffs, NJ: Prentice-Hall, Inc.
10. Heijmans, J. and Pieter, W. (1985), A kinesiological analysis of the taekwondo side kick, Unpublished manuscript, University of Oregon, Department of PEHMS, Eugene, OR.
11. Ingber, L. (1981), *Karate Kinematics and Dynamics,* Hollywood, CA: Unique Publications, Inc.
12. LeVeau, B. (1977), *Biomechanics of Human Motion*, Philadelphia: W. B. Saunders Company.
13. Pieter, F. (1981a), Algemene Grondslagen B-AG2. Les t.b.v. TBN/NTA Niveau Test, Unpublished manuscript, Den Haag: TBN/NTA.
14. Pieter, F. (1981b), Algemene Grondslagen C-AG2. Les t.b.v. TBN/NTA Niveau Test, Unpublished manuscript, Den Haag: TBN/NTA.
15. Pieter, F. and Pieter, W. (1995), Speed and force of selected taekwondo techniques, *Biology of Sport*, 12, 4: 257 - 266.
16. Pieter, F., Pieter, W. and Heijmans, J. (1987), Movement analysis of taekwondo techniques, *Asian Journal of Physical Education,* 10, 3: 45 - 58.
17. Rasch, P. and Burke, R. (1978), *Kinesiology and Applied Anatomy*, Philadelphia: Lea & Febiger.
18. Serina, E. R. and Lieu, D. K. (1991), Thoracic injury potential of basic competition taekwondo kicks, *Journal of Biomechanics,* 24, 10: 951 - 960.
19. Schmidt, R. A. (1982), *Motor Control and Learning. A Behavioral Emphasis*, Champaign, IL: Human Kinetics Publishers.
20. Sung, N. J., Lee, S. G., Park, H. J. and Joo, S. K. (1987), An analysis of the dynamics of the basic taekwondo kicks, *US Taekwondo Journal*, VI, 2: 10 - 15.
21. Vrijens, J. (1988), *Basis Voor Verantwoord Trainen,* Gent: W. Verbessem.
22. Weineck, J. (1980), *Optimales Training,* Erlangen: Verlagsgesellschaft.
23. Wilmore, J. H. and Costill, D. L. (1988), *Training for Sport and Activity*, Dubuque, Iowa: Wm. C. Brown Publishers.

CHAPTER VII

PSYCHOLOGICAL TRAINING FOR TAEKWONDO COMPETITION

Introduction

It is said that martial sports in general "build character" or that they have a positive influence on personality. Funakoshi (11), for instance, observed that karate will develop courage, courtesy, integrity, modesty and self-control. Research in the area of martial sports and personality traits, however, so far has led to rather ambivalent results. Kroll and Carlson (18) did not find any differences between the personality traits of karate athletes and male college students. Masi (23) also found no differences between karate athletes and non-karate students, between beginning and advanced karate students, or between male and female practitioners. On the other hand, Duthie and co-workers (4) found differences in self-confidence, dominance, autonomy, and achievement, among other things, between martial sport practitioners mentioned in *Who's Who in the Martial Arts* and practitioners from local martial sport clubs with the former scoring better on the variables assessed. Layton (19) found that black belt karate athletes scored lower than their colored belt colleagues in extroversion, neuroticism and psychotism as measured by a psychological questionnaire. The question that these studies have tried to answer is, what the effect of training in martial sports is on the individual's personality.

It is also possible to look at the psychological profile of the athlete and how it is related to performance. Given the same physical potential in terms of training facilities, hours of training, level of skill, and so on, it is the psychological make-up of the athlete that in the end is the decisive factor. Competition is often said to be 90% mental (12). As a result, it has long been recognized by sport scientists, coaches and athletes alike that psychological training of the athlete at the elite level will facilitate peak performance. Sport psychologists in the USA and in other countries are currently working with elite athletes in skiing, figure skating, gymnastics, judo, and so on. In some cases, sport psychologists are even members of the coaching staff.

Although elite taekwondo athletes have occasionally consulted with a sport psychologist, it has not yet become regular practice to do so. The preliminary results of our research indicate that elite taekwondo athletes in general, have not incorporated any psychological techniques in their training program. Psychological skills will aid in reducing anxiety levels that can be detrimental to athletic performance. These skills can also contribute to the prevention of overtraining. Elite taekwondo athletes have been found to exhibit signs of (the onset of) overtraining or burnout at the time of testing. It is well known that overtraining will lead to a decrease in performance and eventually even to dropping out. It is recommended, therefore, that taekwondo coaches include psychological training as part of their regular training program or to advise the athletes to work with a sport psychologist.

This chapter will discuss two psychological variables that have been identified by researchers as detrimental to peak performance: competition anxiety and overtraining. The latter will be dealt with in relation to a so-called mood profile of the athletes, the total sum of which has been found to be a good indicator of (the onset of) overtraining. After a discussion of the theoretical background of each variable, results from the Oregon Taekwondo Research Project will be presented. Recommendations will conclude the sections on competition anxiety and overtraining.

The last part of this chapter will then deal with selected psychological skills to help prevent or reduce the athlete's level of anxiety or overtraining. Depending on the country and its specific rules and regulations regarding psychological counseling of athletes, the coach may have to consult or ask a sport psychologist for help. Regardless of how psychological skills are introduced, it should be remembered that in order for these techniques to have any effect, they need to be practiced much the same way physical skills need to be practiced (see below). Consequently, the results will only become apparent after adequate training. Do not expect instantaneous effects, just as one would not expect to see one's aerobic endurance improve after only two days of training. Psychological variables are not the sole determinants of success. As mentioned in a previous chapter, many factors play a role in winning or losing. This implies that it is advisable to integrate information from various scientific disciplines to optimize coaching of taekwondo athletes.

Keeping in mind that the interplay between taekwondo on the one hand and psychological variables on the other is not as clear-cut as one might have assumed, the coach should also be informed that the effect of the environment plays a powerful role on how the taekwondo athlete will react. One such external factor, for example, is competition. Of particular interest to the coach in this regard are anxiety level and mood characteristics to which the discussion will now turn.

Competition Anxiety

Competition anxiety has been hypothesized to have two components: trait and state anxiety (21). Trait anxiety is a predisposition to perceive certain stimuli from one's sport environment as threatening and to respond with varying levels of apprehension and tension. This response, then, is called state anxiety and is associated with activation of the individual. It is an emotional state that will disappear again as soon as the perceived threatening stimuli have dissipated. State anxiety has three aspects: cognitive anxiety, somatic anxiety, and self-confidence (22) (see below).

Competition trait anxiety in elite male and female taekwondo athletes, as part of the psychological component of the OTRP, was tested by the so-called *Sport Competition Anxiety Test* (SCAT) (21), while competition state anxiety was assessed by means of the *Competitive State Anxiety Inventory-2* (CSAI-2) (22). The higher one's score on the SCAT, the more one tends to become tense and nervous for an upcoming competition. The highest possible score for this test is 30 and the lowest is 10. The SCAT is correlated with the somatic anxiety subscale of the *Competitive State Anxiety Inventory-2* (CSAI-2). In other words, the higher the athlete scores on the SCAT, the higher his or her score tends to be on somatic anxiety as measured by the CSAI-2, which is especially true if the CSAI-2 is taken right before (within an hour of) competition (22).

The CSAI-2 represents 3 subscales: cognitive anxiety, somatic anxiety and self-confidence. Each of these subscales has a maximum score of 36 and a minimum score of 9. *Cognitive anxiety* refers to how worried the athlete is about an upcoming competition at the time he/she took the test. A high score indicates that the athlete was worried about that future competition and a low score indicates that he/she was feeling calm and relaxed.

Feeling nervous and worrying about an upcoming competition is a natural response to a competitive situation. Usually, it only becomes a problem if the athlete finds that it is so bothering him/her that it is upsetting his/her concentration prior to competition. Worry usually disappears rapidly once competition actually starts, but if worry persists during competition it may interfere with good performance. In such a case, a sport psychologist may work with an athlete to help him/her develop ways of lowering anxiety and becoming calm during competition.

Psychological skills used to do this may include any or a combination of the following: rather than worrying about the outcome of the competition, the athlete focuses his/her attention more closely on his/her performance (e.g., paying attention to the correct execution of his or her techniques); relaxation exercises (e.g., deep, slow breathing); and talking confidently to oneself (e.g., "I know I can do this"). See *Psychological Skills To Enhance Performance* below for an example of a relaxation exercise.

The *somatic anxiety* subscale measures a person's level of physiological arousal or "nervousness" about the next competition. As a result, the score is a reflection of how somatically (bodily) anxious one felt about one's upcoming competition when the test was taken. A high score indicates the athlete felt very physiologically upset about the event and a low score indicates he/she felt calm before the competition.

Feeling nervous in the body (upset stomach, heart racing) is, like worrying, a natural response to a competitive situation. One may feel nervous and upset without really being worried about the competition (high somatic anxiety, low cognitive anxiety). It only becomes a problem if it is upsetting the athlete's concentration before the event or if he/she feels his/her energy is getting all used up before the competition even begins. In such cases, a sport psychologist may be chosen to work with the athlete to develop ways of lowering anxiety and becoming calm prior to an event. Psychological techniques used may include relaxation exercises (breathing exercises or muscle relaxation exercises), attention and concentration exercises or meditation (an example of a concentration exercise is given below).

The *self-confidence* subscale measures a person's level of confidence about an approaching competition. In this case, the athlete's score indicates how confident he/she felt about the next competition after the test was taken. A high score indicates the athlete felt very confident about the competition and a low score indicates lack of self-confidence about the next event.

A confident approach to competition is generally recognized as being a preferred style of pre-competition preparation. Less well-known is that even world champions often experience a "lack" of confidence before a competition and that the confidence level of many elite athletes fluctuates quite widely. If athletes feel that their lack of confidence is preventing them from reaching their peak, they may desire to work with their coach or a sport psychologist (depending on geographical, local, or personal circumstances) in order to build and enhance a positive attitude toward taekwondo.

Somatic anxiety gradually increases until the beginning of competition and decreases as competition gets under way. Cognitive anxiety, on the other hand, varies depending on the expectation of the athlete regarding his/her success in that particular competition (22). The athlete's expectation may also be based on the coach's or support group's. The exact distinction between these two forms of state anxiety is the topic of ongoing research. There seems to be a relationship between cognitive anxiety and self-confidence, however. It is hypothesized that self-confidence is a reflection of a lack of cognitive anxiety (22). In other words, a high level of cognitive anxiety is indicative of a lack of self-confidence.

Research has shown that athletes in a contact sport (e.g., wrestling) scored higher on somatic and cognitive anxiety, but lower on self-confidence than athletes in a non-contact sport (e.g., track and gymnastics) (22). When comparing subjective (such as gymnastics and taekwondo where the results depend on a person's subjective evaluation of who won or lost) and objective sports (such as swimming where an objective measure, such as electronic time, decides about winning or losing), athletes in subjective sports were higher in cognitive anxiety; they scored lower in self-confidence and were not different in somatic anxiety. Females were found to be higher in cognitive and somatic anxiety than males, but lower in self-confidence (22).

Results from Taekwondo Research

The psychological component of the OTRP for competition anxiety showed that there were no differences in somatic trait anxiety between the adult elite taekwondo athletes and their recreational counterparts. There were also no differences between the males on the one hand and the females on the other (36). Figure VII.1 and VII.2 display the scores for the male and female taekwondo athletes, respectively, relative to somatic trait anxiety.

In terms of competitive state anxiety, the elite taekwondo athletes were found to be more cognitively anxious than their recreational colleagues. The females as a group showed a lower score for self-confidence than the males. Since the elite athletes were tested two weeks before the 1987 Taekwondo World Championships in Barcelona, it should not come as a surprise that they were more cognitively anxious than the recreationalists. Figure VII.3 shows the various components of state anxiety for the male elite and recreational taekwondo athletes, while competitive state anxiety for the female elite and recreational taekwondo athletes is shown in Figure VII.4. A comparison of self-confidence between male and female taekwondo athletes is visually represented in Figure VII.5.

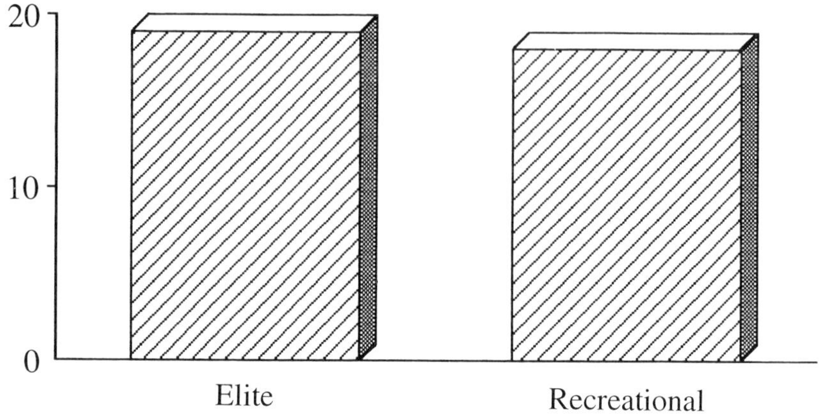

FIGURE VII.1: Somatic Trait Anxiety in Male Taekwondo Athletes

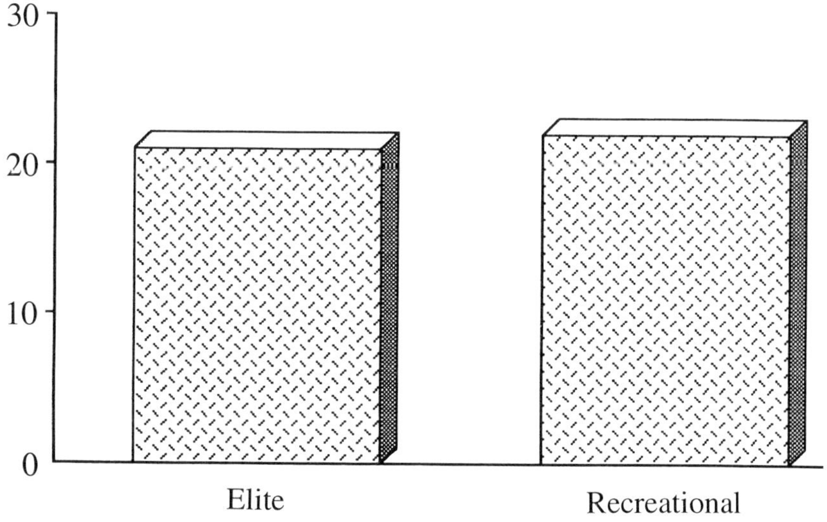

FIGURE VII.2: Somatic Trait Anxiety in Female Taekwondo Athletes

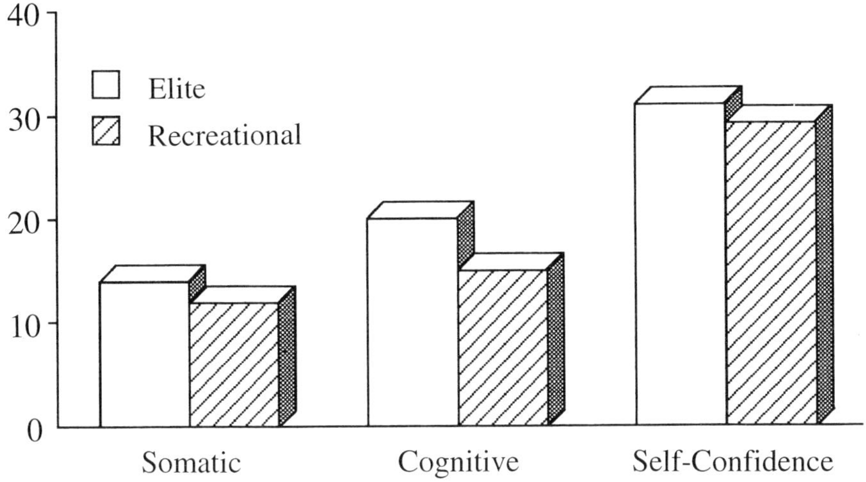

FIGURE VII.3: Competitive State Anxiety of Male Taekwondo Athletes

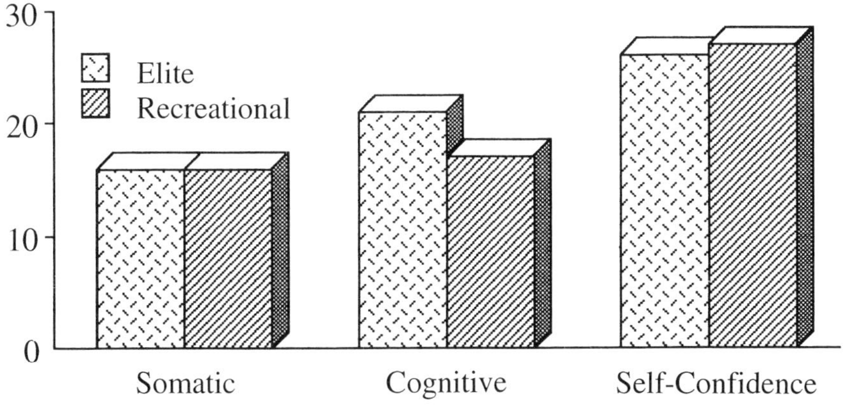

FIGURE VII.4: Competitive State Anxiety of Female Taekwondo Athletes

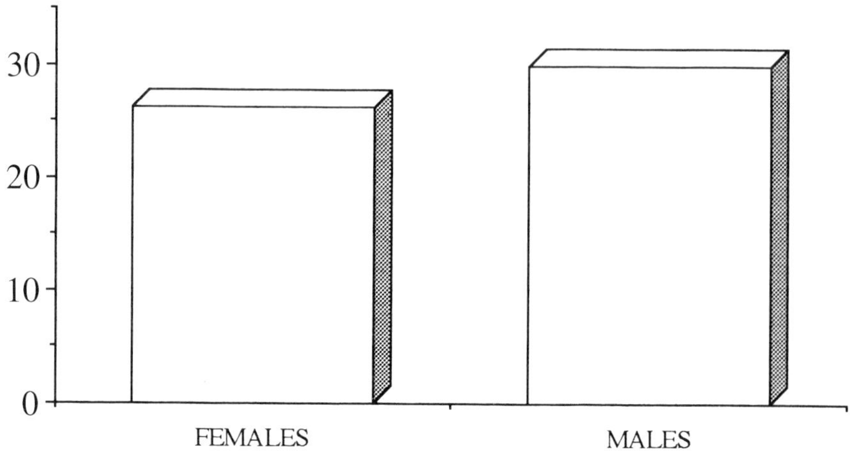

FIGURE VII.5: Self-Confidence of Male vs. Female Taekwondo Athletes

Comparisons with Other Athletes

It is instructive to compare the above results with published norms for other athletes (22). A word of caution seems to be in order, however. Competitive state anxiety is situation-specific. This means that, depending on when the test was taken, the athlete will show more or less state anxiety. At the end of this section, a good illustration will be provided of how components of state anxiety will change subsequent to the time of competition.

When comparing somatic trait anxiety of male recreational taekwondo athletes with wrestlers and college students, it is apparent that the recreational athletes recorded the lowest score (= 18) compared to both the wrestlers (= 21) and students (= 21). The wrestlers and students also scored higher than the male elite taekwondo athletes (= 19). Regionally competitive male taekwondo athletes recorded the highest score (= 23) in somatic trait anxiety (7). The elite and recreational female taekwondo athletes, on the other hand, scored slightly higher than female college students: 21 and 22 for the taekwondo athletes, respectively, versus 20 for the students (see 22). Regionally competitive female taekwondo athletes, similar to their male counterparts, scored highest (= 24) in somatic trait anxiety (7). Remember that the higher the score the higher the physical anxiety of the athletes was.

As far as somatic state anxiety is concerned, wrestlers recorded a much higher score than both elite and recreational male taekwondo athletes. Both female taekwondo groups also scored lower than female elite athletes in general (22). In terms of cognitive state anxiety, however, the elite male taekwondo athletes scored slightly higher than the wrestlers and the elite female taekwondo athletes scored slightly higher than elite female athletes in general (22).

Without the tension of an approaching competition in sight when they took the test, female college age taekwondo students showed more self-confidence than a control group not involved in taekwondo (6), which could be taken as an indication that there seems to be a positive influence on women's self-confidence when they are engaged in taekwondo. The lower self-confidence of women as opposed to men may only be related to self-confidence about competition or about being able to resist an attack as was found in women involved in karate (20). When compared to published norms, both elite and recreational male and female taekwondo athletes recorded higher scores than wrestlers or elite athletes in general (22). Especially the score of the male taekwondo groups is noteworthy (see Figure VII.6, page 160). It is recognized, of course, that more research is needed in this area. Nevertheless, the coach dealing with female taekwondo athletes is advised to expect a lower self-confidence in these athletes and to gear psychological training toward this particular aspect. Keep in mind that self-confidence is related to cognitive anxiety, which calls for cognitive psychological skills to help reduce this component of competitive state anxiety (see section *Psychological Skills To Enhance Performance*).

One of the few studies, if not the only one, in which elite martial sport athletes (male and female judoka) were investigated relative to a variety of psychological variables was conducted by Murphy and colleagues (33). Although comparing the results of that study with those of the psychological component of the OTRP is not entirely appropriate, it is instructive from an educational perspective. Somatic state anxiety for the judo elite athletes at the beginning of the study was comparable to that of the male elite taekwondo athletes, while cognitive state anxiety at the beginning of the judo study was lower than both that of the elite male and female taekwondo athletes. Self-confidence of the judo athletes at baseline was higher than that of the elite female taekwondo athletes, but lower than that of the male taekwondo athletes. It should be remembered that the values for the judo athletes are a composite of both male and female scores. As was alluded to above, there may be a gender difference in self-confidence, which is not reflected in the judo athletes' score.

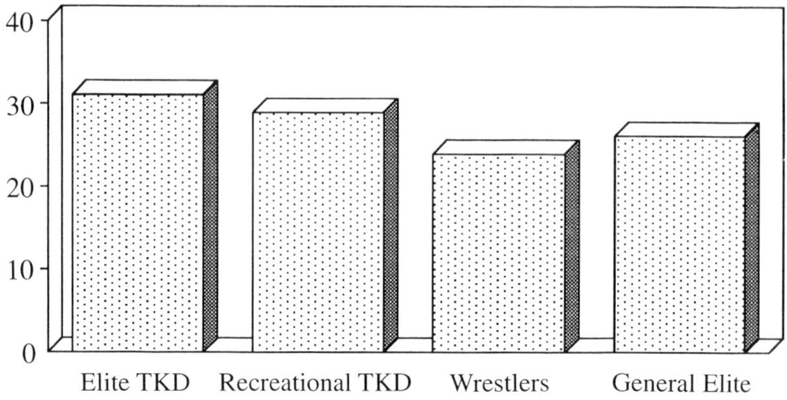

FIGURE VII.6: Self-Confidence of Male Taekwondo and Other Athletes

Research seems to indicate that somatic anxiety increases as competition nears, while cognitive anxiety and self-confidence remain fairly stable (22). Others have suggested that men and women may react differently in levels of state anxiety as competition nears, which may also be dependent on the sport of the subjects under study (16; 17; 22). On the basis of these findings, an initial comparison between elite taekwondo athletes and British male and female intercollegiate athletes (16) showed that the scores for somatic and cognitive anxiety of the taekwondo athletes two weeks prior to a major tournament were higher than the values recorded by the British athletes *30 minutes* before competition (35). Even though the available results are of a tentative nature, the taekwondo coach should be sensitive to psychological intricacies of the athlete and, if peak performance is sought, should do everything in his/her power to optimize the athlete's preparation: from a physical as well as a psychological perspective.

Recommendations

On the basis of results from the psychological component of the OTRP, recommendations to help reduce state anxiety in taekwondo center on lowering the level of arousal of the athletes. Later in this chapter, a number of psychological techniques will be presented to aid the coach and athlete in the latter's psychological preparation for competition. In this section, research will be discussed in which psychological skills have been used to enhance performance in karate. The results are all the more relevant because so far, it seems to be the only research available that deals with improving performance in a martial sport with the help of psychological training.

In an early study by Weinberg and co-workers (43), it was found that for a complex skill such as sparring, a combination of relaxation and imagery seems to lead to better performance. Relaxation refers to trying to relax all muscles in the body in a quiet environment, while *imagery* refers to seeing oneself performing the movements in one's mind. Examples of both strategies will be given at the end of this chapter.

Follow-up research showed that practicing psychological skills, such as relaxation and imagery, should be done from the beginning of the season if improvements in performance are to be noticed (42). This also implies that the coach should monitor the psychological component of the training program on a regular basis by administering psychological tests, such as the ones discussed in this chapter. It is not sufficient to only tell the athletes to practice psychologically. Similar to physical training, the coach should periodically assess the athlete's progress. The longer the athlete is given the chance to practice his or her psychological skills, the better the results will be, especially when these psychological strategies are tailored to the individual (39).

Mood Profile

It has been suggested that a positive mental health state is related to success in sport. In other words, "success in sport is inversely related with psychopathology" (27, p. 71). Mental health state refers to the athlete's response to training rather than his/her baseline psychological profile, which is the profile before the effect of training becomes apparent. Compared to less successful athletes and the general population, the successful athletes show lower levels of anxiety, neuroticism, and depression (28).

Overtraining, or burnout, is the negative outcome of overloading, i.e., increasing the training load of the athlete to provide an optimal stimulus to the body's adaptive capability in order to improve performance (30). Increasing the training load indiscriminately without giving the athlete sufficient time to recover will eventually lead to overtraining, which in turn will lead to a decrease in performance. Overtraining will also increase the athlete's susceptibility to injury, which is detrimental to performance as well. Although overtraining is a long-term product of overloading, it can also be brought about, on a short-term basis, by abrupt changes in the training load (e.g., 30; 33) (see also chapter II).

The most often used psychological instrument to assess (the onset) of overtraining and global mood disturbance is called the *Profile of Mood States* (POMS) (26). The POMS is a scale that measures how one is feeling at the time the test is taken. In the case of the elite taekwondo athletes tested for the OTRP, the POMS measured how they were feeling the week before completing the test.

The POMS measures the athlete's level of tension, anger, depression, confusion, fatigue, and vigor. A score of 50 on each subscale of tension, anger, depression, and so on, is characteristic for the general population but not for (elite) athletes. Athletes and other active people have been found to score higher on vigor and lower on the other levels than the general population, resulting in the so-called iceberg profile (27) or inverted V-profile. A disturbance in this profile is associated with overtraining, staleness, or being burnt-out, which, as alluded to above, will eventually result in a decrease in performance. Stale athletes, then, score lower on vigor and higher on the other subscales compared to the general population. When this is the case, it is said that the athlete's global mood is disturbed. A score of 60 or higher on any of the negative moods is a cause for concern. An effective way to prevent overtraining is a reduction in the training load or complete rest. In addition to its psychological aspects, it should be realized that overtraining also has physiological dimensions, but they are outside the scope of this chapter (e.g., 3).

The *tension subscale* of the POMS measures the level of tension and anxiety of the athlete and any score over 60 indicates that the athlete is feeling very tense, which is not conducive to performance. High levels of tension can sometimes be relieved by learning how to handle stress better. Techniques that can be learned to lower tension include breathing techniques, meditation and biofeedback. Some of these may be used prior to and during competition.

The *depression subscale* measures feelings of sadness, guilt, and loneliness. There is a multitude of reasons why people have these feelings, including the loss of loved ones, personal setbacks, or perceptions of inadequacy. Continued depression can often be relieved by personal counseling or medication. A (sport) psychologist may be contacted for help in this area.

The *anger subscale* is a reflection of feelings of anger and hostility toward others that may be due to many different circumstances. If an athlete experiences intense anger for prolonged periods of time, performance may deteriorate and health may suffer. Most of us experience a number of temporary episodes of high anger and this is generally not a problem. Anger may cause the greatest trouble when it is acted upon, that is, when an individual gets into trouble for impulsive or assaultive acts. Professional help should be sought in such circumstances.

Vigor refers to feelings of great energy and activity. As mentioned earlier, athletes generally score higher on this scale than the general population. If an active athlete has a vigor score below 50, this may be a warning sign that the athlete feels burnt-out. In such a case, it would probably be a good idea for the athlete to discuss the situation with someone, e.g., the coach or a sport psychologist.

Fatigue is indicative of a mood of weariness, inertia, and low energy. For athletes, a high score may be obtained on this scale during periods of intensive or heavy training, which is usually not a problem. However, if fatigue levels are high just prior to important competitions, this may be a serious concern, since intense competition usually requires a great deal of energy. Fatigue levels should be monitored carefully during a training season, as they are good indicators of possible overtraining.

The *subscale of confusion*, finally, measures feelings of confusion and bewilderment. Athletes, who score over 60 on this scale are advised to try to find out what may be happening in their life to cause confusion and uncertainty. These feelings, as with any of the other negative mood states (tension, depression, anger and fatigue) can interfere with performance and can result in poor decision-making.

Results from Taekwondo Research

Figure VII.7 (females) and VII.8 (males) depict the mood profiles for the elite and recreational taekwondo athletes. Both male and female recreational groups scored significantly lower on depression, anger, fatigue, and confusion than the elite taekwondo groups. Although the recreational groups scored higher on vigor than the elite athletes, this was not scientifically significant. The recreational taekwondo athletes also scored lower on total mood disturbance (see Figure VII.9). A possible case of overtraining is displayed in Figure VII.10.

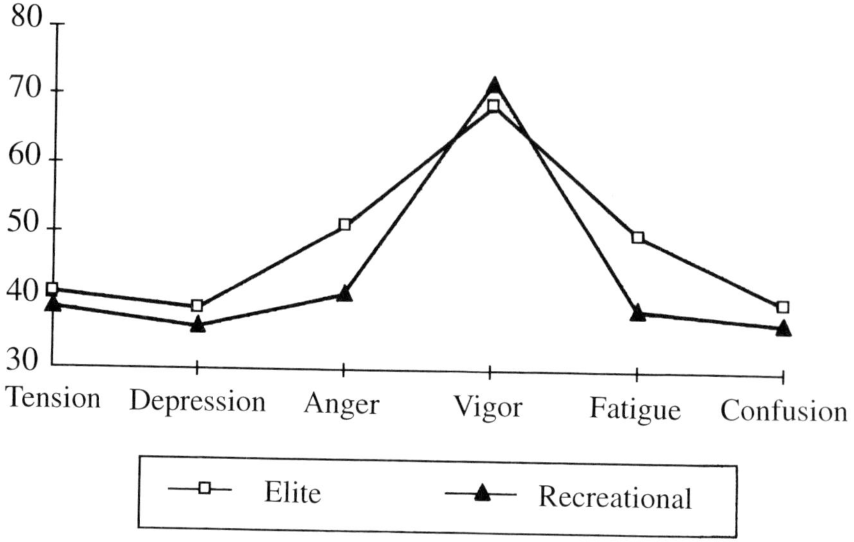

FIGURE VII.7: Mood States of Female Taekwondo Athletes

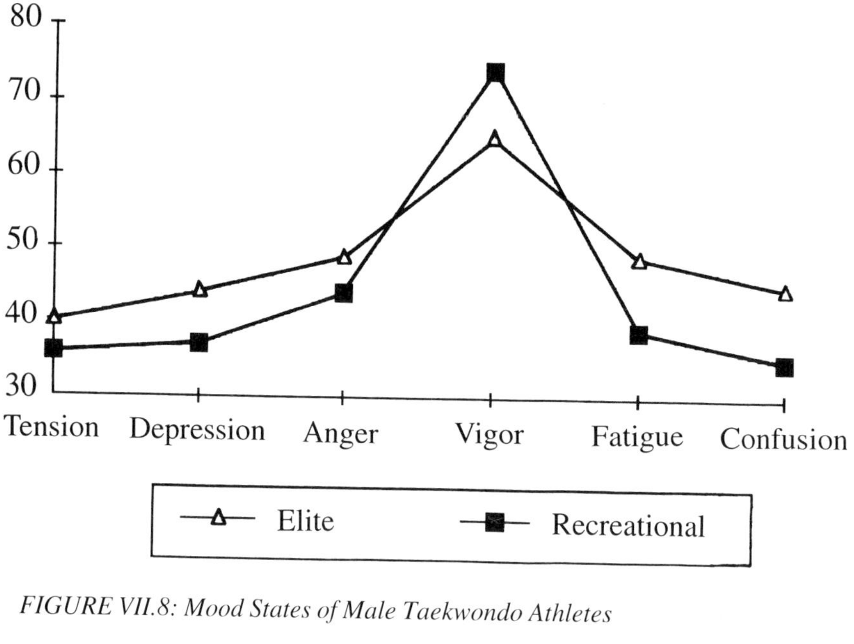

FIGURE VII.8: Mood States of Male Taekwondo Athletes

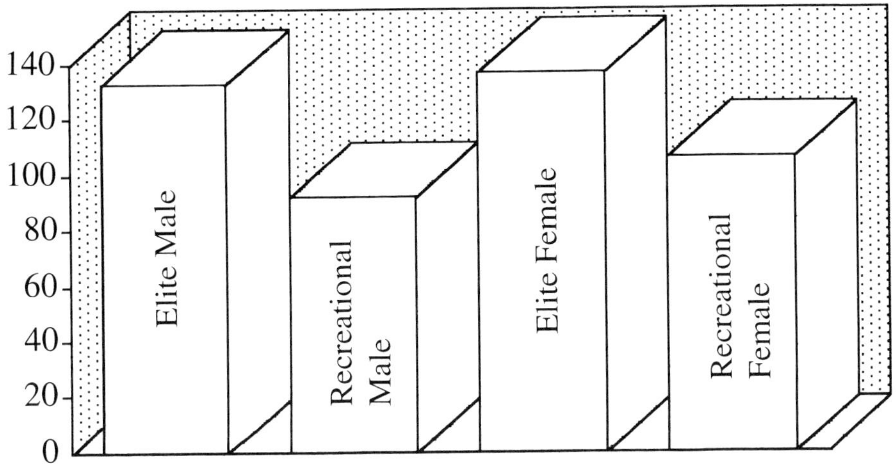

FIGURE VII.9: Total Mood Disturbance of Taekwondo Athletes

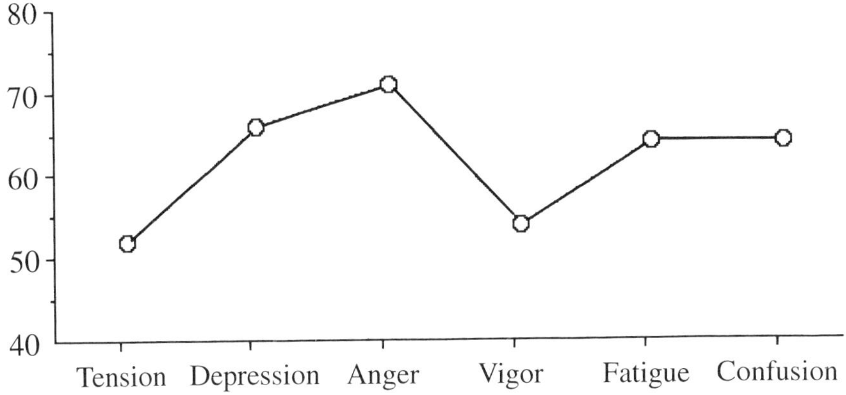

FIGURE VII.10: Mood Profile of Potentially Overtrained

Comparisons with Other Athletes

Several studies have shown the effects of intensive training or competition on the mood profile of a variety of athletes (e.g., 13; 32; 41). Although both elite male and female taekwondo athletes possessed the so-called iceberg profile (see Figure VII.7 and VII.8), as was also found in other elite athletes (e.g., 10; 27; 32; 40), individual athletes within the men's and women's teams showed signs of overtraining with higher than average scores on such negative factors as anger, depression, fatigue, and confusion and a lower than average score on vigor (see Figure VII.10). McGowan and Miller (24) found that more successful karate athletes scored higher on anger than their less successful colleagues. They hypothesized that the successful karate athletes used anger to "psych" themselves for competition. As mentioned above, the POMS was found to be able to detect (the onset of) overtraining if used for regular testing of athletes (28). Staleness is commonly seen as a product of a long-term process of overtraining, but can be induced on a short-term basis by abrupt increases in training load (30; 31).

Increased volume of training in elite male and female judo athletes resulted in changes in anger and, understandably, fatigue, but no disturbance in total mood (33). The reason for the latter finding, according to the authors, may be related to the fact that the judo athletes were nationally ranked elite athletes, whereas the subjects in most other studies were not. The elite taekwondo athletes tested for the OTRP were also nationally ranked athletes, and yet a disturbance of total mood was observed. The difference in this case may be due to other factors, such as the relationship between coach and athletes, length of time during which increased volume of training was applied, and so on. It is highly recommended, therefore, that taekwondo coaches closely monitor their athletes' mood profile, so that precautions may be taken to prevent overtraining, injuries, and a decrease in performance.

Recently, Morgan (27) has suggested a mental health model that relates success in any given sport to a positive psychological profile as measured by mood states. A more negative mood profile, on the other hand, will most likely lead to a decrease in performance. Several studies have shown this relationship to hold at both the elite and non-elite levels (e.g., 9; 30; 31; 40).

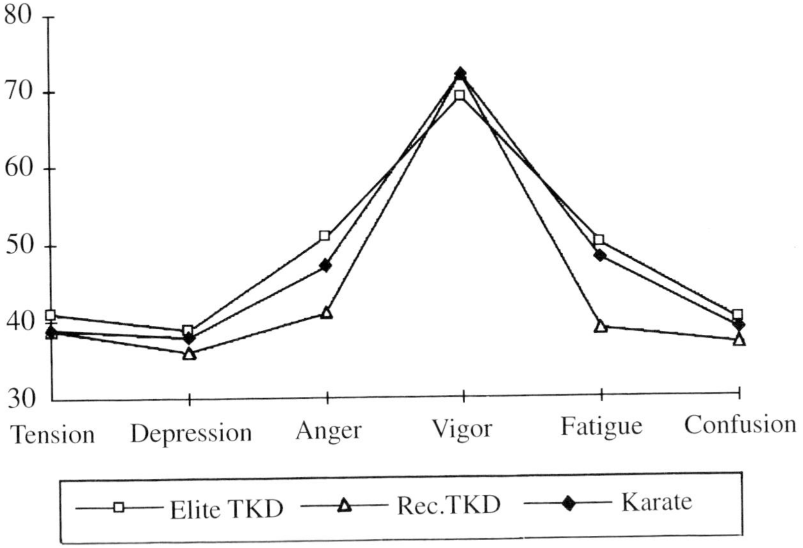

FIGURE VII.11a: Mood States of Taekwondo and Karate Athletes: Females

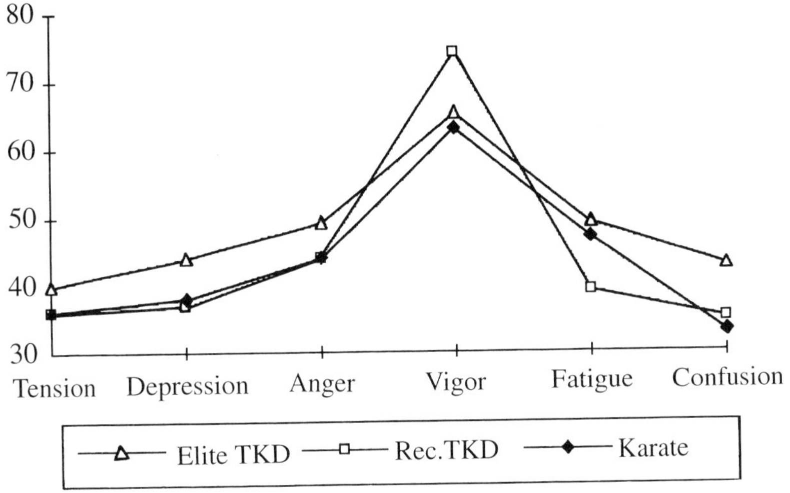

FIGURE VII.11b: Mood States of Taekwondo and Karate Athletes:Males

Figure VII.11a and VII.11b show a comparison of mood states between elite and recreational female and male taekwondo athletes on the one hand and, on the other, nationally competitive karate female and male athletes (25). The female elite taekwondo athletes scored much higher on anger than the female karate athletes, while their tension, depression, fatigue and confusion scores were also higher. On vigor, however, they scored lower than their karate counterparts. In the male elite taekwondo athletes, tension, depression, anger and confusion were all much higher than in their karate colleagues, but their vigor score was also higher. The recreational female taekwondo athletes scored lower on depression, anger, fatigue and confusion than the karate athletes, but similar on tension and vigor. Compared to the male karate athletes, the recreational male taekwondo athletes scored similarly on tension, depression and anger, lower on fatigue but higher on confusion, while their score on vigor was much higher.

Raglin et al. (38) found that when the intensity of training of female rowers peaked, the increase in mood disturbance became significant. Unsuccessful rowers still had an elevated global mood profile after the taper-off, whereas the global mood score of the successful rowers returned to the baseline value. In other words, the successful rowers showed an improvement in global mood with a reduction in training, which is in accordance with the mental health model suggested by Morgan (27). Regularly monitoring of global mood and mood states are again indicated by these results and for taekwondo coaches to help improve their athletes' performance, it is advised to work with a sport psychologist.

Although rest is usually recommended as a cure for overtraining, which could persist for as long as six months (e.g., 37), several measures can be employed to prevent the onset of overtraining. The following recommendations may be used as a guideline for coaches to help prevent overtraining in their taekwondo athletes. Adjusting the training to how the athletes feel at that moment is the decision of a wise coach. Alternating heavy and lighter workouts, as mentioned in chapter II, will also go a long way in the prevention of overtraining.

Recommendations

Preventing overtraining should be part of the taekwondo athlete's training program. This implies that psychological skills to prevent overtraining should be practiced, just as physical skills are practiced. One should realize that, similar to physical skills, it will take time to reap the benefits of psychological training as has been reiterated all throughout this chapter. Do not expect results on a short-term basis. Successfully performing at the elite level in sport takes years of practice, both physically and psychologically.

Taekwondo coaches should be aware that 'the more, the better' is not necessarily conducive to optimal performance. For athletic performance to improve, "less" instead of "more" will often do the trick. Some possible measures to prevent overtraining are suggested below (see 15).

Integrating time-outs in the program. Similar to holidays, days off from work in daily life, taekwondo athletes need time off from their workouts. In this way, they will be able to "recharge their batteries" and find the motivation to work out again, which will be conducive to peak performance.

Give the taekwondo athlete the chance to make his/her own choices. Make sure the athlete has a say in decisions concerning the team, the conditioning and training programs. The athlete will then feel more responsible for whatever happens to the team, the program, and his/her performance. Research has found that sharing decisions and responsibilities will motivate the athlete better and for a longer period of time (5). Goal setting is a good strategy to keep both the athlete and the coach motivated and to optimize the interaction between the two. By setting realistic and attainable goals, both the coach and the athlete know what to expect and what to strive for. Do not hesitate to modify the goals with time and/or if needed. Inflexible coaches will most likely contribute to the athlete getting burnt out and becoming stale (5).

Mental training. Introducing variation in the training may be used to prevent overtraining. The taekwondo coach could vary the physical skills to be practiced, but could also incorporate periods during which the athletes are mentally training these skills. In this way, the monotony of the training will be interrupted and the athlete is given the chance to physically recover from the strenuous workouts without losing practice time. Mental training is also an excellent method to use when injured (see chapter X).

Monitoring heart rate/body weight. Although not a psychological skill per se, this measure has been found to be a very practical and viable option (2). The athlete is advised to take his/her morning heart rate everyday and to write this down in the training log. An increase in morning heart rate is believed to be an indication that the body has not fully recovered from the stress placed on it during training. It could also be a sign that a virus is about to do its unwelcome work. Regardless, closely monitoring the athlete's heart rate and other physical signs, such as restlessness, fatigue, but also fluctuations in the athlete's body weight would be yet another strategy to help prevent overtraining. As far as body weight is concerned, daily instead of weekly monitoring of body weight is indicated if this were to be used as a preventive measure.

Some of the above mentioned psychological skills and others have been successfully employed in different sport settings (e.g., 15; 34). The taekwondo coach who is not familiar with these psychological techniques is advised to consult a sport psychologist to help optimize his/her athlete's performance. Only when working together as a team, coaches, athletes and scientists will be able to make full use of the athlete's potential.

Psychological Skills to Enhance Performance

The psychological skills to enhance performance in taekwondo competition are based on Orlick (34). They will be divided into skills that will address cognitive and somatic state anxiety as well as self-confidence. Some of them, such as relaxation, may also be used as a preventive measure for overtraining. Prevention of overtraining is a combination of the delicate balance of training load and recovery periods in addition to employing one or more psychological skills. Mental training, of course, was already mentioned in the previous section. Whatever the specific psychological strategy(ies), start out with easy exercises and make them more difficult as you go along. For instance, one may choose to concentrate on the down block *(arae makki)* and move up to the spinning hook kick *(twit tollyo ch'agi)*.

Cognitive Skills

One way to help reduce cognitive state anxiety is to practice concentration, which is also useful in other areas of taekwondo training, such as technique training (see previous chapter). There is a number of ways to improve one's concentration. One may focus on an object, on one's own body or body parts, the sky, and so on. One way that the present authors would like to suggest is to use taekwondo forms *(p'umse)* to practice concentration. For example, find a quiet place to sit down. You may choose to close your eyes or to keep them open. Pick a form that you would like to concentrate on. Focus on how it feels when you do that form. Do not let other thoughts enter your mind. As soon as you notice that you are thinking of other things, tell yourself "focus" or "let go" or whatever works for you and return to the form. In the beginning, you may want to do this exercise for about three to five minutes. As you get better at concentrating, you may increase the time you spend on concentration exercises.

Another psychological skill that you can use to decrease your cognitive state anxiety level is called *mental imagery*. Mental imagery is simulating reality in your head before you are dealing with it when you step out of the door. In other words, reality for the taekwondo athlete is training and competition. In mental imagery, the athlete will simulate (parts of) training and/or competition in his/her mind. Mental imagery is when the athlete sees and feels him/herself performing the skills, such as a kick, a punch, a step, or any other taekwondo technique(s). Some athletes will have a picture in their heads in which they are *looking* at themselves performing. Others are actually *doing* the skills in their mind, while still others are going back and forth between these two images. Whatever works for you is best for you as long as you view yourself performing the skills correctly. "It is important to note that the major difference between mental imagery *working* and *not working* relates to the athlete's ability to vividly imagine himself executing the desired skill or response" (34, p. 89).

One exercise that a taekwondo athlete has successfully used involves imagining the competition area from the time he arrived there all the way through the end of the tournament: the location, the competitors, the spectators, the referees, the rings, and so forth. This image would allow him to get used to the situation that he would find himself in when it would be time for him to compete. He felt more relaxed and was more confident when he left for the tournament, because he already knew what he would encounter.

FIGURE VII.12: Concentrating

Behavioral Skills

Relaxation is one method that has been widely used by a variety of athletes. One way to do this is to find a quiet room and to lie down somewhere. Practice tensing your muscles and relaxing them again to feel the difference between tensed and relaxed muscles. You may want to do it in a systematic way by starting with your feet and working your way up to your head. Once you have reached your head, you start all over again to repeat this procedure for about 15 to 20 minutes. After you are used to contracting and relaxing your muscles that way, the next step is to relax them without tensing them beforehand. Use a key word, such as "relax", "calm", "warm", etc., after you have accomplished relaxation of your muscles. You may want to do this exercise for 10 to 15 minutes. The third step would be to relax upon using your key word. Do this several times per day, as many times as you like and wherever you are. The last step is to use the key word and subsequent relaxation in a stressful situation. You may want to create a situation during practice where you are going to use a rather difficult combination of techniques. From practice, you will then move on to less important competitions and finally to important competitions. Every time you feel anxious, use your key word and relax your muscles. You may use this exercise anywhere you want (school, work, etc.) before trying it out in competition.

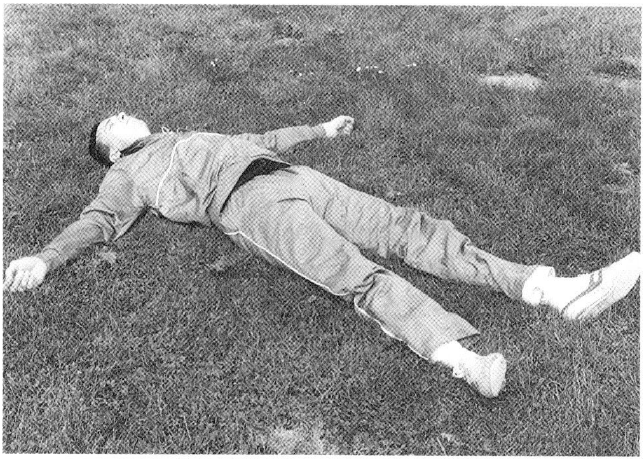

FIGURE VII.13: Relaxation

Self-Suggestion

This technique will help the athlete gain more self-confidence. It is basically positive self-talk and involves creating positive thoughts about yourself. For example, tell yourself that you are in control of your own life and that nobody has the right to live it for you. You could also tell yourself that problems or setbacks are learning experiences and that they will contribute to your growth as a human being. You know that you can do that difficult spinning back kick even with a step prior to it. Tell yourself that you are okay, you know what to do, how to do it and you will. Other people are as nervous as you are before competition, but they do not have the talent that you have. You have set your goals and are fully capable of achieving them. Remember that you are in control, nobody else.

The coach has a very important contribution to make to improve his or her athlete's self-confidence. Use positive reinforcement, emphasize the good things not the errors. Create a positive atmosphere in which the athlete is allowed to experience success, be this because of a properly lifted knee before the kick or a well-executed attack in a sparring bout. A pat on the back will do wonders and will release quite a bit of tension.

The aforementioned psychological skills to help enhance performance may be combined for maximum effect. For instance, mental imagery and relaxation are often used together. The athlete may start out with relaxation exercises and use imagery during the last step in which the key word is to be used in stressful situations. The athlete may simulate a bout in his/her head between him/herself and a very tough opponent. As soon as the athlete squares off, he/she will use the key word to relax.

Periodization of Psychological Training

Similar to endurance, strength and technique training, psychological training can be periodized. Starting out with a few minutes in the pre-season, time spent on psychological training (excluding the time that the athlete would use to practice mentally when injured) may go up to one hour total per session in the competitive period. A possible program for the pre-season and in-season is shown in tables VII.1 (general preparation), VII.2 (specific preparation) and VII.3 (in-season). Psychological training as well as tactical training (see next chapter) will become more important as the athletes continue on to the competition period from the specific preparation phase in the pre-season. In fact, psychological and tactical training will comprise about 50% of the total training time with the other 50% spent on physical and technical training (1).

Obviously, it is not realistic to give a definitive program. As before, the coach will design his/her own program based each athlete's individual circumstances and needs. It should be realized, again, that psychological skills may be combined in one packet. Furthermore, increasing the difficulty of the exercises as the athlete becomes more adept at using these psychological techniques should also be kept in mind. Applying psychological skills during competitions may be one of the goals for a macro-cycle or even one of the goals for a specific competition. For instance, the athlete may want to try out relaxation during a tournament. During the post-competition evaluation, the coach and athlete will assess how many times the athlete was able to relax after the key word and how this affected his/her performance.

If combining relaxation and mental imagery during the specific preparation phase in the pre-season (see table VII.2), the athlete may start with 25 minutes of relaxation and five minutes of imagery. The coach may systematically increase the time spent on relaxation and imagery, in whatever ratio is deemed necessary, during the course of the specific preparation phase to a maximum time of about 45 minutes, for instance, during the in-season (see table VII.3).

TABLE VII.1Program for Psychological Training in Pre-Season: General Preparation Phase

		Week 1 - 2	
Day	**Training**	**Mode**	**Duration**
Monday	-	rest	-
Tuesday	psychological	relaxation	15 minutes
Wednesday	psychological	relaxation	15 minutes
Thursday	psychological	relaxation	15 minutes
Friday	psychological	relaxation	15 minutes
Saturday	psychological	relaxation	15 minutes
Sunday	psychological	relaxation	15 minutes
		Week 3 - 4	
Day	**Training**	**Mode**	**Duration**
Monday	-	rest	-
Tuesday	psychological	relaxation	20 minutes
Wednesday	psychological	relaxation	20 minutes
Thursday	psychological	relaxation	20 minutes
Friday	psychological	relaxation	20 minutes
Saturday	psychological	relaxation	20 minutes
Sunday	psychological	relaxation	20 minutes
		Week 5 - 6	
Frequency	**Duration**	**Intensity**	**Mode**
Monday	-	rest	-
Tuesday	psychological	relaxation	25 minutes
Wednesday	psychological	relaxation	25 minutes
Thursday	psychological	relaxation	25 minutes
Friday	psychological	relaxation	25 minutes
Saturday	psychological	relaxation	25 minutes
Sunday	psychological	relaxation	25 minutes

TABLE VII.2 Program for Psychological Training in Pre-Season: Specific Preparation Phase

Week 1 - 2

Day	Training	Mode	Duration
Monday	-	rest	-
Tuesday	psychological	relaxation/imagery	30 minutes
Wednesday	psychological	relaxation/imagery	30 minutes
Thursday	psychological	relaxation/imagery	30 minutes
Friday	psychological	relaxation/imagery	30 minutes
Saturday	psychological	relaxation/imagery	30 minutes
Sunday	psychological	relaxation/imagery	30 minutes

Week 3 - 4

Day	Training	Mode	Duration
Monday	-	rest	-
Tuesday	psychological	relaxation/imagery	35 minutes
Wednesday	psychological	relaxation/imagery	35 minutes
Thursday	psychological	relaxation/imagery	35 minutes
Friday	psychological	relaxation/imagery	35 minutes
Saturday	psychological	relaxation/imagery	35 minutes
Sunday	psychological	relaxation/imagery	35 minutes

TABLE VII.3 Program for Psychological Training During In-Season

Week 1 - 3

Day	Training	Mode	Duration
Monday	-	rest	-
Tuesday	psychological	relaxation/imagery	40 minutes
Wednesday	psychological	relaxation/imagery	40 minutes
Thursday	psychological	relaxation/imagery	40 minutes
Friday	psychological	relaxation/imagery	40 minutes
Saturday	psychological	relaxation/imagery	40 minutes
Sunday	psychological	relaxation/imagery	40 minutes

Week 4 - 6			
Day	**Training**	**Mode**	**Duration**
Monday	-	rest	-
Tuesday	psychological	relaxation/imagery	45 minutes
Wednesday	psychological	relaxation/imagery	45 minutes
Thursday	psychological	relaxation/imagery	45 minutes
Friday	psychological	relaxation/imagery	45 minutes
Saturday	psychological	relaxation/imagery	45 minutes
Sunday	psychological	relaxation/imagery	45 minutes

References

1. Bompa, T. O. (1983), *Theory and Methodology of Training,* Dubuque, Iowa: Kendall/Hunt Publishing Company.
2. Brown, D. (1986), Stop signs. Stress-proof running by learning when to yield to four telltale signals, *Runner's World,* 21, 5: 72-73.
3. Callister, R., Callister, R. J., Fleck, S. J. and Dudley, G. A. (1990), Physiological and performance responses to overtraining in elite judo athletes, *Medicine and Science in Sports and Exercise*, 22, 6: 816 - 824.
4. Duthie, R. B., Hope, L. and Barker, D. G. (1978), Selected personality traits of martial artists as measured by the Adjective Checklist, *Perceptual and Motor Skills,* 47, 1: 71 - 76.
5. Feigley, D. (1984), Psychological burnout in high-level athletes, *Physician and Sportsmedicine,* 12, 10: 108 - 119.
6. Finkenberg, M. E. (1990), Effect of participation in taekwondo on college women's self-concept, *Perceptual and Motor Skills,* 71, I, 3: 891 - 894.
7. Finkenberg, M. E., DiNucci, J. M., McCune, E. D. and McCune, S. L. (1992), Analysis of the effect of competitive trait anxiety on performance in taekwondo competition, *Perceptual and Motor Skills,* 75, 1: 239 - 243.
8. Frazier, S. E. (1989), A comparison of team mood state profiles utilizing the mental health model, *Journal of Human Movement Studies*, 16, 2: 91 - 99.
9. Frazier, S. E. (1988), Mood state profiles of chronic exercisers with different abilities, *International Journal of Sport Psychology,* 19, 1: 65 - 71.

10. Fuchs, C. Z. and Zaichkowsky, L. N. (1983), Psychological characteristics of male and female bodybuilders: the iceberg profile, *Journal of Sport Behavior*, 6, 3: 136 - 146.
11. Funakoshi, G. (1973), *Karate-Do Kyohan*. The Master Text (translated by T. Ohshima), New York: Kodansha International.
12. Grosser, M., Starischa, S. and Zimmermann, E. (1982), *Conditiegids,* Amsterdam: H. Meulenhoff.
13. Gutmann, M. C., Knapp, D. N., Foster, C., Pollock, M. L. and Rogowski, B. L. (1986), Age, experience, and gender as predictors of psychological response to training in Olympic speedskaters, In: D. M. Landers (ed.), *Sports and Elite Performers. The 1984 Olympic Scientific Congress Proceedings.* Volume 3, Champaign, IL: Human Kinetics Publishers, Inc., pp. 97 - 102.
14. Gutmann, M. C., Pollock, M. L., Foster, C. and Schmidt, D. (1984), Training stress in Olympic speedskaters: a psychological perspective, *Physician and Sportsmedicine,* 12, 12: 45 - 57.
15. Henschen, K. (1986), Athletic staleness and burnout: diagnosis, prevention, and treatment, In: J. Williams (ed.), *Applied Sport Psychology*, Palo Alto, CA: Mayfield Publishing Co.
16. Jones, J. G. and Cale, A. (1989), Precompetition temporal patterning of anxiety and self-confidence in males and females, *Journal of Sport Behavior*, 12, 2: 183 - 195.
17. Jones, J. G., Swain, A. and Cale, A. (1991), Gender differences in precompetition temporal patterning and antecedents of anxiety and self-confidence, *Journal of Sport and Exercise Psychology,* 13, 1: 1 - 15.
18. Kroll, W. and Carlson, B. R. (1967), Discriminant function and hierarchical grouping analysis of karate participants' personality profiles, *Research Quarterly,* 38, 3: 405 - 411.
19. Layton, C. (1988), The personality of black-belt and nonblack-belt traditional karateka, *Perceptual and Motor Skills*, 67, 1: 218.
20. Madden, M. E. (1990), Attributions and vulnerability at the beginning and end of a karate course, *Perceptual and Motor Skills*, 70, I, 3: 787 - 794.
21. Martens, R. (1977), *Sport Competition Anxiety Test*, Champaign, IL: Human Kinetics Publishers.
22. Martens, R., Vealey, R. S. and Burton, D. (1990), *Competitive Anxiety In Sport,* Champaign, IL: Human Kinetics Books.
23. Masi, V. (1975), A Study of the Relationship between Karate Training and Personality Traits, Unpublished Master's thesis, California State University, Northridge.

24. McGowan, R. W. and Miller, M. J. (1989), Differences in mood states between successful and less successful karate participants, *Perceptual and Motor Skills,* 68, 2: 505 - 506.
25. McGowan, R. W., Pierce, E. F. and Jordan, D. (1992), Differences in precompetitive mood states between black belt ranks, *Perceptual and Motor Skills,* 75, 1: 123 - 128.
26. McNair, D. M., Lorr, M. and Dropleman, L. F. (1971), *Profile of Mood States Manual,* San Diego: Educational and Industrial Testing Service.
27. Morgan, W. P. (1985), Selected psychological factors limiting performance: a mental health model, In: D. H. Clarke and H. M. Eckert (eds.), *Limits of Human Performance.* The Academy Papers #18, Champaign, IL: Human Kinetics Publishers, pp. 70 - 80.
28. Morgan, W. P. (1980), Test of champions; the iceberg profile, *Psychology Today,* 13, 7: 92 - 93, 97 - 99, 102, 108.
29. Morgan, W. P. (1978), The mind of the marathoner, *Psychology Today,* 11, 4: 39 - 49.
30. Morgan, W. P., Brown, D. R., Raglin, J. S., O'Connor, P. J. and Ellickson, K. A. (1987a), Psychological monitoring of overtraining and staleness, *British Journal of Sports Medicine,* 21, 3: 107 - 114.
31. Morgan, W. P., Costill, D. L., Flynn, M., Raglin, J. S. and O'Connor, P. J. (1988), Mood disturbance following increased training in swimmers, *Medicine and Science in Sports and Exercise,* 20, 4: 408 - 414.
32. Morgan, W. P., O'Connor, P. J., Sparling, P. B. and Pate, R. R. (1987b), Psychological characterization of the elite female distance runner, *International Journal of Sports Medicine,* 8, Suppl. 2: 124 - 131.
33. Murphy, S., Fleck, S., Dudley, G. and Callister, R. (1990), Psychological and performance concomitants of increased volume training in elite athletes, *Journal of Applied Sport Psychology,* 2, 1: 34 - 50.
34. Orlick, T. (1980), *In Pursuit of Excellence,* Champaign, IL: Human Kinetics Publishers, Inc.
35. Pieter, W. (1991), Performance characteristics of elite taekwondo athletes, *Korean Journal of Sport Science,* 3: 94 - 117.
36. Pieter, W. and Taaffe, D. (1992), The Oregon Taekwondo Research Project. Results and Recommendations, *Journal of Asian Martial Arts,* 1, 1: 73 - 85.
37. Raglin, J. S. (1990), Exercise and mental health. Beneficial and detrimental effects, *Sports Medicine,* 9, 6: 323 - 329.
38. Raglin, J. S., Morgan, W. P. and Luchsinger, A. E. (1990), Mood and self-motivation in successful and unsuccessful female rowers, *Medicine and Science in Sports and Exercise,* 22, 6: 849 - 853.

39. Seabourne, T., Weinberg, R. and Jackson, A. (1984), Effect of individualized practice and training of Visuo-Motor Behavioral Rehearsal in enhancing karate performance, *Journal of Sport Behavior*, 7, 2: 58 - 67.
40. Silva III, J. M., Shultz, B. B., Haslam, R. W. and Murray, D. (1981), A psychophysiological assessment of elite wrestlers, Research Quarterly, 52, 3: 348 - 358.
41. Tharion, W. J., Strowman, S. R. and Rauch, T. M. (1988), Profile and changes in moods of ultramarathoners, *Journal of Sport and Exercise Psychology*, 10, 2: 229 - 235.
42. Weinberg, R. S., Seabourne, T. G. and Jackson, A. (1982), Effects of Visuo-Motor Behavior Rehearsal on state-trait anxiety and performance: is practice important?, *Journal of Sport Behavior*, 5, 4: 209 - 219.
43. Weinberg, R. S., Seabourne, T. G. and Jackson, A. (1981), Effects of Visuo-Motor Behavior Rehearsal, relaxation, and imagery on karate performance, *Journal of Sport Psychology*, 3, 3: 228 - 238.

CHAPTER VIII

TACTICAL TRAINING FOR TAEKWONDO COMPETITION

Introduction

There is not much written information available about tactics for taekwondo competition. Attacking and defending are the basic ingredients of a match, but this is only a simple representation of the many things that happen during the competition as a whole. Some of them include the fear of getting hurt, the will to win, the mental fight, the athlete's motivation, anxiety level, concentration, self-confidence, skill level, and so forth.

All of these and other factors are taken into consideration when the coach and athlete are planning the tactics to be used. Tactics refers to the various ways of preparing and organizing offense and defense to fulfill a goal (2). The goal is to score a point and eventually winning the bout. Preparing and organizing the athlete's offense and defense simply means that certain ways of attacking or defending are practiced to set up the opponent to score a point or to prevent the opponent from scoring one him/herself.

This chapter will deal with the tactical preparation of the taekwondo athlete and will cover selected general principles of offense and defense in taekwondo competition. Every coach has his/her own tactical approach that is based on personal experience, theoretical knowledge and the athletes' potential. Viewed from that perspective, there are as many tactical possibilities as there are people practicing taekwondo. Nevertheless, there are components of a bout that are basic to any match and those are the ones that will be addressed here. Before doing so, however, two related words should be defined first to make sure that we are using the same terminology.

Depending on one's geographical region, the word strategy or tactics may be preferred. For the purposes of this chapter and in accordance with Eastern European literature, strategy refers to the plans the coach has for his or her athletes regarding their competitions throughout the whole annual season or even longer (2), such as the two- or four-year strategy employed to prepare an athlete for the World Championships or Olympic Games, respectively. Tactics, on the other hand, refers to the plans for one competition only and as such is part of a strategy. Tactics is a short-term endeavor, while strategy is a long-term approach. An example of a strategy would be to choose those competitions that the athletes will participate in in such a way, that they will be exposed to gradually more difficult encounters with the most demanding of them all at the end of the road, which would be the one major competition that both the coach and the athletes have prepared themselves for in all those years: the World Championships, for instance, or the Olympic Games.

The next sections, as mentioned before, will deal with tactics, plans for one competition. The success of the tactics utilized in taekwondo, as in many other sports, depends on a high level of technical skill (2). This means that technique is a limiting factor of the athlete's tactics. For instance, if an athlete is not sufficiently proficient in the use of the axe kick, any tactics involving this kick will be doomed to fail. Tactics is also related to physical preparation and psychological readiness. If the athlete's endurance level is poor, any tactics to be developed for him/her will have to consist of very brief offensive and defensive maneuvers to prevent the athlete from getting too fatigued. Similarly, if the athlete lacks self-confidence, for instance, he/she will not be able to execute any of the tactical actions with conviction.

Fighting Distance

The fighting distance is the distance between two athletes, who are competing in the ring. This distance can vary from standing next to each other, making physical contact, to standing as far apart as the boundaries of the ring will allow. It is not only a distance that can be expressed as being so many meters apart from each other. The space between the contenders is not merely an empty, air-filled space. On the contrary, there is much more going on. The space between the competitors is a field of tension, some type of magnetic field, as it were. Emotions expressed by the language of the body, the expression of the face, the eyes (and the voice, when using the *kihap*) fill this space and turn it into an "emotionally loaded" one.

Something similar happens in ballet, for instance, when the dancer appears on stage and his/her presence turns an empty, generic, stage into a "romantic" landscape. The same space suddenly has changed into something else although the space per se has not changed at all. The radiation of the dancer, the way he/she walks, the way he/she holds his/her head, the expression in the eyes and so on, are responsible for the change the spectators go through in terms of how they experience the event. In taekwondo, for example, athlete A moves steadily forward, looking mean and threatening, his/her fists clenched and held in a certain position: the athlete is more than ready to start. The opponent, athlete B, will become influenced by the threatening expression of athlete A and if B is to give A adequate competition, he/she will have to figure out what to do and fast at that, too.

An example of how this emotional distance may influence an athlete's psychological state and, as a result, athletic performance is as follows. At a major competition, the coach noticed that the athlete would not extend his leg to kick, even though he would lift it up and the physical distance to his adversary was optimal. During the breaks between rounds, the coach advised the athlete to complete the kick, but he never did it and subsequently lost the match. The evaluation after the competition revealed that the athlete thought that his opponent was out of reach. Further analysis showed that the athlete was not sure about his ability to perform well under the circumstances of the emotional distance and became so anxious that he could not kick. The physical distance became an emotional distance that could not be bridged.

The ultimate importance of physical distance, of course, is to create an optimal distance to execute techniques. The optimal striking distance is the distance between the athlete and the opponent that will enable the athlete to perform a technique to score a point. If the athlete is too close to the opponent, he/she will not be able to kick properly. This also holds if the distance is too large, in which case the athlete will have to "reach out" to hit his/her opponent. In both instances, the experienced athlete will adjust his or her techniques quickly as the situation arises (see section on Different Kick For Different Striking Distance).

Exercises to Practice the Optimal Striking Distance

Following are some exercises to practice the optimal striking distance. The main goal of these exercises is to develop the optimal distance to strike and not so much to practice the attack itself. The rationale for developing this feeling of the optimal striking distance is related to maneuvering oneself into the best position to score a point. Maintaining one's equilibrium is essential for the proper execution of techniques. If one's balance is perturbed, chances are that the adversary will take advantage of it to score a point.

Exercise 1

The athletes work in pairs and try to touch each other's knees without allowing their partner to touch their own knees. The notion of the striking distance becomes clear now: being able to hit your opponent and not getting hit yourself, which is not easily accomplished. The coach should explain that the focus of this exercise is on creating an optimal distance (see figure VIII.1).

Exercise 2

The athletes place their hands on each other's shoulders and make ballroom dance-like movements. The goal of this exercise is the physical awareness of the partner's body as he or she moves forward, sideways, backward, and so on (see figure VIII.2).

FIGURE VIII.1: Exercise 1

FIGURE VIII.2: Exercise 2

Exercise 3

The same position as in exercise 2, but now one of the partners uses a little force as in pushing and pulling. The goal of this exercise is the same as the previous one, viz., what it is to feel the human body but this time around, with some resistance. It is not the purpose of this exercise to show who is strongest, but to experience the human body as it moves through space, while trying to keep one's balance, following, anticipating.

Exercise 4

This is a punching exercise with a partner. Person A places his/her hands in front of his/her chest, the palm of the hands facing B. B gently punches A's palms. The right punch goes to A's right palm and the left goes to A's left palm. The goal of this exercise is to practice the awareness and feeling of the optimal distance. Do not hit hard, but gently on the right spot (see figure VIII.3).

Variations of this exercise are the following:
a.) Punching while standing.
b.) The partner walks backward and the athlete follows, while punching and keeping the right distance.
c.) The partner walks forward and the athlete goes backward.
d.) The partner moves at random, the athlete follows.
e.) The partner moves at random, while also changing the speed of movement.

FIGURE VIII.3: Exercise 4

Exercise 5

The same exercise as in exercise 4, but this time using roundhouse kicks to the chest. The partners are wearing protective equipment. The goal of this exercise is again hitting gently and accurately, while maintaining an optimal distance to the other (see figure VIII.4). Variations may be done similar to exercise 4.

FIGURE VIII.4: Exercise 5

Exercise 6

For this exercise, an elastic rope is used. The two partners are connected with that elastic rope. While moving, they should try to keep the tension of the rope constant. If they are too close to each other, the rope will hang down and if they are too far apart they will stretch out the rope.

Variations of this particular exercise are as follows:
a.) The athletes move forward and backward.
b.) The athletes move forward and backward at random.
c.) The athletes move forward and backward at random with changing speed.
d.) The athletes move forward, backward and sideways at random and at random speed.
e.) The athletes practice in a semi-fighting situation, while focusing on the optimal distance.

Exercise 7

The athletes practice fighting combinations (for examples of fighting combinations see chapter IV). Again, the focus is on optimal fighting distance. Variations may be done similar to the ones in exercise 6.

Different Kick for Different Striking Distance

Although it is always better to be able to kick from an optimal fighting distance, this is not always possible in a match. The opponent, for example, will try to come as close as possible or keep his/her distance. Therefore, to still be able to score points even though the distance to the opponent is not optimal, the athlete has to adapt his/her techniques. Basic elements of the various techniques used stay the same, but changes are made to meet the new circumstances. Below are two examples to illustrate this point.

Round Kick

Optimal striking distance. Exercises to practice the optimal fighting distance for the round kick are described above. Figure VIII.5 shows the round kick from an optimal distance.

Close-range striking distance. The athletes are standing very close to each other. Performing the roundhouse kick in a normal fashion would mean that the training partner would be hit with the knee, if hit at all. In order to be able to kick at close range, the knee has to be raised high and the leg has to be bent as far as possible in order to bring the foot in the right position (see figure VIII.6).

Exercises to practice close-range roundhouse kicking include the following. One athlete holds two pads on each side of his/her waist. The other athlete, who is practicing the kick, puts his/her hands on the shoulders of the first one and tries to hit the pad from this position. A variation of this exercise would be to hold the pads while moving around.

Long-range striking distance. In this situation, the athletes are standing too far apart and in order to be able to score a point, the gap may be closed by taking a step forward. To be able to score from this position, the athlete has to "extend" his/her technique. It is very important to raise the knee high, bending it at the same time and sliding forward on the support leg to bridge the distance (see figure VIII.7).

FIGURE VIII.5: Round Kick: Optimal Striking Distance

FIGURE VIII.6: Close-Range Round Kick

FIGURE VIII.7: Long-Range Round Kick

The following exercises are suggested to practice this long-range round kick. The partner holds the pad and the athlete who is kicking stands behind a line on the floor from which he/she tries to hit the pad. The goal of this exercise is to increase the distance to the pad by moving the line a little bit further away, and so on. This exercise may be done with a fellow athlete instead of using the pad, or in pre-arranged drills.

Side Kick

Optimal striking distance. Exercises to practice the optimal striking distance were given above and the side kick from this distance is shown in figure VIII.8.

FIGURE VIII.8: Side Kick: Optimal Striking Distance

Close-range striking distance. The distance between the athletes is so close that a normal side kick would be interrupted at the knee/thigh level of the opponent. In order to be able to kick from a close-range position the knee has to be bent as far as possible and the foot, in this instance, has to be higher than the knee (see figure VIII.9).

One way to practice this side kick is as follows. Stand close to a pad held by a partner and try to side kick it. Decrease the distance until it is not possible to hit the pad any longer. Do the same exercise with a partner wearing protective gear (*hogu*).

FIGURE VIII.9: Close-Range Side Kick

Long-range striking distance. In the long-range striking distance, the knee has to be bent, held high and the athlete gains distance by sliding forward on the support leg. While kicking, the athlete has to stretch or reach out as far as possible (see figure VIII.10). One may use the exercises with the pad as the ones described above for the close-range side kick.

FIGURE VIII.10: Long-Range Side Kick

Steps

Stepping in taekwondo is comparable to "footwork" in boxing. According to Ko (3), stepping is at the basis of every change in the body's position, of every change in its center of gravity from one point to the next. It is self-explanatory that stepping is always done in a balanced manner. Steps are used to execute offensive and defensive techniques. Typically, attacks are preceded by steps to confuse the opponent, while defensive maneuvers are preceded by steps to get out of the line of attack by the adversary.

Steps may be done by actually moving forward, backward, sideways, or diagonally but they may also be done "on the spot", without any appreciable change in one's place relative to the opponent's. For instance, the basic, "on the spot", step consists of changing one's leading leg without moving forward, backward or sideways (see figure VIII.11A-C). An example of using a step to close the distance between the competitors is shown in figure VIII.12A-D.

FIGURE VIII.11: Basic "On the Spot" Step

A

B

C

FIGURE VIII.12: Forward Step to Close Distance

A

B

C

D

FIGURE VIII.13: Sideways Defensive Step

A

B

C

D

In this case, the step is followed by a round kick, but could be any (series of) technique(s). A more defensively used step is depicted in figure VIII.13A-D. Here, the leading leg moves sideways first to get the athlete out of the line of attack. Next, the other leg crosses, to finish off with the former leading leg connecting with a kick.

Another way to use steps is to confuse the opponent. For instance, suppose the athlete has planned to execute a series of kicks. He/she may choose to precede the first kick by a couple of steps to confuse the opponent regarding the leg with which the athlete will perform the first kick (see figure VIII.14A-E). Adding a *ki-hap* and intimidating body language, such as facial expressions or extra arm movements will contribute to the confusion and increase the likelihood of a successful attack.

FIGURE VIII.14: Step to Confuse Opponent

A

B

C

D

E

Offensive and Defensive Maneuvers

In taekwondo competition, we can distinguish the basic attack, the fake, the follow-up attack, counterattack, interceptions, blocking and evasive maneuvers. These maneuvers can sometimes be classified as pure attacks or defenses and sometimes as hybrid forms consisting of a combination of offensive and defensive movements. The following breakdown of offensive and defensive tactical maneuvers is based on Barth et al. (1) and applied to taekwondo training/competition.

Basic Attack

A

B

C

FIGURE VIII.15: Sequence of Three Techniques

A basic attack is a direct attack with the aim to hit the opponent and to score a point. Any kick or punch to the legitimate striking areas may serve as a basic attack. The basic attack is very often used in taekwondo competition. It is advised, however, to use a combination of at least three techniques when attacking with a basic attack. Many times during competition, it was observed that an athlete attacked with a combination of two kicks, for instance. The first technique was used to overcome the distance. The second one came close, but no point was scored. If a third technique had been used, the athlete would have had a greater chance of scoring. Examples of kicking combinations were already presented in chapter IV. Figure VIII.15 shows a sequence of three techniques.

Naturally, *the athlete should not telegraph his/her intentions to the opponent.* For example, when punching, the athlete has to move the fist straight from its starting position. If the athlete would pull back the fist prior to the punch to gain more strength, this movement would telegraph the athlete's intentions. Further, the athlete should only attack those body parts, which are *not protected.* Kicking against the opponent's defense will not result in a point, but instead may lead to an injury. Finally, the athlete has to choose the right moment to attack, which refers to when the opponent loses his or her concentration. The athlete has to learn to pick this up and act accordingly. Another right moment to attack is when the opponent makes an unnecessary movement or one that does not serve any apparent purpose. That, for example, could be when the athlete is jumping up and down ("hopping") and changing his/her leading leg position without any tactical intention in mind.

Fake Attack

A fake attack is one where the athlete misleads the opponent by starting a technique to which the opponent reacts by changing his/her defense. As soon as this happens, the attacker subsequently continues with another technique to score a point. An example of a fake attack is initiating a round kick to the middle of the body to lure the opponent into blocking it, while finishing off with a round kick to the face (see figure VIII.16A-C). Other examples of fake attacks are: a front kick to the stomach and a roundhouse to the head; fake side kick to the mid-section of the body followed by a roundhouse kick to the head.

Follow-up Attack

A follow-up attack is one that follows a block. For instance, block a low roundhouse kick by the opponent with a down block and then immediately follow it up with a punch, low roundhouse and spinning back kick combination. It goes without saying that the athlete is supposed to know how to block properly or else there would be no point in following up with the remainder of the series.

A

B

C

FIGURE VIII.16: Example of Fake Attack

Counterattack

The counterattack is initiated while the opponent is attacking. There are two possibilities: the direct and the delayed counterattack. An example of the direct counterattack would be when the athlete counters a middle round kick, for instance, by a round kick of his/her own while stepping sideways and out of the line of attack. In the delayed counterattack, the athlete waits till the last blow in a series of attacks before counterattacking. For instance, suppose the series of attacks consists of a left middle round kick, right middle round kick and a left spinning back kick. The athlete would wait with his/her counterattack until the opponent brings down the kicking leg after the spinning back kick. An example of a counterattack is shown in figure VIII.17A-C.

A

B

C

FIGURE VIII.17: Example of Counterattack

Pointers when executing counterattacks include:

1. The athlete should be able to pick up wrong use of tactics, bad technical skill, breakes in executing techniques, and so on, by his/her opponent in order to be able to perform a counterattack successfully.
2. The athlete should be able to anticipate the techniques his/her opponent wants to use.

Exercises

1. The opponent attacks with a middle right side kick and the athlete counter-attacks with a middle roundhouse. While counterattacking, the athlete has to move slightly forward and diagonally, out of the line of attack.
2. The opponent attacks with a left high roundhouse kick and the athlete counters with a right spinning back kick.

Interception

Interception refers to stopping the attack of the opponent, which may serve several purposes, such as preventing the opponent to take the initiative or to prevent the opponent from taking further action so the athlete can catch his/her breath. The side kick and the pushing kick are two examples of techniques that may be used as interception kicks. During practice, the athlete uses either a side kick or a pushing kick to intercept nearly all the actions by the opponent. The techniques are executed with the leading leg, since this one is closest to the attacker and therefore faster in reaching him/her (see figure VIII.18A and B).

FIGURE VIII.18: Example of Interception

A

B

Blocking

Blocking techniques are defensive movements with the purpose of deflecting an attack by the opponent. In taekwondo, the down block, outward middle block and high block are examples of basic blocks. These and others are mainly used to block kicks. It is much harder to block punches, however. The defense against punches is mostly done by means of protecting the body with both arms, which sometimes is also used against leg techniques.

Evasive Maneuvers

Evading is another defensive technique to prevent the opponent from scoring a point. By stepping back or to the side, out of the line of attack, the athlete avoids getting hit. Pointers to be considered include:

1. Timing, i.e., evading the attack at the right moment is a crucial point, as is the anticipation of the actions of the opponent.
2. The end position after the evasive maneuver must be a position of balance from where the athlete should be able to take over the initiative.

Examples of a Tactical Plan

Based on the aforementioned, the coach will have to select his/her tactics for the next competition. Following are examples using the information presented above. These examples should suffice for now. Every situation is unique, requiring its own tactical approach. However, the selected topics above should provide the reader with material and ideas to design his or her own tactical plan on the basis of the individual's particular situation, needs, possibilities and so on. The first two examples are short tactical plans for specific situations in competition. The third one is more elaborate and spans a whole match at a tournament.

Example 1

During the course of a match, the athlete noticed that his opponent frequently used the jump spinning back kick. He subsequently faked a low round kick to evoke the same response. When his opponent finally did, the athlete was ready for it. He slid back after the fake and counterattacked the opponent upon landing. This little tactical plan worked several times during that particular match.

Example 2

The athlete set up her opponent with the help of steps. She would do a forward step, immediately followed by a backward step with the same leg while making sure to leave an opening in her defense when she stepped backward. After a short while, her opponent noticed the opening and acted upon it by performing a middle round kick. The athlete had anticipated this move and countered immediately with a spinning back kick.

Example 3

The situation for which the third example of a tactical plan will be described is the final match in the women's competition at an international tournament. The athlete had bruised insteps coming into the final, because no instep pads were allowed. She was tired at the end of her semi-final bout, but felt confident and was highly motivated. The referees tended to score for the slightest touch of the head/face area with any kick. The opponent was surprised to be in the final (the athlete's coach had observed her throughout the tournament and had overheard her reactions when she won her semi-final). She was not much taller than the athlete, but had proportionately longer legs. Her techniques were not that fast nor were they as forceful as the coach's athlete. The opponent's preferred technique was the middle roundhouse kick with the right leg.

The tactical plan for the first round of this final was as follows. The athlete was advised to stay as closely as possible to her opponent to offset the potential advantage of those longer legs. She was to use middle side kicks, spinning back kicks and punches after various steps to avoid using the bruised insteps during attacks. For her defense, she would use either interceptions or stepping to the side or backward, for she did not feel as comfortable yet using her arms to block. The middle kicks were used to save energy (remember that the athlete was tired at the end of her semi-final match). After the first round, the athlete felt good, not as tired as she thought she would be. The coach had noticed that her opponent was intimidated by the athlete's punches and the force of her kicks. Both competitors scored one point during this round.

For the second round, the tactical plan was modified somewhat. Since the athlete was not as tired, she would now use the axe kick in addition to the other techniques mentioned previously. The coach reminded her of how to set-up an attack with the axe kick (they had practiced this during the workouts) and told her that she could easily do it to boost up her confidence. Although the axe kick would be difficult to execute when tired, the coach counted on the tendency of the referees to score for the slightest touch of the head/face area (see above). The athlete was also told that she was doing extremely well intercepting her opponent's attacks and that she could use those moments to take a break to catch her breath. At the end of the second round, the athlete was leading by three points.

The athlete again felt good and very confident, which the coach had already noticed during the fight. The plan for the third round was rather simple. It would be the same as the one for the second round and the athlete was given the opportunity to do anything she wanted to do. The coach boosted her confidence even more by saying that she was doing extremely well and there was really no need to change anything in the tactical plan, because everything seemed to "flow". In addition, he also shared with her that her opponent had already given up mentally, which the coach had deduced from the way the opponent moved around the ring and the way she initiated attacks. The athlete eventually won the final.

Training Guidelines for Tactical Preparation

Regardless of each individual's circumstances, there are some basic guidelines that will facilitate the development of the athlete's tactical training. The coach needs to have a thorough knowledge of the scientific foundations of taekwondo coaching and of the competitor him/herself. Insight in the athlete's psychological make-up (is the athlete self-confident? motivated? anxious? and so on) especially will aid in designing a tactical plan. The following guidelines may be used to devise one's tactical plan (based on 2).

Competition rules and regulations. The coach (and athlete as well) will have to know exactly which actions will be penalized and which ones will lead to legitimate scores. It would be quite useless, for example, to include grabbing in the tactical plan, since grabbing is not allowed in taekwondo. It should be obvious why knowing competition rules and regulations is important.

Tactics of champions. It would benefit the coach to study the tactics of those athletes, who are consistent winners or at least be aware of their tactical maneuvers. They do not necessarily have to be taekwondo athletes, but may be from another sport. For instance, one taekwondo coach once used a tactical plan that he knew a champion judo athlete had successfully used in the past. This judo athlete would use one technique exclusively throughout part of a match until he had the feeling that his opponent had gotten used to it. He then waited for a moment to initiate this technique again, but quickly shifted to another one to throw his opponent, who had already started to prepare himself for the technique that had been used so far. Needless to say that the judo athlete would score a point with this maneuver.

Research the tactics of future opponents. This may be done by studying video tapes or watching matches of future opponents. The coach should also include the opponent's physical and psychological potential. An example of this was relayed in the previous section where the coach knew that the athlete's opponent had longer legs, but was psychologically easily intimidated.

Analyze past performances in view of future opponents. For instance, suppose the athlete has the tendency to use a tactical maneuver based on the axe kick. In other words, the axe kick is the technique the athlete scores with after a certain combination of steps or a counterattack, or whatever sequence is applicable. The future opponent happens to be a rather tall competitor against whom an axe kick would not be very effective. In this case, an alternative should be sought in one's tactical plan, such as close-in fighting, middle kicks and so forth. Analyzing past performances also includes one's psychological make-up during a match. If the athlete lacks concentration, care should be taken to develop this aspect (see chapter VII), so that it may be used in the athlete's tactical plan against a very confident future opponent.

Develop a tactical plan while adhering to variations and basing it on personal strengths, while avoiding any weaknesses. During the workouts, the athlete will practice a number of tactical plans to be used in the upcoming competition. For instance, suppose one plan consists of a fake attack with a round kick. One variation would be to use a side kick or an axe kick instead of the roundhouse kick. If the athlete's blocking skills are not up to par yet, his/her tactical plan would not include any blocking techniques. Instead, other options have to be employed, such as backward stepping or side stepping. If the athlete has a rather fast and powerful axe kick, this could be used to his or her advantage by incorporating the kick in the tactical plan.

Practice the athlete's pacing abilities. For instance, do not include a plan for which the athlete will have to go all out during the first round. He or she will be too fatigued by the time the second and third rounds have to be fought. One way to do this is to prolong the number of rounds during the workouts. It would also be possible to use several rested sparring partners, who would alternate to practice with the athlete. This will force the athlete to distribute his/her energy more equally.

Practice a variety of means to solve tactical situations. This will prepare the athlete to perform under circumstances that he/she may encounter during competition. For instance, varying the usual training conditions would be to use spectators during the workouts or to use loud music. Varying the conditions would also be to invite other competitors to work out together or to create situations in which the athlete will have to use his/her own creativity. After all, it is not possible to foresee every situation that one could be faced with during competition. For instance, use a heavier, lighter, shorter or a taller training partner to put pressure on the athlete to use his/her imagination.

Practice switching tactical maneuvers. For instance, the athlete usually has a tactical plan for offense and defense. The coach may ask the athlete to switch back and forth between offensive and defensive maneuvers and to do this at random. For example, one moment the athlete could set up an attack using fake attacks or steps and then switch to a more defensive style by using blocks, side stepping, or a combination of both, such as a counterattack or a follow-up attack. Switching tactics will make it more difficult for the opponent to get a handle on one's tactical plan.

Build up the athlete's confidence. The success of one's tactical plan is partly dependent on the athlete's confidence, or in more general terms, the athlete's psychological make-up. This means that the coach should work on the athlete's confidence (psychological framework) during training as well as during competition. An example was given in the previous section in tactical plan 3. The coach of that particular athlete would stress how well everything was going and would try to build up the athlete's confidence.

Set realistic goals for the upcoming competition. Based on the above mentioned guidelines, the coach and athlete should agree on goals to be set for the competition. For instance, the coach could set two goals for the upcoming competition. One goal is to use the axe kick as part of a tactical plan for offensive purposes and the other one is to use this kick to intercept the opponent's attacks as a defensive tactical maneuver. Naturally, these two goals were practiced during training. Constant feedback will be necessary during the breaks between rounds and throughout the entire competition, so that changes may be implemented in time, if necessary.

Periodization of Tactical Training

Tactical training starts in the pre-season. Since physical training is emphasized during the general preparation period in the pre-season, only a small portion of total training time will be allocated to it. One may start out with exercises to get a better feeling for the optimal striking distance as discussed above. An example of a tactical program is shown in table VIII.1.

TABLE VIII.1 Program for Tactical Training in Pre-Season: General Preparation Phase

		Week 1 - 3	
Frequency	**Duration**	**Intensity**	**Mode**
Tuesday	10 minutes	50% maxHR	distance
Thursday	10 minutes	50% maxHR	distance
Saturday	10 minutes	50% maxHR	distance
		Week 4 - 6	
Frequency	**Duration**	**Intensity**	**Mode**
Tuesday	20 minutes	60% maxHR	offense
Thursday	20 minutes	60% maxHR	offense
Saturday	20 minutes	60% maxHR	offense

The first three weeks of the general preparation period may be used to practice the optimal striking distance. The next three weeks, the athlete may start working on offensive maneuvers. If steps are part of the tactical plan, they may be practiced first. Keep in mind that the goal in this stage is to practice attacking. The overall intensity is low, between 50 - 60% of max HR. As in technique training, the correct execution of the various maneuvers is emphasized. The duration of tactical training as well as the intensity may be increased in the second half of the general preparation period.

During the specific preparation period, defensive maneuvers are first practiced. They include exercises described above or others that the coach deems necessary, depending on each individual's situation. Since the athlete's general endurance and strength will have improved by this time in the pre-season, the duration of tactical training may again be increased in addition to the intensity (see table VIII.2).

TABLE VIII.2
Program for Tactical Training in Pre-Season: Specific Preparation Phase

Week 1 - 3			
Frequency	**Duration**	**Intensity**	**Mode**
Tuesday	30 minutes	70% maxHR	defense
Thursday	30 minutes	70% maxHR	defense
Saturday	30 minutes	70% maxHR	defense
Week 4 - 6			
Frequency	**Duration**	**Intensity**	**Mode**
Tuesday	45 minutes	90% maxHR	offense/defense
Thursday	45 minutes	90% maxHR	offense/defense
Saturday	45 minutes	90% maxHR	offense/defense

The second half of the specific preparation period will subsequently consist of practicing both offensive and defensive tactical maneuvers. The intensity will have to be increased as well as the duration. Both may be done progressively, but the coach should realize that it is during this time (second half of specific preparation period) and the in-season that tactical training (as well as psychological training; see chapter VII) will be emphasized and occupy an increasingly larger part of the total training time (2). As before, each individual situation is unique, but for our purposes, a duration of 45 minutes has been chosen to spend on tactical training in the second half of the specific preparation period in the pre-season.

Table VIII.3 displays a possible program for tactical training during the in-season. The duration may vary, depending on the other components of training (technique, psychological, taekwondo endurance, taekwondo strength). It is during this phase that tactical training will be tried out in test competitions and eventually in the main competition(s). Test competitions are very important during the in-season, because it will give the athlete and coach the opportunity to really see the results of their training. As far as the tactical component is concerned, it is more "complete" during the in-season than it is in the pre-season. In the pre-season, for instance, offense and defense may be practiced separately or even together (second half of the specific preparation period). It is not until the in-season, however, that "complete" tactical training is done because the athlete will practice with real opponents in the various test competitions. Everything will have to fall into place now: the physical, technical and psychological foundations of tactical training culminating in a tactical plan.

TABLE VIII.3 Program for Tactical Training During In-Season

Week 1 - 6			
Day	**Training**	**Mode**	**Duration**
Monday	-	rest	-
Tuesday	tactics	offense/defense	varies
Wednesday	tactics	offense/defense	varies
Thursday	tactics	offense/defense	varies
Friday	tactics	offense/defense	varies
Saturday	tactics	offense/defense	varies
Sunday	tactics	offense/defense	varies

References

1. Barth, B. (ed.) (1979), *Fechten. Ein Lehrbuch für die Grundausbildung im Florett-, Säbel-, und Degenfechten.* 2. stark bearbeitete Auflage, Berlin: Sportverlag Berlin.
2. Bompa, T. O. (1983), *Theory and Methodology of Training,* Dubuque, Iowa: Kendall/Hunt Publishing Company.
3. Ko, E. M. (1980), *Taekwondo (Gyorugi) Kompendium der Wettkampftechnik in Taekwondo nach WTF System,* 1. Auflage, München: Verlag Schramm-Sport Dachau.

CHAPTER IX

ANATOMY OF JOINTS

Introduction

The taekwondo athlete relies on the skeleton and muscles to execute taekwondo techniques. Basic knowledge of the skeleton, particularly the joints and the way they function, is necessary to understand the possibilities and the limits of the human body when performing taekwondo skills. Understanding the anatomy of a joint wil give the coach and athlete better insight in the functions of that joint. This chapter will deal with joints and their practical application to taekwondo training. First, however, general information on the types of joints and the movements they will allow will be presented. After that, a brief description will follow of the joints of the shoulder, elbow, wrist and hand, hip, knee as well as ankle and foot.

A joint is the connection between the bones of the skeleton, which allows movement. It is made up of two ends belonging to two bones. In a ball and socket joint (see figure IX.1), for instance, such as the shoulder joint, one end forms the ball and the other the socket with the ball being able to move within the socket. The ball and socket is covered with cartilage, allowing smoothness of movement. The joint capsule covers and protects the joint, while the ligaments that reinforce the joint capsule contribute to its stability. The muscles running over the joint are responsible for the movement and add to the stability of the joint.

The ball and socket joint allows all kinds of movements, such as flexion, extension, *abduction* (outward and away from the body), *adduction* (inward and toward the body), *inward rotation* (rotation along the long axis toward the body) and *outward rotation* (rotation along the long axis away from the body). Combining all these movements will result in the limb performing a circular motion called *circumduction*.

Depending on the shape of the ends of the bone that form a joint, there are also the hinge and pivot joints. A hinge joint, such as the knee, will only allow flexion and extension. In a pivot joint, such as the elbow joint, one bone rolls over the other, allowing supination and pronation.

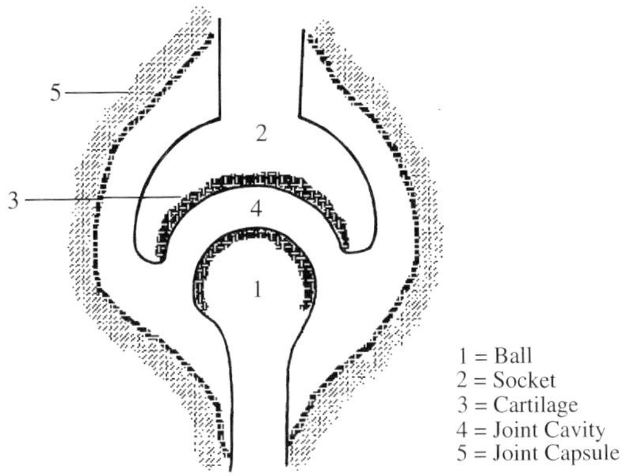

FIGURE IX.1: Basic Scheme of a Ball and Socket Joint

Shoulder Girdle/Joint

The shoulder girdle is formed by the shoulder joint, the clavicle and part of the upper spine (see figure IX.2). The shoulder joint is formed by the connection of the *humerus* and the *scapula.* The shoulder joint is rather unstable, because the larger head of the humerus moves against the smaller *glenoid fossa of the scapula*, while the ligaments of the shoulder joint are not very strong. The many muscles that run over the joint, therefore, contribute a great deal to its stability.

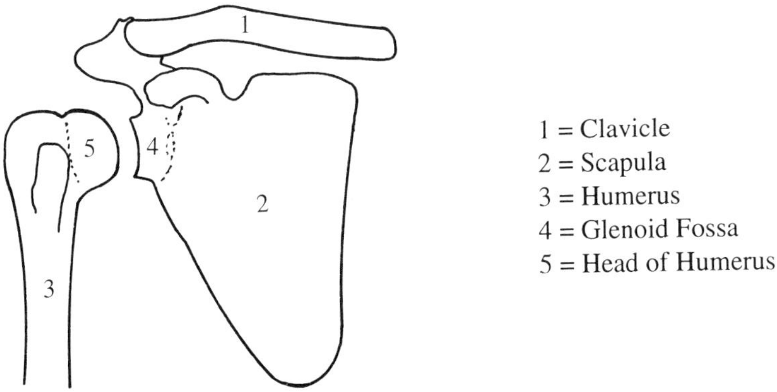

FIGURE IX.2: Shoulder Girdle/Joint

The shoulder joint, as mentioned above, is an example of a ball and socket joint, which makes it possible for the arm to move in many directions. The arm can flex, extend, move sideways and away from the body (abduction) as well as sideways toward the body (adduction). It can also turn around its long axis. When the thumb turns toward the body it is called inward rotation and when the thumb turns away from the body, it is called outward rotation. The shoulder joint can also describe a circle (circumduction).

Implications for the Taekwondo Coach

The shoulder joint depends on a strong muscular system for stability and movement. There are many arm techniques in taekwondo, so having strong shoulder muscles is essential. For exercises to strengthen the shoulder girdle see chapter V. A word of caution is warranted regarding self-defense techniques. While practicing shoulder locks, there is a chance this joint may become (partially) dislocated. Students, who have poor technique, are inexperienced, or are mismatched in terms of age, height and weight, form an increased risk for causing partial or complete dislocations and/or ruptures to the shoulder girdle/joint in their training partners or opponents during competition.

Clear agreements are necessary for the workouts: signaling „stop" actually means stop and not pushing it a little further for whatever reason! The clavicle is the connection of the shoulder joint to the chest. It is a relatively fragile bone and very susceptible to injury, such as fractures. If there is pain, deformation of the natural alignment of the clavicle, loss of function and strength of the arm/shoulder as well as problems when raising the arm above shoulder level, a fracture of the clavicle is very likely.

Elbow and Radio-Ulnar Joint

What is commonly known as the 'elbow joint' is actually a combination of two joints: the elbow and *the radio-ulnar joint* (see figure IX.3). The elbow joint is formed by the connection of the humerus and the ulna. The radio-ulnar joint is formed by the connection of the radius and the ulna. The elbow joint is a so-called hinge joint and makes it possible for the arm to bend (flexion) or extend. The radio-ulnar joint is a pivot joint and allows the forearm to pronate and supinate. *Pronation* is a rotation of the radius along its axis where the thumb moves inward (from lateral to medial), the 'drinking movement' of the forearm. *Supination* is the opposite: the rotation along the long axis of the radius where the thumb moves outward (from medial to lateral).

Implications for the Taekwondo Coach

Extension and flexion of the elbow joint are limited by and dependent on the shape of the joint, the ligaments and the muscles. Extension is mainly limited by the compression of the ulna against the humerus, a bone to bone friction, as it were, and somewhat by the ligaments. When punching, many students have the tendency to extend their elbows, and sometimes even hyperextend them, thereby causing bone to bone friction. In the long run, this will lead to injuries of the involved bones and will impair the joint. For instance, the cartilage that covers the surfaces of the joint becomes damaged and, as a result, will turn into bone over time and after many of these injuries, which will eventually hamper the function of the elbow joint. To prevent this bone to bone friction, the athlete should stop the extension of the arm when punching by contracting the muscles (biceps) that are responsible for elbow flexion just before the elbow is completely extended.

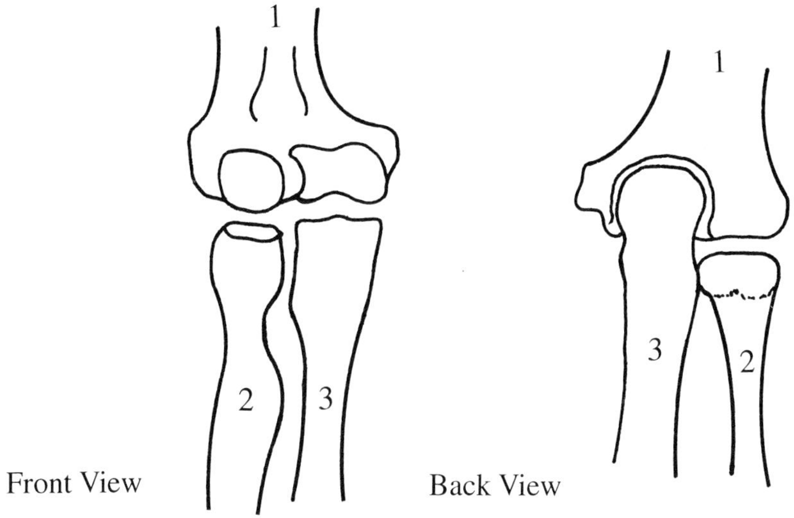

FIGURE IX.3: Elbow and Radio-Ulnar Joint

In self-defense, elbow locks are practiced by hyperextending the elbow. In this case, stress is placed on the ligaments and joint capsule. The ligaments are not very strong and the muscles can contribute little or nothing to the stability of the joint in this hyperextended position. Here again, the danger of rupture/dislocation is present and the stop signal given by the athlete when a partner is applying an elbow lock, really means stop!

Wrist and Hand Joint

The joint of the wrist is formed by the radius and carpal bones (see figure IX.4). The carpal or wrist bones are eight small bones tightly connected to each other by ligaments, only allowing slight movement among the bones.

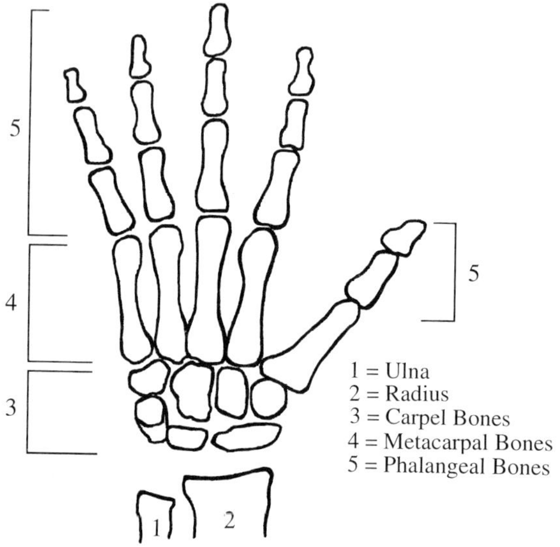

FIGURE IX.4: Wrist and Hand Joint

The wrist joint is a condyloid joint, which resembles a ball and socket joint with round surfaces that are ellipsoidal in shape. The movements of the wrist joint are limited compared to a ball and socket joint and include flexion, extension, abduction, adduction and circumduction. A rotational movement along its long axis is not possible.

The joint of the hand is formed by the wrist bones and *the metacarpal bones*. These metacarpal bones or bones of the hand only allow some gliding movements among each other because of their irregular shape and tight ligaments.

Implications for the Taekwondo Coach

When punching, the wrist joint relies on the muscles for its stability. The muscles on the front and back of the forearm have to maintain the wrist in the mid-position. In the mid-position, the back of the fist forms a straight line with the forearm. When practicing the punch against the heavy bag, the wrist joint can be sprained very easily. Therefore, strong muscles of the forearm are necessary to prevent this from happening. A heavy and hard punching bag will increase the risk of spraining the wrist joint, because this kind of bag will not give way to the energy of the punch and is therefore not recommended. Good technique is as important to prevent injuries. For exercises to strengthen the wrist joint see chapter V.

When punching against a hard, non-resisting surface, the small wrist bones may become contused (bruised). Although contusions are micro injuries, they are cumulative and may lead to increased calcification of these joints, which is another reason a softer heavy bag is advised (see next chapter on injuries). In the long run, calcification will cause the wrist to become stiff, which will result in loss of function and increased degeneration of the joint.

When punching, the striking surface is formed by the first and second knuckles (metacarpal two and three, respectively), which are the ends of the bones of the hand. The tendon of the extensor muscles of the fingers run over the knuckles (see figure IX.5). When hitting an object, the force is first transmitted through these tendons, then trough the metacarpal bones, the carpal or wrist bones and so on. Contusions of these tendons are very likely to happen when striking a hard and non-resisting object. The knuckles will swell and are painful. This injury, once it is sustained, is very difficult to get rid off and even punching gently against a resistance will make the knuckles swell instantly (for treatment of contusions, the reader is referred to the next chapter on injuries). Again, a soft kicking or punching bag is advised and a word of caution when breaking boards or bricks.

The knife-hand strike as used in breaking, is performed with the side of the hand. There seems to be a misunderstanding regarding the exact striking surface, in that the blow is thought to be executed with the little bone at the base of the hand. This is not so! This small bone, called the pisiform bone, is weak and serves as the attachment of a muscle. It is not strong enough to withstand the forces involved in breaking. The striking area for the knife-hand strike should be the whole base of the hand formed by metacarpal number five and the small muscles of the hand that run along this bone. The fingers, especially the little finger, do not make contact with the surface of the object the athlete wants to break.

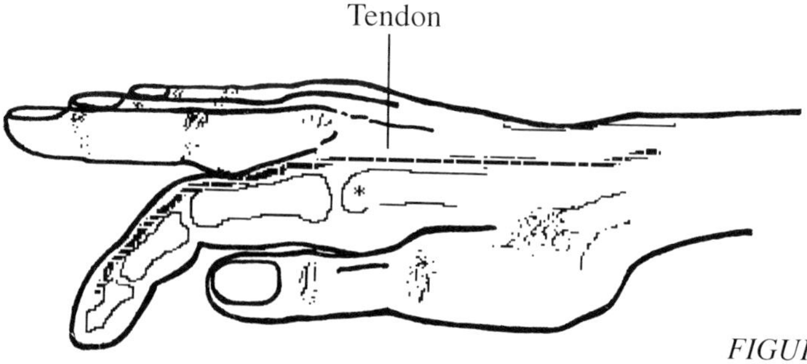

FIGURE IX.5: Tendon of Extensor Muscle of the Hand

Hip Joint

The hip joint (see figure IX.6) is formed by the head of the *femur* and the acetabulum of the pelvis. The hip joint is a ball and socket joint. The socket is larger and deeper than the socket of the shoulder joint. Since the hip joint is also a weight-bearing joint, it has a strong joint capsule, making it a stable joint. Being a ball and socket joint, it also allows for all kinds of movements. The leg can move forward (flexion), backward (extension), sideways away from the body (abduction) and toward the midline of the body (adduction). Along its long axis, the leg can rotate inward and outward (the foot of the extended leg moves inward or outward). Similar to the shoulder joint, circumduction is also possible.

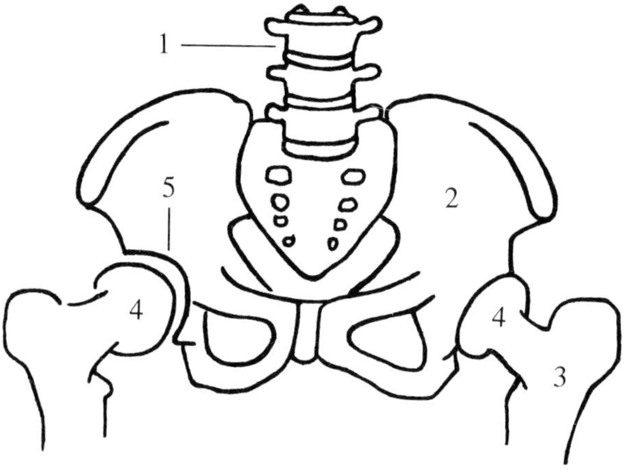

1 = Lower Spine
2 = Pelvis
3= Femur
4 = Head of Femur
5 = Acetabulum

FIGURE IX.6: The Hip Joint

Implications for the Taekwondo Coach

The muscles that run over the hip joint are strong and contribute to the stability of the joint. Since flexibility is very important in taekwondo, flexibility of the hip joint is emphasized, especially that of the hamstrings because this muscle group will be stretched when performing high kicks.

Knee Joint

The knee joint is also a large and weight-bearing joint and is formed by the femur and the *tibia bones*. The round ends of the femur connect on a flat surface of the tibia. This construction is very unstable (see figure IX.7).

Nature has tried to solve this problem by increasing the contact surface area by means of two menisci in each knee joint to add to the stability of the knee joint. The menisci have the form of half (medial menisci) and three quarters of (lateral menisci) a circle and are made of cartilage. In addition to the menisci, the knee has a strong joint capsule, reinforced by the lateral and medial ligament, and the cruciate (anterior and posterior) ligaments that add to its stability. The muscles that cross the joint play a very important role in its stability as well. The *patella* or knee cap is not part of the joint. It serves as a bone that increases the angle under which the quadriceps attach to the tibia by means of a ligament. By increasing the angle of insertion of one of the front thigh muscles, more force can be generated. The cartilage of the knee cap runs over the cartilage of the femur, which means that injury or damage to the knee cap can have its effects on knee function. Pain, loss of function and strength may result. The knee joint is a hinge joint and therefore can only flex and extend. A little rotation in the flexed position is possible, however.

Implications for the Taekwondo Coach

Being a hinge joint, the anatomy of the knee has very important implications relative to the execution of taekwondo kicks. If the foot of the support leg is fixed to the floor while kicking, the knee joint will be twisted, which may lead to severe knee injury. To avoid this, the support foot has to rotate on the floor, which should be done on the ball of the foot. As a result, kicking with running shoes or while standing on a soft surface may very likely cause knee injuries because it will be more difficult for the foot to pivot.

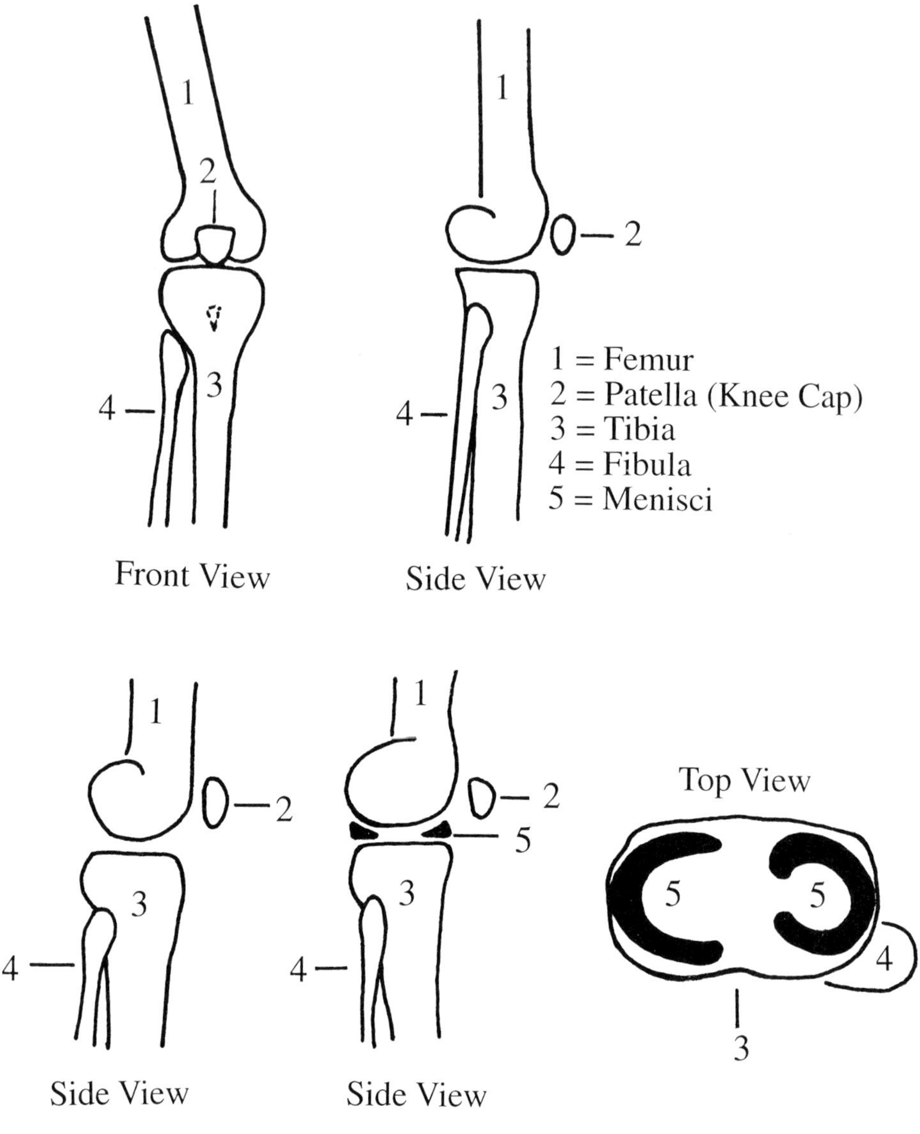

FIGURE IX. 7 The Knee Joint

The extension of the knee joint during kicking is stopped by the ligaments and muscles. Kicking in the air will cause severe tearing actions to these ligaments, which may lead to micro injuries and, if repeated many times, may cause damage to the stability of the knee joint. This effect is especially apparent when the athlete expects to kick against a pad that is pulled away without warning, which will result in a severe blow to the capsule of the knee joint. For this reason, while kicking in the air, it is advised to pay attention to the repeated extension of the knee and to stop this movement by the hamstrings muscles. The stronger these muscles are, the better they will be able to break the extension of the leg at the knee joint and the less chance there is for injuries. Another way to prevent these tears to the ligaments of the knee is not to kick all out while kicking in the air, but to do so against a pad or kicking bag. Pulling the pad away just for the fun of it right before impact, should be avoided.

Ankle and Foot

The ankle joint is formed by the *tibia* and the *fibula* with the talus bone of the foot (see figure IX.8a). The stability of the joint is increased by the joint capsule and by ligaments. The muscles that run over the joint also add to its stability. The ankle joint is a hinge joint and allows pointing (*plantar* flexion) and pulling up of the toes (extension).

The 'joint' of the foot (see figure IX.8b) is a combination of several joints and consists of *tarsal and metatarsal bones*. These joints allow inward *(inversion)* and outward rotation of the foot sole *(eversion)*.

Implications for the Taekwondo Coach

When performing a roundhouse kick with the instep of the foot, the force of impact is first transmitted through the tendons of the extensor muscles of the foot and then through the metatarsal bones. As in punching, the tendons will get irritated. Swelling, pain and loss of function are the results, with an increased risk for this injury to become a chronic one if it does not heal properly. Therefore, using *safety pads for the instep* is strongly recommended.

FIGURE IX.8a: Ankle Joint

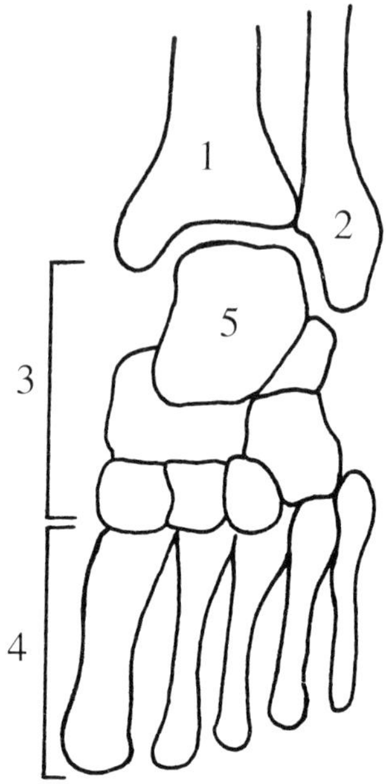

1 = Tibia
2 = Fibula
3 = Tarsal Bones
4 = Metatarsal Bones
5 = Talus Bone

1 = Tarsal Bones
2 = Metatarsal Bones
3 = Phalangeal Bones

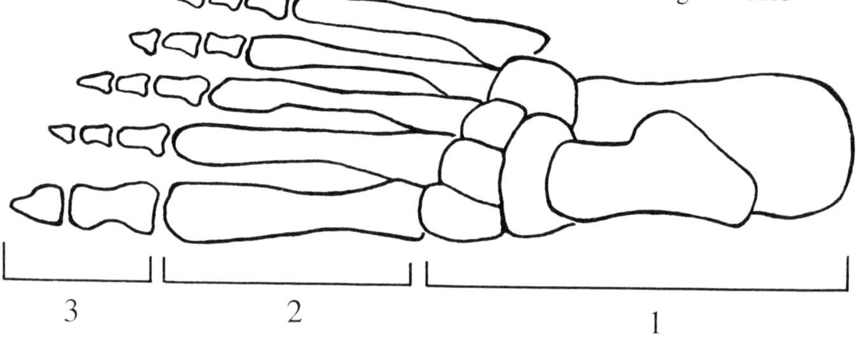

FIGURE IX.8b: Foot "Joint"

Chapter X

INJURIES IN TAEKWONDO

Introduction

For every taekwondo athlete it is very important to be able to continue to work out all year around. Continuity in a training program is an essential contributing factor to the success of the athlete. An injury is therefore undesirable and will interfere with the athlete's training program and may cause a setback in the program or, even worse, make the athlete lose a whole season.

Some of these injuries, such as a contusion or an injury to the attachment of the hamstrings to the hip, could have been prevented if there had been some insight by the athlete, coach, referees and tournament director in how they occur. Although information on injuries and guidelines for first aid treatment of certain types of injuries will be presented in this chapter, the following recommendation should be adhered to: ATHLETES AND COACHES SHOULD BEAR IN MIND THAT FOR DIAGNOSIS AND, DEPENDING ON THE INJURY, TREATMENT OF INJURIES, THE ATHLETE SHOULD BE SEEN BY A PHYSICIAN. Under no circumstances should the coach or other unqualified people decide what is best for the injured athlete, especially when dealing with a serious injury, such as a brain concussion or fracture.

Research on injuries in Junior (6 - 16 years) and Senior (17 and older) taekwondo competitors has shown that about 36% of all reported injuries were serious enough to cause time-loss from participation of one day or more (46). Approximately 30% and 46% of reported injuries in the Senior and Junior competitions, respectively, involved time-loss injuries. This difference may be related to physicians being more conservative in their recommendation of non-participation when dealing with children and adolescent athletes. The majority of injuries of Junior and Senior athletes combined was to the lower extremity (44%), followed by the head and neck with 31% of all injuries. The remaining injuries were to the upper extremities (15%) and trunk (9%).

The following sections will discuss types of injuries and body parts injured in both taekwondo training and competition. In addition, this chapter also will deal with injury prevention, warming-up and stretching exercises, cooling down and

the effects on performance of dehydration techniques to lose weight. An alternative training program will be suggested for those who are injured, so that any training decrements may be minimized.

Types of Injuries

Contusion (Bruise)

Contusions are caused by a sudden, hard impact of a softer body part with a harder object. For example, kicking with the instep of the foot against the elbow of an opponent may cause a contusion to the instep. In most instances, the skin is still intact, although it may also be grazed. A swelling will develop and, depending on the severity of the contusion, an internal hemorrhage, in which case the swelling will develop faster. Again depending on the severity, partial or complete loss of function may occur.

A severe bruise to the shin may lead to a complication known as the *anterior compartment syndrome*. This syndrome is caused by a blow to the shin or the muscles of the leg and may result in an intense swelling. Since the muscles are located in a compartment, the increased pressure, due to the swelling, will cause the muscles to "suffocate". So, in case of severe swelling, intense pain and progressive loss of function of the foot, the athlete should go to a hospital.

The injury component of the OTRP revealed that contusions were the most frequently occurring type of injury during competition (e.g., 29; 31). In fact, both during training and competition, contusions occurred most frequently in taekwondo or in related martial sports, such as karate (2).

Sprain

A sprain is an injury to the ligaments of a joint. There are several degrees of severity varying from a light sprain, due to hyperextension of the joint with nearly no consequences, to a complete dislocation. The symptoms vary with the degree of severity, starting from tenderness, pain, swelling, loss of function to deviations of the involved joint due to complete rupture and dislocation. The ankle joints, for example, are very susceptible to sprains.

Sprains and strains (see next section) are common injuries in taekwondo training (2) as well as in competition (2; 31). They are usually reported together in the (sports)medical literature and may be considered types of injuries that occur quite frequently in taekwondo as well as karate training and competition (e.g., 2; 4; 21).

With contusions often ranked first in terms of frequency, sprains and strains are usually found in the top ten of frequently occurring injuries, together with lacerations/abrasions and nose bleeds (see below) (e.g., 4; 29; 41).

Strain

A strain is a rupture of a muscle or tendon by which the muscle is attached to the bone. Strains occur due to a sudden forceful stretching of the involved muscle or muscle-tendon transition whereby the involved muscle does not give way to this stretch. Partial or complete rupture of the involved tissues may be the result of this action. A complete rupture of the tendon from the bone is also possible, especially during extreme forceful contractions of the muscles. Ruptures are very likely to occur due to incomplete warming-up and stretching exercises, especially if the temperature of the environment is low. It may vary from a minor one involving only some muscle fibers to a partial or complete rupture of the muscle or muscle-tendon transition. Pain is the most frequently occurring symptom. Swelling is usually seen in case of a partial or complete rupture. The pain, even secondary to a minor rupture, can cause the athlete to cease his/her activities. The sites where the muscle changes into the tendon are vulnerable to injuries. In most instances, these areas are less well supplied by blood vessels. Injuries tend to heal more slowly then and may re-occur, turning into chronic ones.

An example of a muscle strain or muscle-tendon transition strain is that of the attachment of the hamstrings to the hip bone. Due to sudden forceful stretching of the muscles or the forceful downward movement of the kicking leg (e.g., during the execution of the axe kick), this area may get injured rather easily. Mediating factors may include poor warm-up and stretching exercises as well as an apparent imbalance between the quadriceps and hamstrings muscles.

Tendinitis/Bursitis

Tendinitis is an inflammation of the tendons and bursitis is an inflammation of the bursae. Bursae are special sacs with fluid between tendons, ligaments, bones and skin in places where there is an increase in friction, for instance. These structures may become inflamed mainly by overuse and/or wrong use of the joints involved. Once they develop, they tend to last for a very long time. The symptoms of tendinitis and bursitis include tenderness, pain, loss of strength and swelling.

Although tendinitis or bursitis has been recorded as a result of taekwondo competition (29), the nature of the research precludes any definitive conclusions regarding the exact rates of this injury. It seems logical to assume that this type of injury will occur quite frequently in taekwondo, since the requirements of the activity seem to put much stress on the tendons, which may eventually lead to tendinitis/bursitis. In training, tendinitis may be incurred to the tendon of the extensor muscles of the fingers (see previous chapter on anatomy of joints). In karate, for example, tendinitis was reported as a result of hand-conditioning (10), which may even damage blood vessels of the hand (43).

First Aid

Although certain injuries should be treated by qualified personnel, the coach and athlete may contribute to the healing process by applying the ICE-R rule for less severe cases of bruises, sprains, strains and tendinitis/bursitis. In this way, the coach and athlete will be actively involved in the rehabilitation process after an injury and it will also contribute to an understanding of the importance of injury prevention. If one is not aware of what it takes to recover from an injury, the tendency may develop to underestimate the impact of an injury on the athlete's training program and subsequent performance.

The treatment of a contusion, sprain, strain and tendinitis/bursitis takes place according to the ICE-R rule (1). I stands for *Ice*. The injury should be cooled with cold water or ice packs for 10 to 20 minutes, to reduce the swelling as well as the inflammation process. This procedure should be repeated every four to six hours. The tender spot should be cooled by rubbing it with an ice cube until it feels numb, which will take about five to ten minutes. Do not hold the ice cube on one spot, since this may cause freezing and permanent damage to the tissues. Be careful when using cold sprays, however, for there is the danger of overusing them, which may result in freezing spots.

C stands for Compression. Compression can be in the form of a bandage or tape administered by an athletic trainer or physical therapist. The compression will also prevent the injury from further swelling as well as immobilize the injured body part to facilitate healing.

E stands for Elevation. Elevating the injured body part will prevent the blood from pooling and swelling to occur, which will enhance the healing process.

R stands for Rest. A complete rest for 24 - 48 hours is necessary in case of severe contusions, sprains, strains and tendinitis/bursitis, with shorter rest periods in less severe and even longer periods in more severe cases. The athlete will have to decide for him/herself when the injury has healed completely. In case of tendinitis/bursitis, special attention should be paid to taping for immobilization and rest for healing.

If it is possible to work out, the cooling should be done just before and right after the workout. The athlete should listen to his/her body and avoid performing techniques that cause pain. He/she should also avoid the use of the injured body part for the time being. If the instep is bruised, for instance, the athlete ought to avoid kicking against the heavy bag, kicking pad and partner exercises where there is a chance for contact, until the instep has healed completely, for it is possible that the healing process may be delayed and the injury may become a chronic one.

Warming-up and stretching exercises are very helpful and can aid in the active healing process. The pain caused by the injury, such as a strain, sets the limit to the stretching and warming-up exercises.

Fractures

A fracture is the sudden breakage of a bone. Fractures in taekwondo have been found in both training (3) and competition (34; 46). In fact, fractures occurring in competition, regardless of body part injured, were about three times as high as seen in American college football when expressed in minutes of competition (46). This injury rate for fractures incurred during taekwondo competition is a minimum number, since there were several cases of suspected fractures that could not be confirmed by means of an X-ray until after the competitions were over. Logistically, it was not possible to follow up on these injuries for the OTRP researchers and, as a result, suspected fractures were categorized as either contusions or sprains at the competition site where injury data collection took place.

Fractures to the hand and fingers in taekwondo are hypothesized to be related to the frequent use of open hands in competition instead of the use of fists (46). As in karate (9; 23), fractures to the hand during taekwondo practice may be the result of hand-conditioning, breaking or blows delivered or received as in blocking a kick with the knuckles (3). Given the frequent use of the feet in taekwondo, it should not come as a surprise that fractures to the foot and toes are among the injuries in the lower extremities. A major concern with fractures in young taekwondo athletes is related to the possibility of stunted growth in the involved area, although most fractures do not seem to result in growth deformities (28). Extra caution is nevertheless warranted when dealing with young, growing, taekwondo athletes.

Muscle Soreness

Muscle soreness as a result of training is a sign of overuse. If muscle soreness occurs after a workout, the workout was probably too hard. Muscle soreness is caused as a result of the contents released by damaged cells in the muscle fibers (see figure X.1). Muscle soreness mostly occurs in beginners, at the beginning of

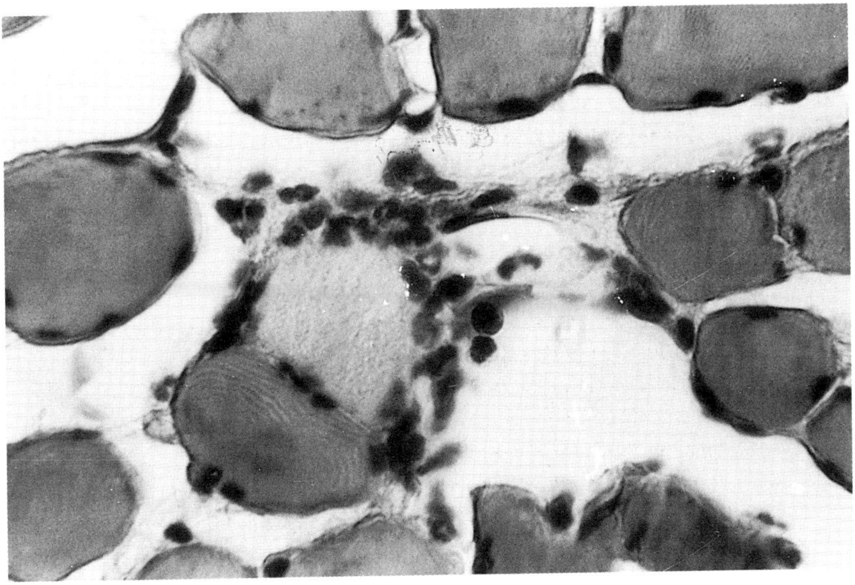

FIGURE X.1: Damaged Cells in Muscle Fibers
Courtesy of Prof. Dr. H. Kuipers, Human Movement Studies Program, Faculty of Health Sciences, University of Limburg, Maastricht, The Netherlands.

a new training season (regardless of skill level), due to a workout that was too intensive and lasted too long, starting new or different exercises (e.g., strength training, running) and if the athlete is about to get sick with the flu. If the athlete senses muscle soreness, the training load should be decreased for the next workout(s), so the body can adjust more gradually to the increased levels of the work load. Muscle soreness reaches its point of maximum pain on the second or third day, after which it subsides. During these 'painful' days, light workouts with the emphasis on warming-up and stretching exercises are recommended.

Injuries to Body Parts

Head Injuries

Blows to the head in taekwondo may lead to brain concussions, which in turn may lead to chronic brain damage. The athlete does not have to be knocked out to incur long-term brain damage, for the number of bouts fought may be more related to brain damage than knockouts per se (e.g., 6; 25). As a matter of fact, occasional knockouts may be less damaging on a long-term basis than repetitive subconcussive blows to the head (22). The rate of concussions in taekwondo competition has been found to be about three times as high as that in American college football and when expressed in terms of competition time, it was about eight times as high (46).

The following mechanisms have been thought to cause brain damage or concussions (22):

1.) rotational acceleration
2.) linear acceleration
3.) deceleration upon impact
4.) blow to the side of the neck (this will be discussed in the next section).

Rotational Acceleration. A rotational blow to the head will cause more acceleration to the brain than a linear one (22; 37; 45). In addition, the duration of the blow is also involved (24): the longer the impact time of the blow, the greater the chance of incurring a brain concussion. Research has shown that, after rotational blows, the head will accelerate to such an extent that brain injury will most likely occur (16; 37; 38). Punching speeds in boxing of 8 m/s were found to give the head an acceleration that was sufficient to cause a brain concussion (16). As was shown in chapter VI, the round kick, as an example of a rotational technique, produced an average speed in excess of 8 m/s, with a range of 13 - 16 m/s, which was much higher than the more linear side kick. It should be clear that the chance of sustaining brain damage after a round kick to the head is greater than it is after the side kick.

Linear Acceleration. Straight blows to the head may cause lesions in part of the brain, which may develop a few days after the blow occurred and may become increasingly more serious after subsequent subconcussive blows (22). Sudden linear acceleration may also lead to hyperextension of the neck, which will damage nerves in the cervical spine and result in a knockout.

Impact Deceleration. After a knockout or a blow to the front of the head, the athlete may fall on the back of his/her head, which will produce a rapid deceleration of the head and result in a so-called *contrecoup contusion* of the front of the brain (22), which simply means that the contusion in the front of the brain is the result of an impact on the opposite side, the back, of the brain (contrecoup), which will lead to injury as well. In addition to brain injury, the sudden deceleration may also result in a fractured neck (18). Contrecoup contusions also occur secondary to linear or rotational acceleration.

An insidious complication of a head injury is the slow internal bleeding of the blood vessels of the brain. The injury may start as a concussion with a depression of the level of consciousness, for instance. After some time, the athlete apparently recovers and a period of no complaints will follow, which is deceiving. Due to the slow accumulation of blood caused by damaged blood vessels, a second and progressive phase of depressed consciousness will result. If no medical attention is sought, the outcome of this progressive deterioration will be fatal.

There is no generally accepted classification of brain concussions in the (sports)medical literature (33). In the Oregon Taekwondo Research Project, the classification system as suggested by Nelson and co-workers (26) was used.

Grade 0 Concussion. After receiving a blow to the head or after the head has moved rapidly, he/she is stunned or dazed initially and subsequently complains of headache and has problems concentrating.

Grade 1 Concussion. The athlete is stunned or dazed and complains of having his/her "bell rung". No loss of consciousness or memory and normal sensation returns in less than one minute.

Grade 2 Concussion. The athlete complains of headache and "cloudy" or fuzzy consciousness, lasting more than one minute. There is no loss of consciousness, but there is ringing in the ears and memory loss. The athlete may also be excitable, irritable, confused and dizzy.

Grade 3 Concussion. The athlete loses consciousness for less than one minute without coma, where psychological and physical responses to stimulation are impaired. He/she may demonstrate grade 2 symptoms during recovery, such as irritability, confusion, dizziness.

Grade 4 Concussion. There is loss of consciousness for more than one minute without coma. During recovery, the athlete may demonstrate grade 2 symptoms. Sawa (33) has suggested the following recommendations for coaches in case of a brain concussion:

Grade 0 and 1: the athlete may be allowed to return to training or competition when his/her senses clear. Regular check-ups for symptoms should be carried out during the remainder of training or competition. If symptoms develop, the athlete should be removed from training or competition.

Grade 2: Remove the athlete from training or competition for a minimum of one week. After symptoms disappear, the athlete should not be allowed to return to training or competition for a minimum of one week.

Grade 3: The athlete should be removed from training or competition. Consult with a neurologist immediately and do not allow the athlete to return to practice or competition until after clearance by the neurologist.

Grade 4: The athlete should be transported immediately to a neurological trauma center or emergency room of the nearest hospital.

Although the OTRP has used the above mentioned classification for brain concussions for research purposes, one should be aware that hospitals may utilize a different categorization to accommodate very serious injuries that may occur in traffic accidents, for instance. As alluded to above, the results from the injury component of the OTRP showed that the injury rate for brain concussion, regardless of grade of severity, was about three times as high as that seen in American college football and when expressed in minutes of competition, it was about eight times as high (46). When expressed in grade of concussion, the rates for grade 0 and 1 were about three times as high as well, but for grade 4 it was even higher (more than eight times!), especially in Senior and Junior male taekwondo athletes (30). Regardless of grade of brain concussion, over a four-year span of injury data collection there was about one brain concussion for every 100 competitors.

Gronwall and Wrightson (11) showed that the capacity to process information in concussed individuals is reduced immediately after concussion and that this reduction is not only greater in those, who have had a concussion before, but that it would also last longer before returning to normal. The reduced ability to process information was especially related to complex tasks, such as driving a car, studying, working, and so on. There were also problems remembering material or storing information in memory to be retrieved at a later date (13). Recent results demonstrated that even after one match, boxers showed diminished brain function, although they had not been knocked out (14). Concussed individuals usually complain of concentration problems, irritability, poor memory and fatigue easily (12).

A helmet, such as worn by taekwondo competitors, will do more in the way of dissipating the force of the blow (32) than offsetting the acceleration of the head (37). On the other hand, it will provide some protection to the head if it hits the mat upon falling (19). However, wearing protective equipment also has its disadvantages. For one thing, the life span of fist or foot padding is limited (e.g., 39; 42), which would require regular testing of the protective gear. It was also found that higher accelerations were recorded of the head after impact with the protected fist or foot (37; 39). It was concluded that pads will protect the wearer more than the one punched or kicked.

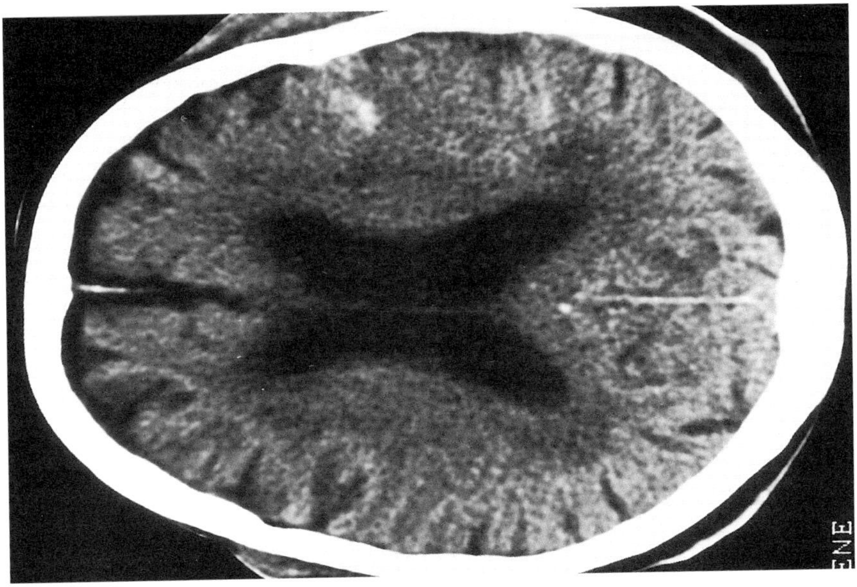

FIGURE X.2: CT Scan of Brain Concussion
Courtesy of Prof. Dr. J. F. Wilmink, Department of Diagnostic Radiology, University Hospital Maastricht, Maastricht, The Netherlands.

A head injury may involve more than what is visible to the naked eye. Figure X.2 shows a cross-section of a concussed brain with internal bleeding. The white spots in the upper right side of the brain depict the bleeding as a result of trauma to the head and should be compared to the left side of the brain, which shows normal brain tissue. Also notice the swelling on the outside of the skull (bump on the head) due to the injury. Proper medical attention is always indicated in case of a head injury.

Neck Injury

Neck injuries are very likely to happen due to a kick or punch to the throat. The danger of an injury to the throat lies in the fact that the larynx composes part of the upper airway. Due to internal damage such as a hemorrhage, swelling of soft tissue or deformation, the air passage may become obstructed and breathing may become a problem. If the athlete is not able to breathe sufficiently, the obstructed airway creates a life-threatening situation. In this case, an open airway has first priority and immediate medical attention is necessary. The accumulation of liquid (swelling) may take awhile before it is severe enough to block off the airway, which makes it necessary to observe the injured athlete for a longer period of time after the injury occurred.

A fractured neck as a concomitant of a blow to the head has already been mentioned above (see section on head injuries). There, it was also observed that a blow to the side of the neck may result in brain damage. A taekwondo kick to the side of the neck may cause an injury to this area that will lead to a decreased blood flow to the brain (22; 27). It may cause a rupture of the blood vessel in the side of the neck that leads to the brain, or form a blood clot that will restrict the blood flow to the brain. Although no separate injury rates were calculated for the neck, head and neck injuries in taekwondo competition were found to occur quite frequently (29; 31).

Injury to the Eyes

A blow to the eye can bruise and cause a hemorrhage of the soft tissue lying directly under the skin. This injury will result in the typical appearance of the so-called "black eye". Besides icing, this injury does not need any further attention.
In case of a more severe injury, the eyeball and/or the socket of the eye can become damaged. The base of the eye socket is made of a very thin bone that is fractured easily. If fractured, the eyeball can move downwards and the athlete can complain about symptoms such as pain, double vision, deformation and hemor-

rhage. This injury is called a 'blow out' fracture and needs immediate medical attention. Between 1988 and 1991, only a few fractured eye sockets were recorded in the OTRP (W. Pieter, unpublished data), although no separate injury rates were calculated for fractures per body part. "Black eyes", on the other hand, were more often seen in taekwondo competition.

Wrestler's or Boxer's Ear

A kick to the ear can cause a hemorrhage of the outer ear. If the hemorrhage is severe and no medical attention is sought, this might lead to a serious complication, the so-called wrestler's or boxer's ear. The complication is due to the hemorrhage that, over time, may lead to a deformation in the form of a cauliflower of the outer ear. Before medical attention is sought, applying ice to the injured area is the first thing to do. As of this writing (1995), no wrestler's ears have been found in the OTRP, but the injury may not reveal itself until much later.

Nose Bleed

In sports in general, nose bleeds happen very easily. So, in taekwondo, a punch or kick to the nose can very readily cause the nose to bleed. The nose, as part of the head-face-neck area, was one of the body parts that was frequently injured during taekwondo competition. In addition to nose bleeds, fractured noses were also reported as well as contusions to the nose (29).

First Aid

The athlete should blow his/her nose, bend the head slightly forward (like the writing position of the head) and pinch the nose just in front of the bony part with finger and thumb. In general, the bleeding stops within ten minutes or so. The athlete will be able to continue, but should avoid blowing the nose for the next two hours. In case the bleeding is severe, cotton tampers can be placed in the nose. Examine the nose for swelling, deformation or deviation from the midline, since the nose may be fractured. If so, a physician should be consulted (1).

Injury to the Teeth

A kick or punch to the teeth can fracture or dislocate one or more teeth. If it is a dislocation, repositioning the involved tooth in its socket should be done first before attending a dentist. If this is not possible, the athlete should carry the tooth under the tongue until he/she arrives at the dentist's. The best way to prevent dental injuries is to wear a mouth guard, both during practice and competition. It will reduce the occurrence of lacerations of and within the mouth, injuries to the upper jaw as well as provide limited protection against fractures of the lower jaw (33). A mouthpiece was also found to reduce the risk of brain concussions following a blow to the lower jaw in rugby (7). The mouth guard acts as a shock absorber against fractures of the teeth and prevents the jaws from being forcefully pressed against each other after a blow (33). In cases where a mouthpiece was worn, no teeth injuries were recorded in the OTRP. However, if no mouth guard was used, lacerations to the lips, broken teeth and other injuries were found to the mouth/lower face area.

Solar Plexus

The solar plexus is located just below the point where the rib arches meet the chest bone. The solar plexus is a spot from which many nerves radiate. A blow against the solar plexus can cause a temporary paralysis of the diaphragm (1). Symptoms include a temporary stopping of breathing, increase in perspiration, instant decline of blood pressure and heart beat. The athlete can also be confused and there is an increased chance of panic, because the athlete is unable to breathe for a few seconds.

If the abdominal pain continues after the blow, the abdomen stays tender and/or becomes hard, the athlete looks pale, feels nauseated, weak and clam and has a high and weak pulse, something else may be the matter and he or she may have a shock. A hard blow to the abdomen may cause bleeding of the internal organs, such as the spleen. In this case, the athlete has to be transported to the hospital as fast as possible. Injury to the spleen may sometimes even lead to death (36).

No blows to this body part were reported to the OTRP, but that may have something to do with the fact that only competition injuries were collected for the project and that the effects of a blow to the solar plexus are transient. During training, this body part may be hurt more often, since the chest pad is not always worn then.

First Aid

Calm the athlete down by telling him/her to relax. Put the athlete in the supine position and loosen his/her clothing around the abdomen and chest areas. Raise the legs of the athlete above head level in order to increase the blood supply to the brain. Encourage the athlete to breathe in a relaxed manner by short and firm inhalation and by exhaling slowly and gradually.

Groin

A kick in the groin causes a very painful and nauseating sensation. Depending on the severity, swelling, bleeding, fluid production and muscle spasm may occur (1). These symptoms may be caused by internal damage or internal bleeding. A kick in the groin in a woman is also a very painful and nauseating sensation. Just as in male athletes, shortness of breath, etc., may happen as well. A swelling may also be caused by internal bleeding. The injury component of the OTRP has recorded only a few groin contusions, indicating that injuries to this body part do not occur frequently and are probably related to the use of groin protectors.

First Aid

Put the athlete in a supine position, bend his/her knees and bring them to the chest. This position is supposed to relieve the muscle spasms. Check the groin for swelling or bleeding. Ice may be applied to reduce the swelling. In case of a severe swelling, internal or external bleeding, the athlete should be brought to the hospital.

Weight Loss, Dehydration

As in any other weight-categorized sport, taekwondo athletes sometimes subject themselves to rather stringent diets to lose weight, so that they can compete in a lower weight division. Similar to some sports, such as wrestling, boxing, judo, gymnastics or figure skating, taekwondo athletes usually try to "make weight" by what is commonly known as dehydration techniques to lose weight, including the use of saunas, working out in plastic suits or in double layers of clothes, fluid restriction and even food deprivation. Unfortunately, these methods are potentially hazardous to the athletes' health. For female athletes, these practices may cause menstrual problems.

A decrease in performance is especially apparent during a tournament, although not necessarily during a single bout (40). It was found, for instance, that a forced reduction in body weight of about 5% by dehydration had deleterious effects on strength, anaerobic peak and mean power, and aerobic power (44). Several hours of rehydration did not result in bringing the body up to pre-dehydration levels. A significant decrease in muscle glycogen concentration and a concomitant decrease in dynamic strength was found after an 8% loss of body weight through fluid and food restriction over a four-day period (15). Since glycogen is the fuel source mostly relied upon in predominantly anaerobic sports, such as taekwondo, it is clear that performance will suffer. The taekwondo athlete also will be more susceptible to injury, because he/she will fatigue easily due to glycogen depletion.

When dealing with young taekwondo athletes, dehydration methods to lose weight are of special concern relative to their negative effects on the growth and development process (35). Tournament directors and coaches are advised to make sure that plenty of opportunity be provided to eat and drink before and during the course of competition. DO NOT hold them in a WAITING AREA without any food or fluids, so that they will not dehydrate, which will not only be counter-productive to performance but it is also hazardous to their health and may lead to (serious) injuries.

In general, when the athlete wants to "make weight", eating less with adequate physical activity is recommended. Eating less refers to decreasing the caloric intake relative to energy expenditure through physical activity. It does not mean that the athlete should abstain from eating and drinking, as is sometimes done! It does, however, include banning candy bars and "junk food" from one's menu. Aerobic workouts of a certain duration and intensity are usually recommended for active individuals to lose fat, which may be monitored by their sum of skinfolds. Typically, a minimum of three days a week at 70% of max HR for at least 15 minutes each training session is usually advised to lose fat without the loss of lean body mass (muscles) at the same time (5).

Alternative Training Program for Injured Athletes

Staying without injuries in a contact sport, such as taekwondo, is wishful thinking. When an athlete becomes injured, this may mean a setback in his/her training program. The injury needs time to heal and the athlete will be unable to work out as planned. If it is not given enough time, it may become chronic and this will interfere even more with one's training progression or will force one to stop working out altogether for the current season. To make up for this lost time, some alternative training possibilities are presented below. We hope that this will keep the athlete from engaging in her/his regular training program until she/he has recovered completely, while at the same time providing for the continuation of her/his daily training routine. Depending on the kind and the severity of the injury and the stage the athlete is at in his/her training program at the moment of injury, the coach may design a new or alternative schedule.

Endurance Training

If the athlete is unable to continue his/her workouts to improve the aerobic, anaerobic or taekwondo-specific endurance, he/she has to look for alternative activities to be able to continue to work on this training component. Alternative activities include cycling (on the road or on a stationary bike), cycling with the arms on a modified stationary bike, swimming, running in water, and so on. As was said before, to train endurance, one has to perform the actual competition activities or activities that resemble the sport skills as closely as possible. However, we now are dealing with a different situation and it is deemed more important to choose for the continuation of the training program instead of adhering to a taekwondo-specific timetable. Engaging in non-taekwondo related activities or activities that may not have the ideal carry-over in terms of muscle groups used will enable the athlete to do exactly this.

An example of an alternative training program for anaerobic endurance could be as follows. Suppose the regular program during the pre-season calls for four times a 400 m-run on Tuesday, Thursday and Saturday at an intensity of 95% HR_{max} with adequate rest periods in between. The approximate time for one 400 m-run is set at 80 seconds, for example. As a consequence, the alternative training program has to consist of an activity that should also be done for four times 80 seconds at an intensity of 95% HR_{max}. If swimming is the mode of training for the alternative program, the athlete will have to swim a distance (a 100 m, for example), that will take him/her about 80 seconds at the same intensity of 95% HR_{max} on Tuesday, Thursday and Saturday. The same rationale may be applied to the other activities mentioned in the first paragraph of this section. The duration, the intensity and the rest interval of the originally planned activity, which in this case was running, will be used as the starting point for the activities of the alternative training program.

Flexibility

During the period of inactivity after an injury, the athlete should keep working on his/her flexibility as before, provided that the injury will allow the athlete to do so. A good warm-up is essential, which may pose a problem, since the athlete is injured.

Strength Training

Again depending on the kind of injury and of its severity, the athlete should try to continue to work on those strength exercises he/she is able to do. A change in the intensity, weight, repetitions and so on, are some of the possibilities to adjust one's strength program. For special rehabilitation exercises, the advise of an athletic trainer or physical therapist is required to gradually regain the previous level of training.

Taekwondo Exercises

There are some techniques in taekwondo that can be used when modified to accommodate the injury. For example, the athlete may practice arm techniques while sitting or even lying down. He/she may also practice kicking while sitting or kneeling on the floor (see figure X.3).

A *B*

FIGURE X.3: Alternative Taekwondo Exercises

Psychological Training

Psychological training is part of the regular training program for the non-injured athlete (see chapter VII). While injured, the time spent on psychological training may be increased.

Evaluation

Extra time is available to talk about competition, strategy, tactics, long-term goal setting and so on, with one's coach or fellow athletes. There is also time to read and study this book and other books that deal with taekwondo or related subjects. Time has also become available to evaluate one's performance by means of video tape recordings. The following questions may serve as guidelines to assess your performance on video: How was your own performance? When did you score a point and when did you not after an attack, counterattack or otherwise? You will also be able to analyze your opponents: What are his/her strong and weak points? What is his/her favorite leg? What are his/her favorite techniques? The answers to these questions may provide the athlete with clues to prevent the opponent from scoring a point or how he/she him/herself may be able to score. Analyzing one's technique or the adversary's may also aid in the prevention of injuries. For instance, if one has the tendency to kick against the other competitor's elbow with the instep of the foot, one may want to change this during the next kick or match.

Testing Data

Baseline data on the profile of the injured athlete that were collected at the beginning of the pre-season and maybe even during later assessments, may be used to evaluate the improvement in performance after the injury. If his or her performance is below par, the athlete is probably not fully recovered yet compared to pre-injury levels. Secondly, this implies that the athlete is not ready yet to continue with his/her regular training program. As a result, the workouts will be too hard and will most likely result in increased risk of re-injury.

Injury Prevention

Warm-up and Stretching Exercises

Every workout should start with warm-up and stretching exercises. They are very important to prepare the body for the demands that will be put upon it by the workout that is to follow, enabling the athlete to perform at high levels as well as help in the prevention of injuries (17). In addition, this preparatory period serves as a time to get ready psychologically for the upcoming training.

Warm-up and stretching may be divided according to their general or specific nature and may be categorized as follows:

1.) general warm-up,
2.) general stretching,
3.) specific warm-up,
4.) specific stretching.

General Warm-Up. The purpose of the general warm-up is to activate the muscles, heart and lungs (see figure X.4). All main muscle groups should be included and all kinds of exercises may be used to serve this purpose, such as running, lifting the knees up while running, kicking the butt with the feet while running or swinging the arms in a circular motion. The exercises should start at a low intensity (around 35 - 50% of max HR) and slowly progress to a higher intensity (about 65 - 75% of max HR). Ball games or warm-up exercises to music are welcome changes to the daily routines.

FIGURE X.4: Example of General Warm-Up

General Stretching. The purpose of general stretching is to stretch all main muscle groups. Here, too, all kinds of exercises may be used, such as stretching the calfs, hamstrings and triceps. The stretching exercises should be static as opposed to dynamic or ballistic, so that no muscle injuries may occur. Each stretch may last for approximately eight to ten seconds. Examples of general stretches are shown in figure X.5A - D.

Specific Warm-Up. The specific warm-up focuses on taekwondo and taekwondo-related exercises, such as lifting up the leg to the level of the chest, to warm-up those muscle groups that are used in taekwondo kicks. They should also be performed at a low level of intensity. Other examples of specific warm-up exercises are: low front kick, low side kick and punching (see figure X.6).

FIGURE X.5: Examples of General Stretching Exercises

A

B

C

D

A *B*

FIGURE X.6: Examples of Specific Warm-Up Exercise

Specific Stretching. Specific stretching exercises involve those muscle groups for which flexibility is needed in order to execute taekwondo techniques. Examples of specific stretching exercises are: the front or side split and exercising with a partner raising the leg in a side kick position (see figure X.7).

A B

FIGURE X.7: Examples of Specific Stretching With Partner

When doing warm-up and stretching exercises, the following pointers should be kept in mind:

1. Raise the level of intensity gradually. As long as the athletes are able to talk while they are running, for example, the intensity level is just right. The beginning of perspiration, a slightly increased frequency of breathing and the change toward a reddish color of the face indicate that the body is warming up. Another way of pacing the level of intensity is to check the athlete's heart rate.
2. While alternating the warm-up and stretching exercises, make sure the stretching exercises do not last too long, so that the athlete will not cool off too much and the effects of the warm-up lost, which may lead to damaged muscles and hence injuries.
3. The recommended time for warm-up and stretching exercises is at least 20 minutes up to 60 minutes, depending on the time available to work out.

Cool-Down

Cooling down after a workout or competition is as important as warming up. The cool-down may consist of similar exercises and stretching as the ones used during the warm-up. Similar to the warm-up, the cool-down is thought to be related to injury prevention (17). It will allow the muscles to return to their pre-exercise temperature and the blood vessels to gradually contract slower to prevent fainting as a result of pooling of blood in the leg muscles after cessation of training. It is also believed that the cool-down exercises and stretching contribute to the prevention of muscle soreness after exercise.

Heavy Bag

The heavy bag is a device that is often used in taekwondo workouts. A bag that is too heavy or too hard may cause injuries. If the bag is too heavy, the athlete may sprain his/her ankle when performing a roundhouse kick, for instance. If the bag is too hard, the athlete may bruise or otherwise injure his/her feet or wrists. These injuries can be prevented by using a bag that is not as hard and as heavy, which may be accomplished by filling the bag with rags or old clothes, for instance. When executing all-out techniques on the bag, no injuries whatsoever should result.

Chest Protector (hogu) and Padding

An important source of injuries as well as injury prevention may be the equipment utilized in taekwondo: the *hogu*, arm and shin pads. Research on hand (safe-T punch) and foot padding (safe-T kick) (38; 39; 42), as mentioned above, has shown that the lifespan of the material used is rather limited. After only a few blows, it was found that the forces of the punches with the hand pads were within the zone of concussion (38; 39), which would make these pads very unsafe for repeated use. Although the so-called safe T kicks had a longer lifespan (42), it would certainly be wise to renew them regularly if they are part of the athlete's equipment.

No research has been done yet on the *hogu* and the helmet. In one study (8), it was suggested that the *hogu* would only protect the wearer against certain types of kicks and not against others. If the helmet is made of the same material as the hand pads, it should come as no surprise that brain concussions will very much stay a reality in taekwondo. To help reduce the occurrence of serious injuries and prevent such injuries as bruises, it would certainly be advisable to renew the equipment on a regular basis. Finally, as was mentioned in the previous chapter, padding for the instep of the foot is highly recommended. As of this writing (1995), no padding is required (yet) for the foot. All too often, the instep is injured during kicking, especially when the roundhouse kick is used. It would make logical sense to protect this area.

Ring Mats

Using ring mats will certainly help in reducing the number of brain concussions as a result of falls. A blow to the head may not necessarily lead to a concussion, but the athlete may fall on his/her head with the risk of incurring a brain concussion or a neck injury. Preferably, the mats should be of one piece with no folds in the cover. In addition, make sure to have the mats all around the ring with plenty of room beyond the borders of the ring. DO NOT use carpets or other substitutes. The mats should not be too soft, for this may lead to ankle or knee injuries.

References

1. Arnheim, D. D. (1985), *Modern Principles of Athletic Training,* St. Louis, etc.: Times Mirror/ Mosby College Publishing.
2. Birrer, R. B. and Birrer, C. D. (1982), Martial arts injuries, *Physician and Sportsmedicine,* 10, 6: 103 - 108.
3. Birrer, R., Birrer, C., Son, D. S. and Stone, D. (1981), Injuries in taekwondo, *Physician and Sportsmedicine*, 9, 2: 97 - 103.
4. Birrer, R. B. and Halbrook, S. P. (1988), Martial arts injuries. The results of a five year national survey, *American Journal of Sports Medicine*, 16, 4: 408 - 410.
5. Brownell, K. D. (1988), Weight management and body composition, In: S. N. Blair, P. Painter, R. R. Pate, L. K. Smith and C. B. Taylor (eds.), *Resource Manual for Guidelines for Exercise Testing and Prescription*, pp. 355 - 361, Philadelphia: Lea & Febiger.
6. Casson, I. R., Sham, R., Campbell, E. A., Tarlau, M. and Didomenico, A. (1982), Neurological and CT evaluation of knocked-out boxers, *Journal of Neurology, Neurosurgery and Psychiatry*, 45, 2: 170 - 174.
7. Chapman, P. J. (1989), Players' attitudes to mouthguards and prevalence of orofacial injuries in the 1987 U.S. Rugby Football Team, *American Journal of Sports Medicine*, 17, 5: 690 - 691.
8. Chuang, T. Y. and Lieu, D. K. (1991), A parametric study of the thoracic injury potential of basic taekwondo kicks, In: K. Min (ed.), *USTU Instructors Handbook.* Third Edition, Berkeley: USTU Instructors Certification Committee, pp. 118 - 126.
9. Crosby, A. C. (1985), The hands of karate experts. Clinical and radiological findings, *British Journal of Sports Medicine*, 19, 1: 41 - 42.

10.Gardner, R. C. (1970), Hypertrophic infiltrative tendinitis (HIT syndrome) of the long extensor, *JAMA,* 211, 6: 1009 - 1010.

11.Gronwall, D. and Wrightson, P. (1975), Cumulative effect of concussion, *Lancet*, II, 7943: 995 - 997.

12.Gronwall, D. and Wrightson, P. (1974), Delayed recovery of intellectual function after minor head injury, *Lancet*, II, 7881: 605 - 609.

13.Gronwall, D. and Wrightson, P. (1981), Memory and information processing capacity after closed head injury, *Journal of Neurology, Neurosurgery and Psychiatry*, 44, 10: 889 - 895.

14.Heilbronner, R. L., Henry, G. K. and Carson-Brewer, M. (1991), Neuropsychologic test performance in amateur boxers, *American Journal of Sports Medicine,* 19, 4: 376 - 380.

15.Housten, M., Marrin, D., Green, M. and Thomson, J. A. (1981), The effects of rapid weight loss on physiological functions in wrestlers, *Physician and Sportsmedicine,* 9, 11: 73 - 78.

16.Johnson, J., Skorecki, J. and Wells, R. P. (1975), Peak accelerations of the head experienced in boxing, *Medical and Biological Engineering,* 13, 3: 396 - 404.

17.Jones, B. H., Rock, P. B. and Moore, M. P. (1988), Musculoskeletal injury: risks, prevention, and first aid, In: S. N. Blair, P. Painter, R. R. Pate, L. K. Smith and C. B. Taylor (eds.), *Resource Manual for Guidelines for Exercise Testing and Prescription*, pp. 285 - 294, Philadelphia: Lea & Febiger.

18.Jordan, B. D., Zimmerman, R. D., Devinsky, O., Gamache, Jr., F. W., Folk, F. S. and Campbell, E. A. (1988), Brain contusion and cervical fracture in a professional boxer, *Physician and Sportsmedicine,* 16, 6: 85 - 88.

19.Jorritsma, L. S. M. (1987), *Veiligheid Boksen.* Rapport van de Commissie Veiligheid Boksen, Rijswijk: Ministerie van WVC.

20.Kelly, D. W., Pitt, M. J. and Mayer, D. M. (1980), Index metacarpal fractures in karate, *Physician and Sportsmedicine,* 8, 3: 103 - 105.

21.Kurland, H. L. (1980), Injuries in karate, *Physician and Sportsmedicine*, 8, 10: 80 - 85.

22.Lampert, P. W. and Hardman, J. M. (1984), Morphological changes in brains of boxers, *JAMA,* 251, 20: 2676 - 2679.

23.Larose, J. H. and Kim, D. S. (1968), Knuckle fracture, *JAMA*, 206, 4: 893 - 894.

24.Lissner, H. R., Lebow, M. and Evans, F. G. (1960), Experimental studies on the relation between acceleration and intracranial pressure changes in man, *Surgery, Gynecology and Obstetrics*, 111, 3: 329 - 338.

25.McCunney, R. J. and Russo, P. K. (1984), Brain injuries in boxers, *Physician and Sportsmedicine*, 12, 5: 52 - 67.

26.Nelson, W. E., Jane, J. A. and Gieck, J. H. (1984), Minor head injury in sports: a new system of classification and management, *Physician and Sportsmedicine*, 12, 3: 103 - 107.

27.Nyst, M. and Laundly, P. (1987), Injuries incurred in the practice of karate, *Sport Health*, 5, 2: 7 - 10.

28.Pappas, A. M. (1983), Epiphyseal injuries in sports, *Physician and Sportsmedicine*, 11, 6: 140 - 148.

29.Pieter, W. (1995), Sportletsels, naar tak van sport: taekwondo (Injuries by sport: taekwondo), In: F. J. G. Backx and B. Coumans (eds.), *Sportgezondheidszorg in de Praktijk* (Practical Sports Health Care), Houten/Zaventem: Bohn Stafleu van Loghum, pp. 3205-1 - 3205-42.

30.Pieter, W. and Taaffe, D. (1992), The Oregon Taekwondo Research Project. Results and recommendations, *Journal of Asian Martial Arts*, 1, 1: 73 - 85.

31.Pieter, W. and Zemper, E. (1990), The Oregon Taekwondo Research Project: part II - preliminary injury research results, *Taekwondo USA*, 3, 1: 24 - 26.

32.Ryan, A. J. (1983), Eliminate boxing gloves, *Physician and Sportsmedicine,* 11, 12: 49.

33.Sawa, D. L. (1990), Head injury in sports: classification and management of concussion, *Sports,* 10, 6.

34.Siana, J. E., Borum, P. and Kryger, H. (1986), Injuries in taekwondo, *British Journal of Sports Medicine*, 20, 4: 165 - 166.

35.Saris, W. (1986), Nutritional concerns for the young athlete, In: R. Rutenfranz, R. Mocellin and F. Klint (eds.), *Children and Exercise XII*, Champaign, IL: Human Kinetics Publishers, Inc., pp. 11 - 18.

36.Schmidt, R. J. (1975), Fatal anterior chest trauma in karate trainers, *Medicine and Science in Sports,* 7, 1: 59 - 61.

37.Schwartz, M. L., Hudson, A. R., Fernie, G. R., Hayashi, K. and Coleclough, A. A. (1986), Biomechanical study of full-contact karate contrasted with boxing, *Journal of Neurosurgery*, 64, 2: 248 - 252.

38.Smith, P. K. and Hamill, J. (1985a), Karate and boxing glove impact, In: J. Terauds and J. N. Barcham (eds.), *Biomechanics in Sport II. Proceedings of ISBS 1985,* Del Mar, CA: Academic Publishers, pp. 114 - 122.

39.Smith, P. K. and Hamill, J. (1985b), Karate and boxing glove impact characteristics as functions of velocity and repeated impact, In: J. Terauds and J. N. Barcham (eds.), *Biomechanics in Sport II. Proceedings of ISBS 1985,* Del Mar, CA: Academic Publishers, pp. 123 - 133.

40.Steen, S. N. and McKinney, S. (1986), Nutrition assessment of college wrestlers, *Physician and Sportsmedicine*, 14, 8: 100 - 116.

41.Stricevic, M. V., Patel, M. R., Okazaki, T. and Swain, B. K. (1983), Karate: historical perspective and injuries sustained in national and international tournament competitions, *American Journal of Sports Medicine,* 11, 5: 320 - 324.

42.Thomas, M. and Prince, P. (1987), Capacité d'atténuation d'impact et durée de vie des protecteurs de pied utilisés dans la pratique de sports de combat, *Canadian Journal of Sport Sciences*, 12, 3: 136 - 143.

43.Vayssairat, M., Priollet, P., Capron, L., Hagege, A. and Housset, E. (1984), Does karate injure blood vessels of the hand? *Lancet,* II, 8401: 529.

44.Webster, S., Rutt, R. and Weltman, A. (1990), Physiological effects of a weight loss regimen practiced by college wrestlers, *Medicine and Science in Sports and Exercise,* 22, 2: 229 - 234.

45.Whiting, W. C., Gregor, R. J. and Finerman, G. A. (1988), Kinematic analysis of human upper extremity movements in boxing, *American Journal of Sports Medicine*, 16, 2: 130 - 136.

46.Zemper, E. D. and Pieter, W. (1991), A two-year prospective study of taekwondo injuries at national competitions, presented at the International Congress and Exposition on Sports Medicine and Human Performance, Vancouver, BC, Canada, April 16 - 20.